The HOT SHOT
Heard 'Round
the World

For information, address:

BearManor Media
P. O. Box 71426
Albany, GA 31708

www.bearmanormedia.com

Book design by John Gummere • Studio 264
www.be.net/JohnGummere

Published in the USA by BearManor Media

ISBN: 978-1-62933-404-2

The HOT SHOT Heard 'Round The World

A Musical Memoir by
ANDY KAHN

Commentary by
Bruce Klauber

I dedicate this book to the multitude
of talented individuals responsible for
creating The Great American Songbook,
the wellspring of countless musical styles
that took their cues from this
incredible musical genre.

— *Andy Kahn*

FOREWORD

I have known Andy Kahn, personally and professionally, for more than 50 years. Through all that time, he has never failed to amaze me with his range of talents—all of them first-rate. Even before we first played music together at the age of 9, he already helped helm a pirate radio station in suburban Philadelphia, was an acclaimed actor/singer in local area theater and, as I recall, had an encyclopedic knowledge of meteorology. When we met, I found out he was an extraordinary pianist who knew just about every popular song ever written. When he first sat down to play for me, I had to bring out my drums and start banging along. (Some years later, we managed to parlay our musical talents into one of the most popular jazz groups Philadelphia has ever seen or heard, due in no small measure to Andy's talents as a player, improviser, showman and charismatic leader.) As a boy, Andy just had no fear. As rudimentary as we may have sounded in those days, his enthusiasm helped, as they used to say in vaudeville circles, "put it across."

Eventually, we became immersed in modern music by way of Bill Evans and other jazz innovators. Andy Kahn internalized that music and made it his own. It was easy for him. I won't detail his years as a bandleader on the society circuit. The money was good and the music was, shall we say, fun, especially Andy's crowd-pleasing "bump circle" dance routine and our bass player's quite individual version of the "Hokey Pokey." The escapades of the boys in the band could fill a separate book. All I'll say is that during a road gig at a restaurant/hotel in Greenville, Maine, a certain band member ended up on the hotel's roof, minus some of his clothing. How Andy put up with us, I will never know.

My friend's visions and aspirations were always high. When he became involved in Philadelphia's Queen Village Recording Studios, with his brother Walter, it appeared that there was no limit to what they could accomplish. And accomplish, they did. There was the discovery of the Gipsy Kings, recording the likes of Princess Grace and Astrud Gilberto, the production

1

of "Hot Shot," the number one disco record of 1978, and other marvelous musical milestones and technical innovations.

Nothing was beyond Andy's grasp and, to his credit, he managed to play great jazz piano through it all. Andy Kahn is among the select few to have made substantial contributions in both the jazz and pop fields as a performer, producer, engineer and composer. He stands among giants like Dave Grusin, Bob James, Mike Mainieri and Quincy Jones as not only a pop hit-maker, but as a singular jazz improviser. Some jazz purists may claim that it's impossible to do both. Look at the record. As just one example, jazz pianist Bobby Scott, who backed up Gene Krupa, Louis Prima and Lester Young among others, served with Quincy Jones as a pop producer at Mercury Records and ended up writing "A Taste of Honey" and "He Ain't Heavy, He's my Brother." Along with those legends, Andy has proven that one can do it all.

I have had the great fortune of knowing Andy Kahn through many of his various entertainment guises over the years, so I've taken the liberty of contributing some commentary, anecdotes and observations here and there throughout this narrative. My comments are in italics throughout.

There are some incomparable tales told within. Andy's story tells of the rise and fall of disco, the inside goings-on of the record business, of jazz, world tours, pianos, politics, family disputes, recording studios owned, singing, double-dealing, female singers, summer stock, pirate radio stations, songs written, industry prejudice and fear, tragedy, heartbreak, recordings produced and engineered and handling mega-success and changing times with grace.

I continue to be overjoyed at Andy's every success and to marvel at how he has dealt with everything. I look forward to at least 50 more years of the same.   — *Bruce Klauber*

INTRODUCTION

This memoir is in two parts. Part One: "Off The Record" covers my first two decades on this planet and explains how I became involved in the field of entertainment. Part Two: "On The Record" details events leading me into the recording industry and follows my career from the early 1970s to the present.

A significant portion of my destiny was firmly anchored at the intersection of 4th & Catharine Streets in South Philadelphia, a place where my family's first, second and third generations resided and earned livings over many years. Southwark Paint Company, which my grandfather founded in 1918 at 801 South 4th Street, is where my father was raised, above the store, until he married my mother. He worked at the paint store all his life until he died in 2005. My uncle lived and worked in that building his entire life. As a child, my mother lived around the corner, less than a block away. Queen Village Recording Studios was built across the street at 800 South 4th Street. My older brother lived above the studio. I lived next door to the studio in a small three-story home I renovated in 1975. My younger brother Billy lived at 807 South 4th Street for a few years. These locations represent my family's three generations of staking its claim at this crossroad. In 1982, I took over ownership of Southwark Paint, our third generation to control that edifice and business. At the end of 2010, the Kahn family ceased operating any commercial enterprises or owning residential property along the 800 block of South 4th Street.

The following pages are filled with the extraordinary events I've experienced. The stories, varied and often connected, detail many fascinating personalities, portraying situations that seem, even to me, incredible. Of particular note is my accounting that chronicles the final chapter of my family's 92-year association with a single street corner in Philadelphia, one that served both as a witness to, and nurturer of, a great many magical and musical events in my life.

PART ONE

Off the Record

TAKE IT FROM LETTER "A": A WORLD OF ENTERTAINMENT

In the corner of our living room on Drexel Road in Overbrook Park, a neighborhood west of central Philadelphia, lived a typical early-1950s model DuMont black and white television. The TV component was hidden within the real-wood cabinet behind a pair of doors, ensuring it would blend in like any other piece of furniture. It shared its residence in this room with a wood-case record player that was always cranking out popular music from the mid-20th century. A walnut grand piano occupied another corner of this room harboring what would now be considered vintage appliances. Together, the wood trio of entertainment inventions provided the wellspring for my career in music. They served as bait for me, offering an endless supply of musical sounds I would first absorb and then immediately reproduce on the keyboard. Always playing with both of my hands, documented in a photo of my playing that big, grand piano at the age of 7 and a half months, I dazzled three living grandparents, both of my parents, their friends and an army of relatives. All of them were entranced by this young boy who had discovered a surefire method for attracting attention to himself.

Living with a seriously jealous brother five years my senior, I was forced to create unique interest in me. His sour attitude is corroborated in a tell-tale eight-millimeter film clip shot the day I was brought home from the hospital following my birth on July 23, 1952. Walter Kahn pointed a toy machine gun into the carriage where I'd been drawing a lot of attention. He then gave the lens a thumbs-down, registering his keen disapproval at having his thunder stolen by way of my arrival. I should have known right then that there would always be contention between us. Born on the first day of Leo, it always seemed natural I should be a performing artist. I demanded attention whenever the chance presented itself. I played the piano all the time. When I was five, I suggested I play a somber version of "Pray for the Dead" on the day of my paternal grandmother's funeral. This remains one of the very few occasions when I was asked not to perform. It would be a dozen more years before another such request occurred, that time in a nightclub.

In my early years, I would examine sheet music my mother would purchase for me. These were usually basic Piano/Vocal collections containing the most popular songs from well-known Broadway shows. With a little help from private teachers along the way, and from what I learned in music classes at school, I taught myself how to read melody notes on the G-Clef music staff. The chords I played in my left hand, which provided the harmony, came naturally for me. I'd experiment with chords on the piano until I found those that sounded like the ones I heard on records or themes on television and radio broadcasts. I became readily able to make associations between my chords and those written above the melody line on the printed music. Most of my early chordal harmony was developed by ear. It was my ability to play what I heard, which only improved throughout my childhood, that astonished both my teachers and me. This extraordinary gift has always served me well whether playing solo piano, as a member of a musical group and/or accompanying a soloist or vocalist.

Later, whenever I was introduced to new jazz pianists, I immediately wanted to play like them. Hearing Oscar Peterson for the first time was an overwhelming and illuminating experience. For years I tried to emulate the man and his sheer ability to dazzle. After hearing Art Tatum, like many others before and after me, I aspired to cultivate even a tenth of the virtuoso's musical prowess and artistry. When I was first introduced to Bill Evans and Thelonious Monk, following Bruce Klauber's insistence that I broaden my pianistic aspirations, I strove to learn as much as I could about the way these two jazz giants performed—and thought—musically. Encountering the genius of Lennie Tristano, thrust on me by my dear childhood pal David Kay, I was instantly bowled over by Lennie's intuitive and original style. He demonstrated a never-ending inventiveness when playing American standards. I believe that Tristano's ability to employ substitute chords whose voicing he'd already inverted and/or altered has never been attained by anyone else. I've never stopped trying to approach his mantle, though.

How was it that I could simply hear a musical phrase and then play it "by ear" on the piano? Such was the case, resulting in the piano and me becoming lifelong partners. Nothing exhilarates me more than sitting at my piano and getting lost in its vast orchestral universe. Give me a piano in good shape, properly tuned, and I become enraptured as it responds to what I have to "say"—transmitted from my fingers through its myriad wooden moving parts, springs, screws, felt hammers and wire strings. A piano's mechanical action is the conduit for music first created in the player's mind. Through its metal plate and the soundboard below it, the results resonate. Nothing sounds like a piano. I love playing the piano. This was a good thing, as the piano would certainly figure prominently in my future.

Grand pianos have become impractical for many people and locations, because of their size, lack of portability and cost to produce. As with so many other natural, acoustic instruments, it didn't take long for the "rocket scientists," geniuses who inhabit the digital realm, to create a satisfactory substitute. Grand pianos are large instruments made of cured hardwood, metal foundry components, strings, screws, brass and, hopefully, a generous quantity of pride and love. Today, we have keyboards at our disposal that digitally reproduce recorded "samples" of these fascinating, historic, oversized instruments.

The digital keyboards are much smaller and lighter, offering a decent alternative to a musical object that otherwise insists on taking up a great deal of space. The better digital pianos produced today have keyboards offering the advantage of a weighted, graded "action," meaning that the physical feel of the keys changes as it is played from the bottom, lower section toward the top, higher section. In a traditional acoustic piano, either in a grand or vertical style, the wire strings for the bass notes at the extreme left are very long. Gradually, they become shorter over all 88 keys as they approach the treble notes at the extreme right of the keyboard. The lower notes require more force from the player to produce enough energy for the felt hammers to strike and resonate the long bass strings. In contrast, the higher notes require less force from the player to produce enough "strike" from the hammers onto the short treble strings. Digital keyboards now compensate for this "feel." Their keys simulate those of the keyboards in an acoustic piano. Combine that with the digitally-reproduced "sampled" sounds recorded from an authentic Yamaha, Steinway, or Bosendorfer grand piano, and one gets an amazingly realistic experience while playing one of these new, electronic instruments. Before long, the player forgets that he is not playing a 9-foot acoustic piano. Considering the piano-like sound being reproduced, actually, he is.

I never thought playing on a digital keyboard was for me—and rejected countless opportunities to do so. It wasn't until I owned one that I signed on to the experience. As the intelligence of computers continues to duplicate yet another basic area of our human experience, high-quality digital keyboards now offer decent substitutes for the real deal. However, for me, there is still nothing like a grand piano. They thunder. They roar. They make the floor tremble as they provide orchestral dynamics when played. They are instruments created like no others on our planet. But, today's digital keyboards offer some serious advancements, providing an experience similar to playing an acoustic piano. I assume they will only get better. This, sadly, will eventually cause the demise of acoustic grand and upright piano manufacturing altogether someday. I hope I will have been long-gone by the time that happens!

UNCLE LLOYD

My father's younger brother, Lloyd Kahn, was an enigma to both his parents. Uncle Lloyd always perceived things with a slightly different slant from the rest of his family and the other "normal" children in the thriving community of Philadelphia's South 4th Street where he was born and raised. In the 1920s, this crowded street where Lloyd and my father lived hummed with commerce and was filled with the aromas of ethnic foods and a constant clamor created by its inhabitants. My father Kenneth, the first-born son, was athletic, genuinely handsome and very popular. He embodied the all-around normal, white, Jewish kid growing up in South Philadelphia during that time. Lloyd, also very good-looking, while affable and generally well-liked, on the other hand, was clearly cut from a different cloth. He demonstrated early signs of authentic artistic talents, the ability to draw and write creatively. He even mastered playing the harmonica, a seldom-appreciated musical instrument.

The neighborhood was dominated by parlor pianos and violins, instruments subjected to students' lessons that rarely produced more than agony for their players and the families forced to endure the practicing—more often than not, irritating screeching and the banging of strings. Lloyd's harmonica, not the last one he would own, was a birthday present from his Aunt Fannie. She recognized that this little boy had talent. And she believed he should have a creative outlet on which to develop it—something about which my grandparents were not in concert, let alone prepared to encourage.

Lloyd loved listening to big-band music. He and the other boys in the neighborhood, one whom he revered and who'd eventually become his brother-in-law Stanley Weiss, couldn't accumulate enough recordings of the swing bands fronted by Glenn Miller, Tommy Dorsey and Harry James. Lloyd flipped for the big bands of Count Basie, Stan Kenton and Duke Ellington. He knew every song, vocal artist, composer and arranger for these bands. He became a human encyclopedia on them and was known throughout his neighborhood as the authority on this "new" music. Mention a song title and my uncle would tell you which bands recorded it and the vocalists who performed it. "Tenderly," a gorgeous ballad, both lyrically and musically, was his all-time favorite, especially as performed by the Kenton band. You could see tears in his eyes whenever he whistled it.

I had no knowledge about the intervalic relationships that exist within musical compositions. "Tenderly" introduced me to the Flat 5 interval (also known as the Sharp 11) in musical harmony. It is commonly used in modern chord structure. A major scale's natural 5th chord (a Dominant 7) gets altered through chromatically diminishing by a half-step the dominant 5th chord's own 5th interval. The effect produced by this one-note deviation intoxicated me at an early age. When it was first introduced in Classical music, this type of chord produced a similar effect on humanity—causing an uproar. Today, what is universally referred to as the "Tritone Interval," was once widely known as "The Devil's Interval," when it first appeared in composition. Its sound purportedly stirs up sensual and erotic feelings in the listener and, therefore, it was considered inappropriate by many factions in society. Ah, some things never change.

Whistling was one of Lloyd's favorite pastimes. His method of whistling was unlike anything anyone had ever seen. He curled his lips to form a hole in the corner of his mouth, not the center, through which the notes would emerge. The look on his face as he emitted a melody from his repertoire was both angelic and demonic. He embodied a life-form positioned somewhere between "the devil and the deep blue sea." If you showed even the slightest interest, Lloyd's face would brighten up considerably as he provided the name of the arranger of a band's musical charts, many of whom went on to become famous. Unless you were prepared to settle into his ensuing, mandatory lecture on the importance of any composition's musical arrangement, and the personnel making up a bandleader's organization, you would have to think up a clever way to excuse yourself politely. And no matter how you managed to secure your exit, Lloyd's quirky smile would turn upside down into a disappointed frown. Often, that scowl would then lead to his unleashing a tirade of unpleasant rumination regarding the lack of interest my grandparents and my father showed toward him and the music he loved so dearly.

Fully enraged, Lloyd progressed onto ranting and raving about the ineptitude of the United States government, the municipal government of Philadelphia, the military branches of government and then all governments in general, along with authorities on any level, who were in charge of a world that clearly was "going to Hell." Your best choice was to sit back and let Uncle Lloyd play his music for you, absorbing what he had to say, if only for a few moments, allowing it all to escape from your memory when this session was finally over. Or, as it was in my case and in deep contrast to the rest of my family, one might actually learn something from this man.

Lloyd Kahn was an authority on American standards and Big-Band Swing music. If you could get past his childishness and innocent neediness to impart some of his knowledge so someone else might also become enlightened about the importance of this musical genre, his presentations could actually be worthwhile. On the other hand, were you one to have little patience or tolerance for such things, you were sentenced to suffer an interminably miserable time with him, either enduring his lecturing or, by turning away, having him unleash a fireball of fury upon you and anyone else who happened to be within earshot. This would be his way until his last days on Earth. Uncle Lloyd, upon whom my parents bestowed the distinct honor of being my godfather, would continue to be an influence on me and the musical career I would later pursue. I just didn't know at that point how important those early years I spent with him would be.

Lloyd Kahn was certainly a man conflicted. But he also was one who had been clearly misunderstood. He lived during a period in history when most people chose not to invest much effort in comprehending individuals demonstrating rare, pure and natural talent. Aunt Fannie fell into a different category. She had enough heart and keen perception to do something for her nephew, whom she realized was different. She did so in a loving and caring way, having recognized that little Lloydie was wired uniquely from the other kids on the block. She hoped that her small gesture of giving him a toy harmonica when he was a youngster might help him find his way, whatever that might be. And he did—though it was a bumpy road that

13

most people in his neighborhood, especially his family members and school chums, found difficult to ride on. The local gentry and his relatives elected to take an easy route, simply shunning him in the process.

An exception was a man destined to become one of my other uncles. Stanley Weiss is the younger brother of my mother Janice. He lived right around the corner from my uncle and my father. He saw Lloyd's usefulness right away, deeming him the perfect "fall guy" for any scheme that Stanley could dream up. "If there was a party your Uncle Stanley wanted to crash, I'd be the one to go up to the front door and ring the bell. If someone was going to get a pie thrown in his face, it was always me!" I heard this story from Uncle Lloyd my entire life.

Despite this lopsided arrangement between two friends, Uncle Lloyd deeply admired my future Uncle Stanley and would have "taken a bullet for him," no questions asked. In fact, once, when Stanley was being threatened by a gang of local hoodlums, Lloyd, witnessing this from inside the paint store, came running out with a rusty pipe and chased them away, demonstrating heroics to Stanley. I've been told that he performed in a like manner time and again.

Lloyd carried a very deep appreciation for Stanley's friendship, one of only a few he was ever able to maintain. Lloyd expressed over and over how crazy he was about Stanley Weiss. Stanley has acknowledged that Lloyd also made a profound impression on him, telling me many times that a truer friend than Lloyd Kahn could never be found. These words of honor and trust between two men with extremely different personalities had a major effect on me—one that would serve as my guide in developing relationships with special people who came into my life, several of whom remain very dear to me to this day.

Here, on this street of dreams that ran north and south between South 3rd and South 5th, immigrant merchants laid out their wares daily on pushcarts in front of their buildings. Storefronts served as the center of a family's livelihood. When they were not running the store or hawking merchandise to customers out front, these families would usually be found upstairs, where they lived. In the residence above the paint store, Lloyd played music on his small tube radio day and night. He boasted to me years later, that each night he pretended to be asleep when he heard my grandparents coming up the steps to look in on him. He'd turn down the volume so they wouldn't know he'd been up all night listening to live radio broadcasts of the bands he loved so much. My grandfather would put his hand on the radio and feel that it was still warm from the heat emitted by the vacuum tubes inside. When he asked Lloyd if he was asleep —a story recounted to his three nephews no less than a half-million times—he answered, "Yeah, Dad, I'm asleep!"

Uncle Lloyd was driven by the music. I sometimes think the swing and jazz he absorbed helped make him crazy, because my grandparents showed absolutely no understanding of his passion for this music or any of the other creative talents he demonstrated. Unfortunately, they never allowed him to blossom naturally in areas that possessed his daily thoughts. Stifled by his recalcitrance, they elected to ignore him. They chose to sweep him "under the rug." It was too time-consuming to pay attention to his needs or attempt to inspire him. That would have helped him develop into the artistic person he surely could have been. "Artistic people never amount to anything," they believed, as did many of their contemporaries. In this neighborhood, lives were carved out through a work routine enabling one to make a living while raising a family and educating the children. Art certainly was not in any way considered an education or a living! These people saved up resources for that proverbial rainy day, which many saw as already upon them. "Just loos (leave) him alone!" my grandfather said often with regard to the younger of his two sons.

My father was the normal one. My grandparents were proud of having produced one decent, hardworking individual to carry on the family tradition. Everyone viewed my father as the archetypal adolescent who would go to a good college, marry the right girl (my mother Janice, of course!) and take over the family business, providing perpetuity to our family name. That was every parent's dream on South 4th Street, one repeated on all the streets east, west, north and south of theirs, spreading out onto byways and avenues across the country. The American Dream would be a piece-of-cake achievement for Kenny Kahn; of this my grandparents were certain. Lloyd, conversely, would continue making their hearts ache. So why should they bother encouraging, or worse, try to rehabilitate him? In their opinion, he would always be a foul ball, no matter what they did. So "loos him alone," was their choice. And my father, the dutiful and respectful first-born son, expected to carry the torch to the Finish Line, followed suit when it came to handling his younger brother. My father was ashamed of Lloyd's behavior, so he never gave him the much-needed nurturing and support that only a brother could offer.

My uncle was drafted into the United States Army at the age of 18. Private First-Class Lloyd Kahn had his harmonica with him (a newer model, substantially advanced over the one Aunt Fannie had lovingly given him) during the years he served in the army. Overseas during World War II, he always referred to his location as The European Theater. He suffered greatly during his time on the front lines with the 84th Infantry Division, an outfit known as The Railsplitters. He spent most of his enlisted days stationed in France. It was there that my uncle was wounded by flying metal shrapnel, surviving an explosion during which he also witnessed a close Army buddy from his troop get blown to pieces. Lloyd recuperated in a hospital located in Nancy, France, before heading back into combat. I'd heard the words "Nancy, France" many times as a child, initially believing this was the name of some girl he met while fighting in the war. That life-changing, emotional event involving his fellow soldier dying led to Lloyd being awarded The Purple Heart and The Bronze Star. He often said it was his harmonica that got him through those tough times.

My father, who became a Captain in the United States Army, learning that Lloyd had been wounded in combat, requested special orders allowing him to rendezvous with his younger brother stationed several hundred miles away. Those orders were granted. I treasure the photo of my father and Lloyd being reunited while they were serving in France, following Lloyd's recovery from his wounds. Gorgeous smiles on their two handsome faces, in their khaki uniforms, shaking each other's hands (hugging—are you kidding?) all indelibly etched deep in my consciousness. I'm certain that had my father demonstrated anywhere near such simple affection and concern for his younger brother while Lloyd was alive, my uncle's life would have been very different.

Upon returning to America, Lloyd went into treatment with a psychoanalyst, courtesy of the United States Army—a GI Bill benefit afforded him because of the physical and emotional experiences he suffered during the war. Reports from the therapist informed my grandparents that Lloyd was deeply injured emotionally during his time overseas, and that only time could heal the wounds inflicted on his psyche. My uncle was hostile toward the therapist, often accusing his doctor of being the one who was sick. Lloyd Kahn was one of many thousands of soldiers who went into that second Great War one way and came out another. In defense of the doctor, he likely treated Lloyd in the best way known, based on his training. The current approach toward an individual demonstrating such stifling behavior patterns is lightyears ahead of the medical profession's knowledge 65 years ago. This is especially true for those possessing creative talent, which was alluded to in Lloyd's doctor's reports that stated he suffered from Schizophrenia, Depression and other manic disorders.

In today's world, I believe Lloyd's behavior would be classified as Obsessive Compulsive. He was forever compelled to wash his hands, run water in a sink, measure and record on paper the capacity of any container that held liquids. He hoarded every paper clip, rubber band, envelope, nail, nut and bolt that came his way. He rummaged through alley trash cans looking for the simplest things people would discard, squirreling them away in jars and cans, which he piled all the way to the ceiling in the tiny space of a former closet where he slept at the rear of the paint store. How my grandfather, and then my father, ever permitted an immediate family member to live like that bewilders me. The reason I was told, when inquiring early on about Lloyd's living conditions, was that he "wanted" to live there that way. So, I was led to believe also, Lloyd was a lost cause. I didn't know any better until years later, when I'd taken over management of our family paint business and began to deal with this awful abomination firsthand.

From the beginning of my experiences with my uncle, I assumed that my grandparents and father had done everything possible to help him. And they certainly believed they'd done just that. I learned that my grandmother Mary tried desperately to "save" Lloyd, taking him to doctors, one of whom arranged for him to spend time at an institution in Coatesville, PA, where he received extensive psychological treatment. She was repaid with a tirade of hostility from her vitriolic son who carried a boiling-hot resentment toward her for the rest of his life. Because my grandfather and father demonstrated little or no understanding of Lloyd's mental condition, my grandmother was forced to shoulder the brunt of his deep anger over being sent away to be cared for by doctors—whom he hated. He blamed her for being forced to stay in that mental hospital, far away from his family and his familiar life centered at 4th and Catharine Streets. When my grandmother died in 1957, Lloyd was left with only his father and brother to care for him. They continued to treat him as an embarrassment to our family, preferring to dismiss or hide him away. Even so, Lloyd's resentment stayed mostly directed toward my late grandmother for the rest of his life. Whenever her name came up, he managed to work the conversation into a well-rehearsed statement: "Your grandmother, she was buried six feet under the ground. Well, she should have been buried sixty feet under!" I remember vividly the pained look on his face whenever he said that.

That rage toward his mother later developed into a deeper resentment toward my father, which endured until Lloyd's own death. I don't recall his ever saying anything derogatory about my grandfather, however. Lloyd held Abraham Kahn in reverence, often relating a humorous anecdote or two about his old man's character and idealism. My grandfather amazingly managed to escape his second son's wrath, despite the substantial negative actions he took toward him with regard to the difficult social issues Lloyd was forced to confront. Those issues influenced Lloyd's life every day.

On weekends, Uncle Lloyd would stay at our suburban Philadelphia home in Penn Valley, where we'd moved from Overbrook Park in 1958. In the back of his red Ford Falcon station wagon, he'd cart paint boxes, stuffed with record albums, which he'd play for his nephews on a regular basis. He wanted us to know all about the bands, their singers, the leaders, the arrangers. It was the first time I'd ever heard the word "arrangers," those incredibly gifted musicians who wrote the individual musical parts for the band's players. I imagined it might be quite satisfying if someday I might be able to arrange music for a band or orchestra; about a dozen years later I brought great fervor to accomplishing this.

Uncle Lloyd had grown up mesmerized by the creative spirit these bands brought to their performances during the 1930s and 1940s. And he was intent on passing his interest in this music on to his nephews Walt, Andy and Billy. Walt was old enough to appreciate Lloyd's era but he was more interested in the new rock and roll music ferociously sweeping the nation. My younger brother Billy was not old enough to appreciate any of the stories that Uncle Lloyd foisted on us every weekend. I was, perhaps, just the right age to "hear" what was going on. I perceived that "drive" within the bands, as they swung in 4-4 time—the ever-present sizzle of the drummer's high-hat on each up-beat and the sheer excitement of the huge, screaming horn sections, all making this music electrifying to me.

I didn't get the essence of the lyrics in the songs while I was age five through ten, but I did sense a special spirit about them. It certainly seemed to me even at such a young age, presumably from some of the stories Uncle Lloyd told, that this music had played an important role in creating the national pride that helped get our country through the traumatic years of the severe economic depression leading up to World War II—and those energized years during that Great War itself. It's been suggested that the music of the big bands played a defining role in maintaining the morale of our soldiers entrenched in a war that took them far away from the safety of American soil. Nobody would have any problem convincing my uncle that this was so.

Despite the effects the war had on him, Uncle Lloyd always spoke with a tremendous amount of pride regarding his own service to the United States of America. The medals bestowed on him as a result of his actions were some of his proudest possessions. While his experiences left him permanently scarred, both physically and emotionally, that terrible war, those two medals earned while engaged in conflict and especially the intense camaraderie he had with his fellow servicemen ruled his conversations every single weekend.

Serving as the babysitter for his three nephews, Lloyd believed he was really "stationed" there on the weekends to entertain and teach us, through his stories and music, many endearing things I have never forgotten. He strongly influenced my development of an appreciation for the music of the big bands, swing and jazz. My uncle played the musical "Kiss Me Kate" incessantly, and that's how I was introduced to Cole Porter. Had I not heard Lloyd's worn-out vinyl recording of "The Pajama Game" at least a thousand times, how else would I have learned who Hernando or Lola was? I became familiar with timeless songs that would later hugely influence my musical career, setting the standard for my own endless appreciation of The Great American Songbook.

Uncle Lloyd helped set the musical bar very high for me. By the time I steered my way onto a path leading to a career in music, a foundation of American standard songs had already become integrated into my DNA. I owe a great deal to my Uncle Lloyd, a man accustomed to being sneered at and ridiculed throughout his life. He was different, that's for certain. But he introduced his nephews to "the greatest period in American popular music, an era producing the finest songs ever written," and that has always meant a lot to me. He guided my music appreciation at a very early age in ways that would benefit me greatly in the future as an artist who'd be performing many of the marvelous compositions played for me every weekend. From my Uncle Lloyd, I absorbed the songs that told the stories of our lives, songs that influenced not just me, but my fellow countrymen's lifestyles and attitudes.

FRANK, ELLA AND KENNY

Besides the musical influence of my Uncle Lloyd, I can't ignore the fact that I grew up in a house where both my parents were die-hard fans of Frank Sinatra and Ella Fitzgerald. They didn't own a ton of record albums, but most of what they did have had been recorded by these two prolific vocalists. On weekends, my father, not much of a singer, well-known for substituting nonexistent words for lyrics he couldn't remember, sang along with Frank, grabbing my beautiful mother and dancing her around the living room. If they entertained their friends, Frank and Ella were always the performers whom they "hired," distinctive voices coming from our record player in the den. I heard Sinatra swing his way through "Come Dance with Me" and "Baubles, Bangles and Beads" so many times, I memorized his every utterance in these songs. Often, I'd put his records on the turntable in my bedroom and sing along with Frank into a fake microphone. Sometimes, I must admit, I even became Ella!

I learned their phrasing and mimicked their styles, growing to appreciate the driving force coming from those swinging, fantastic bands always backing up these terrific singers. I learned that the arrangements helped make certain songs definitively a singer's own. Cole Porter's "I've Got You Under My Skin" has been recorded by an untold number of vocalists. But its signature version, arranged by Nelson Riddle, belongs to Frank Sinatra. Could Rodgers and Hart's "The Lady is a Tramp" ever really belong to anyone other than Mr. Sinatra? While Ella's version holds a close second, Frank really "owns" that song. And what would "How High the Moon" or George Gershwin's "Oh, Lady Be Good!" be without Ella's personal stamp on those classic compositions? These musical renditions filled my head. It wasn't long before I was overtaken by the same infectious spell that they'd cast over the rest of our country, albeit usually affecting much older people.

My father was totally sold on Frank. Though he showed no technical abilities when it came to operating any appliance, be it a television or a 1960s stereophonic sound system, my father—while driving his car— somehow managed to learn how to get Frank Sinatra to perform for him. First, it was cassette tapes he had to master. Then it was compact disks—the latter being much easier for him. Pop in a disk, wait a few seconds and Frank was right there in the car alongside him. Don't like that song too much, Dad? Push this button here and the device jumps instantly to the next song. What could be easier or more rewarding?

His rides home from the paint store to Penn Valley and trips to his condominium after the house was sold a few months following my mother's death in 2001 were mobile "concerts on wheels." Frank Sinatra was Dad's trusted companion. I know my father sang the whole way home, listening to the man he believed to be, without question, the best vocalist the world had ever known. And he wasn't wrong.

In late 2004, my father developed a serious blood disease. It wasn't leukemia, though we were told that it could eventually turn into that disease. But that was only if my father lived long enough, something his doctor told him was unlikely. Having contracted myelodysplasia, he asked the specialist how long he had to live. Her answer was vague, but not hopeful. He inquired, "A year?" Her answer: "Perhaps."

Meanwhile, his regimen of regular, outrageously expensive weekly injections would continue to ensure he was full of red blood cells, which this villainous disease did a great job of eliminating from his body. Still, he cheerfully went to his sessions at Pennsylvania Hospital, making friends with all the patients. I'd take him there, drop him off at the entrance, park the car and meet him at the office, usually filled with people awaiting their own blood transfusions. There he'd sit, so many times with me by his side, lots of other patients around him looking a whole lot worse than he did, in a huge, overstuffed chair, a needle attached to his arm. He often asked me, "How the Hell did this happen to me? What did I do to get this? How long will I be able to work?" I gave him the same answer I'd heard from a surgeon 15 years earlier, when my partner Bruce's mother asked her surgeon if she was going to die. Each time my father posed that one question to me, I'd answer: "I am not the Lord, Dad. Only he knows the outcome."

While he was undergoing this blood therapy for myelo-dysplasia, my father continued to drive himself to work four days a week. He kept his cherished Thursday Day-Off for himself. That was the weekday reserved for playing golf, tennis or working out at his swim club. For several decades he was part of a long-established foursome that played golf at his beloved Spring-Ford Country Club in Royersford, PA. My father and those other three men had the distinction of being the club's first four Jewish members. This was not the result of an existing discrimination policy restricting Jews from joining—something still being practiced then at other clubs—when they applied to Spring-Ford. These four golf buddies were merely the first Jews to seek membership at this remote country club, far away from the city, way out past Valley Forge. (One of the foursome, Carl Kahn, was my father's first cousin, the son of my great uncle Aaron Kahn.)

Spring-Ford boasted a terrific, award-winning golf course these guys loved to play. For years, the foursome was my father, Carl, Dick Weisz and Sy Katz. When Sy died, his cherished spot was inherited by another close friend, Jay Toll. And after Jay, it was Bernie Tissian. These men got to be well-known and liked by many other members at Spring-Ford. This marvelous golf club began attracting a diverse and well-heeled membership.

My father gave up his longtime membership around 2001, following my mother's sudden death. And by the time he contracted his fatal illness, he had stopped playing golf altogether. But Thursdays, he told me, were still going to be his day off. The paint store was closed on Saturdays and Sundays, so none of us worked on the weekends. I told my father that he could have every day off if he wanted. But that would not have been Kenny Kahn at all. He'd worked continuously at Southwark Paint since returning from overseas service in World War II. This is where he would deploy his professional talents until he was unable to work.

By the middle of January 2005, he began to look rundown and pale. He started calling periodically, saying he thought it best to skip that day. Days like those began occurring more frequently. The sense that my father was beginning a rapid descent took hold of me. I couldn't imagine what life without work was like for him. I also couldn't imagine what Southwark Paint would be like without his presence, his dynamic, his personality, his face. His image was stamped all over our company's long reputation for being "the place to buy paint in Philadelphia." The sadness I felt was more for him than for me. I tried to envision how helpless he felt, how he was dealing with knowing he was dying and that his ability to stay connected to his lifelong career in our family business was rapidly slipping from his grasp.

On February 1, after driving to the paint store, he could barely get himself out of the car and decided to return home. I was frightened he wouldn't be able to drive back, even with Frank Sinatra inspiring him along the way. He insisted he could make it. I'd learned long ago it was better to let this somewhat stubborn and always proud man do as he wished. He would do it his way, so I never interfered with whatever was his intent to pursue. I did insist that he call me when he got home—something he neglected to do. I phoned his condominium desk and asked if they'd check to see if he had arrived—and that he was all right. After knocking on his unlocked door, the doorman found him sitting listlessly, slumped back on a swivel chair in the living room, his coat and cap still on. He assured them he was okay and that he was just very tired. When they reported back to me, I sensed I'd better take that 15-minute drive from Southwark to check on him myself. I needed to be convinced that he'd be okay staying there alone, with no one to help him if he got into real trouble. I also knew that it would take a lot for him to call me, or anyone else, for help. Proud? You bet, he was.

My father had been seeing a woman during the five years after my mother died. Though he referred to her as his girlfriend, I never understood their odd relationship. Ironically, this was the same person my father had dated before marrying my mother. During my parents' 54-year marriage, they ran into her occasionally. My mother remarked to my father, more than a few times, that if something were ever to happen to her, he had her full blessing to "Go back to her."

There were many single, mature women available to this

suddenly-widowed, handsome man who was physically active and, if nothing else, was still able to walk. So my father followed my mother's advice. Return to his old flame, he did. A woman long since divorced, she lived alone in a comfortable condominium complex. The company my father kept with her was sporadic—and strictly on her terms regarding when they'd be together. This was something my father complained about many times to me, saying that he just didn't understand the distance she kept.

Once, he was sitting in his condo watching television, and she called him. She proceeded to describe a "juicy steak and delicious baked potato" she'd just cooked for herself, yet she did not invite him to join her. I hated when he related such trivial, yet hurt-filled stories about the way she treated him. I felt embarrassed for my father, and he was truly humiliated by her callous treatment. She insisted on maintaining her independent status with him. It was perfectly fine for my father to conveniently escort her to a social event or for them to go out for dinner together. But she insisted on maintaining a barrier with this lovely man who made himself completely available to her. Here was a great guy who'd remained faithful and devoted to his wife, a man who was still clearly a "catch."

I considered calling his girlfriend to have her check on him after he headed home from the paint store. But the reality of their quirky relationship changed my thinking. I figured she'd probably be cooking a nice chicken dinner for herself, with no intention of sharing it with my father. I expected she wouldn't come to his aid, as she never offered to assume any responsibility for him, especially following his worsening health issues. Then I realized she was still in Florida at her winter home. She didn't see him again until returning to Philadelphia in the spring. And so, on this fateful day, I needed to go to my father myself. I had to make sure he'd be okay staying home alone, following the report I'd just received from his building. This was a job for Andy Kahn.

When I got to his unit door it was still unlocked. I went right in, expecting to see him still on his chair in the living room. I called out for him but got no response. Nervously, I went toward his bedroom. With a trail of used tissues he'd dropped that led me right to him, I found him collapsed on the floor just outside his bathroom. He glanced up at me, clearly upset and frightened—a look I'd never seen before on this strong man's face. He asked me again, "How did this happen to me?"

I called the front desk in a panic. Instead of asking them to call an ambulance, I decided to do something more heroic. I would deliver him personally to the hospital with which his doctor was affiliated, which was back in the city. An ambulance would have taken him to a hospital closer to his building. Calling 911 was an option I decided against. I chose instead to somehow maneuver him into my car.

I enlisted the help of the doorman who'd checked on him earlier. He brought up a wheelchair. I was determined to get my father to Pennsylvania Hospital. The only thing I remember during the 20-minute ride was trying to keep him engaged in conversation and prevent him from passing out on me. Arriving at the Emergency Room loading area, we were refused entrance! The sign clearly stated that this portal was for ambulances only. Cars and Walk-Ins were not permitted to use that entrance. I couldn't fathom the idea that hospital staff would not open those doors. I pleaded with them on the intercom at the door. I was ordered to get the man slumped over in my car to the walk-in Emergency entrance around the corner. There was simply no way I could do this alone. I'd have to leave him there and get someone to help me.

A police officer walking down the street noticed I was in a predicament. He offered to help me by running around the corner. He retrieved a hospital wheelchair and assisted me in lifting my father's limp and seemingly dead-weight body out of the car's passenger seat and onto the wheelchair. Together, we wheeled my broken father into the Emergency Room entrance, which was about a block away from my car. The officer said he would stay with my father while I parked. I told him I didn't care about the car, which was sitting in a Tow-Away Zone. He grabbed me by both of my shoulders, looked squarely into my eyes and said "I'll watch your father. Get settled down. Stop freaking out. Go park your car! Then come back here, and we'll arrange to get your father seen right away."

It hit me right then. An angel had arrived on the scene to help me. One should never argue with an angel. So I followed the angel's instructions. When I got back to my father, I found a hospital attendant standing next to him, waiting for me to provide information to the admissions agent. No angel was in sight. I never got to thank him for saving the day. I realized that angels always have work to do elsewhere and, therefore, are in no position to wait around for gratitude or extraneous conversation. I followed the angel's advice, calming myself down in preparation for the upcoming events that would define my father's waning days on this planet.

He spent fifteen days in the hospital where he was tested, monitored and given a new regimen of medicines. About a week into his stay, I noticed he wasn't wearing his wedding ring, which had NEVER been off his finger since he married my mother—something he'd told me years back. While he was attempting to watch the Super Bowl on television, I asked about it. My father, wearing his 2004 Super Bowl hat from the previous year's Philadelphia Eagles/New England Patriots game he had attended, would likely have been in that stadium right now were he not ill and in the hospital. At one point, I demanded he take his eyes off the television and tell me why his wedding ring was not on his finger. A sheepish, embarrassed look came over his face, a visage I'd never seen before. After pressing him hard about the ring's location, he told me it was in the night table drawer in his condominium. Why, I asked, was it there? Had it gotten too tight because his fingers became fleshier in his later years? No, was his curt reply. Because he'd continued to wear it for the four years since my mother's death, I again prodded him to explain why he'd taken it off. Finally, he conceded that his girlfriend had asked him to remove it.

I sat there staring at him with nothing to say—something uncharacteristic for me. He stared back, also not speaking. Breaking the silence, I finally demanded to know the reason. He said that because they were not a married couple, she felt he should not be wearing his wedding ring when they were in public or when he was with her alone. The pregnant pauses in this conversation were unlike any I'd ever had with him—or that I'd experienced with anyone else, for that matter. Was it that she was embarrassed being with him? No, he said. She told him that by his wearing the ring, she felt it implied to other people that they were a married couple. This made her uncomfortable.

I then asked him if there was something wrong with people perceiving that the two of them could be married? Did she feel that appearing to be married to Kenny Kahn was a bad thing? He had no answer for me. I, on the other hand, had plenty for him. I was furious, and I told him so. I vehemently said that it was disgusting that she found it offensive, his honoring the 54-year marriage to my mother by wearing that ring. If he married her, then of course, he'd wear a new ring associated with their union. But in this case, her attitude toward his continuing to wear that wedding ring was truly a low blow to my darling father. I was in total shock that he had acquiesced to her demand. And this, coming from a woman who didn't have the decency to share her homemade dinners with him! Presenting my father with her opinions over wearing his wedding ring took a lot of nerve, overstepping what I considered to be any form of an acceptable boundary.

As I was getting all fired up, he also began to get angry. There was only one solution to this abomination, I told him. I left his hospital room, drove to his condo and retrieved the ring. I then drove right back to the hospital and wiggled it back onto his finger, where it belonged. He smiled broadly, and then he began to weep openly. We both did. I told him he never should have taken that ring off, especially for the unconscionable reason she gave him to do so. Only a marriage to his girlfriend would provide him with an alternative. He said he felt the same way and admitted he was embarrassed he'd ever agreed to take it off the finger on which it had been nestled safely for 54 years! My father never felt the same about her after that moment in his room in Pennsylvania Hospital. He reconciled his truest feelings about her with me, admitting he'd had a lapse in his judgment. He'd allowed this person to influence the memory of his marriage to my mother—a life-long relationship that he was extremely proud of and cherished deeply.

My father's doctor conferred with us often while he was in the hospital. After two weeks, she suggested that nothing more could be done there and that he needed to enter rehabilitation. On February 15, he was transferred to The Watermark of Logan Square, a well-respected facility near my home in downtown Philadelphia. There, he continued his decline despite the staff providing him the most excellent care imaginable. My older brother Walter, younger brother Billy and I concluded that there was nothing anyone could do to save our father. Not even Frank Sinatra could rescue him from his inevitable demise now. Together, we faced the new, extremely tough emotional hurdle of accepting this facility's recommendation to transfer his care to their resident hospice organization. His health had deteriorated to the degree that all the expensive blood transfusions and powerful medications were no longer accomplishing anything for him. There was little else they could do other than make his remaining time alive comfortable. His stay there amounted to five short weeks.

During the last few days of my father's life, he was surrounded by the voice of Frank Sinatra singing all of his favorite songs. I brought a CD boom box to his room, instructing the nurses to keep Sinatra's voice playing at all times during the day, even while my father was sleeping. His lips mouthed the lyrics, as he was clearly delighted to hear the music that had served as his own life's soundtrack. "A Foggy Day" was playing on March 18, 2005. I was singing along, standing at my father's bedside, just as I'd done for several weeks. A number of close friends and family had come to see him on what would be his last day of listening to Frank Sinatra. It became a large gathering of people, as if these close associates sensed that time was indeed about to run out. My father loved "A Foggy Day," perhaps more than any other song Mr. Sinatra ever recorded. He'd sing along with it, without fail, every time he heard it. He even knew ALL the words of this particular 1937 classic American standard. George Gershwin composed it with his brother Ira, close to the time of his own tragic, sudden death in 1938.

Sinatra started to deliver the lyrics through the speakers in the CD player positioned right beside my father's bed. At the phrase *"Then suddenly I saw you there, and in foggy London town, the sun was shining....everywhere"* I noticed my father was not breathing. I grabbed his hand and couldn't feel a pulse. About a dozen people whom he loved, and who loved him right back, were now surrounding his bed as I choked on the words, "My father is gone."

I ran from the room to find his nurse. She came, checked his vitals and confirmed to all of us gathered around him that Kenny Kahn had indeed just left us. And it all happened during the crooning of one of my father's absolutely favorite compositions by the "world's greatest male vocalist." It was a touching way for this wonderful and special man who happened to be my dad, to say goodbye to all of us here on Earth. He left our presence while taking a musical journey like no other he'd participated in before. I picked up his left hand, removed his gold wedding band and placed it onto my own finger—on a digit where it has remained since that moment when my father died.

I cannot listen to "A Foggy Day" or play it anymore without tears welling up in my eyes. I usually choke on some of the words—all in remembrance of my father's last moments. This marvelous song will always bring my father to mind. It was Frank Sinatra who took him personally by the hand, leading him off on a farewell trip by way of London Town, then on to his eternity. That famous city in the United Kingdom will always hold a unique distinction for me. I often wonder if my father might be in London Town right now. Maybe he was overwhelmingly inspired by Frank's singing wistfully and dreamily about the magic that exists there, on that final day, when he was standing in line and they called his number.

BROADWAY BOUND...
IN THE ROUND

I was introduced to musical theater at age nine. My mother took me to see "My Fair Lady." I came home from Philadelphia's Shubert Theater with a burning desire to learn all the words sung by the leading man. I began to practice speaking in a British accent. It was not a very good one. But I was pleased at my ability to create a brand new accent—in a style one might find somewhat reminiscent of the King's English. I fashioned myself playing the role of Professor Henry Higgins someday. I really got a kick out of portraying this character, first to my parents and then to family members who were all clearly amused. This delighted me even more. My mother, discovering her middle son possessed an artistic leaning quite different from both his older and younger brother, suggested we go see another play together. This time, though, she decided that we'd go to New York City—to see a Broadway show.

Professor Harold Hill in "The Music Man" on Broadway threw me right off the bridge. I immediately knew what I wanted to do with my life. I figured I ought to be able to sing and act. So, while perfecting my skills portraying the roles of two professors, the pivotal characters in each of the musicals I'd been exposed to, I decided to pull some additional tricks from up my sleeve—performing in another role before an audience. I was adept at performing magic tricks.

Through an acquaintance of my parents, I managed to land an engagement at Inglis House, a Philadelphia institution for incurable patients, not far from our home. Under the pseudonym "Marvello the Magician" and nattily dressed in sport jacket and tie, I performed a routine of stock magic tricks for an audience that ate it all up and applauded loudly after each trick. They made me feel like a true star. Of course, these unfortunate souls were really just thrilled to have any form of live entertainment.

Suddenly, one of them grabbed a prop of mine and smashed it on the floor. Being just nine years old, I became terribly upset. I started crying and ran off the stage. An understanding counselor there saw how disturbed I became and swung into action. He heaped a carton full of his own magic tricks on me. He declared he was a frustrated magician and wanted me to have these tricks for my developing magic act. Developing magic act? I'd never considered having to change it, but he insisted that magic shows get stale—really fast. The counselor said I'd have another opportunity to try out some new shtick on a familiar audience with the props he'd given me—despite the mishap with the patient unable to control his actions.

They asked me to come back to perform my magic act, and I happily agreed. When I came the next time, though, I'd ceased being Marvello the Magician. I had the new pseud-onym of Andy Stevens, believing that I was on the road to becoming a stand-up singer of Broadway show tunes. I sang over instrumental recordings of well-known tunes, doing my best to project myself as a lead star vocalist, fronting an or-chestra. The Inglis House residents were expecting a magic show. And they got one; just a different kind of magic this time.

These two appearances were my first experiences doing charity work—offering my talents for the benefit of others. My magic show and subsequent singing act heralded the start of an era—one that saw me performing benefits for lots of chari-table organizations in the years to come.

From these early experiences, I discovered an over-whelming satisfaction in lending my talents to others who were less fortunate. I was able to see past the wall, that vapid look in the eyes of the institutionalized patients. Within those eyes, I found love, warmth and understanding that shined beyond their otherwise listless facial expressions. I sensed that they could truly feel what I was feeling. Not yet in my teens, I felt compassion, and I knew I was supposed to share my talents with those who could never do what I could do. It made me swell with pride each time they applauded when I completed a magic trick successfully or sang a song with passion. They actually inspired me to perform for them. I feel that today, as I continue to offer my talents and creative abilities at venues where I bring some happiness to others less fortunate. It spills over into those audiences that are disadvantaged. Knowing that I'm having a positive effect on people who hear me perform, lecture or share my knowledge keeps me doing this time and again.

It's not so much to bolster my ego, which I'll admit happens. Any artist who claims otherwise is out of touch with their talent! Rather, the true purpose is to achieve satisfaction that comes when one shares their wealth with others—being the catalyst for that special give and take that occurs between a performing artist and an audience. They might be individuals who rely on wheelchairs and nurses to navigate down a hallway before returning to a lonely, small shared room. Or they might be well-heeled patrons of the arts who arrive in limousines and then go home to lifestyles abundant in opulence. It's the same, from one extreme to the other—and every type of audience falling in between. I've learned that as an artist, my objective is to bring joy to those who attend. And I make sure that this objective is always achieved, something I uncovered how to do while I was very young. Having been blessed with special and unique talents is something for which I am extraordinarily grateful.

My mother, recognizing how determined I was to become an actor, approached our synagogue about doing a production of "The Music Man" in their small auditorium. This 1961 event would sport an all-child cast; I would naturally play the lead—Professor Harold Hill. I had memorized every word and nuance of Robert Preston's immortalized characterization of this musical's leading con-man. I invited all my friends to join our production. In no time, a cast of players was assembled. My closest friend Fred Reinhart played River City's Mayor Shinn, and Dinah Brein, my real first girlfriend, played Marian the Librarian. Another pal from school named Paul Cooper played Professor Hill's sidekick Marcellus Washburn. (Paul was a budding bassist and guitarist with whom several years later I would form, along with Bruce Klauber, my first jazz trio.) A bunch of other neighborhood kids joined the cast in smaller roles as townspeople. My mother held weekly rehearsals in our home, teaching and coaching us on our parts.

Assuming the role of Director for this youthful production, my mother's own passion for the arts found its creative outlet in a bunch of enthusiastic kids. Before long we had put together our small-fry interpretation of Meredith Willson's legendary musical. A wanna-be actress for most of her life, my mother found particular delight in presenting her version of "The Music Man" at Beth David Reform Congregation in Wynnefield, PA. And its star, of course, was her son Andy. We performed the show twice to packed houses, the synagogue filled with our cast members' parents and relatives, all of whom kvelled proudly. If a seed had been planted early in my life, meant to develop into a burning desire to become a performer, "The Music Man" certainly was an event that nourished it well— stimulating its rapid growth ahead.

Regarded as a precocious nine-year-old, always ready to ham it up, my third-grade school teacher Mrs. Finkel selected me to participate in a program at Philadelphia's Temple University, where she was studying for her Master's degree. The university's "Psychology of the Gifted Child" program centered on its graduate students interviewing children selected from a list of candidates each student submitted. The "fortunate" child would engage in a deep discussion in front of the graduate students, placing him under a great deal of personal scrutiny. The child was expected to respond quickly to each question asked.

I remember having the group's moderator fire questions at me as I sat alone on a chair in front of about 20 graduate students. I was asked to define what it felt like performing in front of an audience. They wanted to know how I became so well-versed in the music of Frank Sinatra and Ella Fitzgerald. I acknowledged my parents and did so regarding many social associations they inquired about, for which I was expected to provide relevant answers. They wanted me to describe my interactions with family members and the other students I was friendly with in my third-grade class. What did it feel like being able to play the piano as well as I did at such a young age? Did I watch much television? What radio stations did I listen to? Who taught me how to fix electrical appliances and do wiring around the house? Why didn't I enjoy participating in athletics or want to attend ball games like my two brothers? What career would I pursue after finishing school? There were also questions involving math computations, comprehension, memory retention and vocabulary quizzes—all to which I apparently responded well.

My answers to these and what seemed to be hundreds of other questions during the sessions with the moderator and students seemed to entertain those listening intently. For me, it felt like just another event in which I was being given the opportunity to perform; the difference here was that I was sitting alone in a university classroom. But to me, I was merely acting in another show and, once again, I was its Leading Man. I was, ironically, aware that I was actually helping to educate others. This experience set an early precedent for my mentoring other creative people, which I pursued, albeit much later in life.

My mother, in attendance during these sessions at Temple, was clearly proud of me, as was my father. When he got home from work, he had to endure hearing every detail of each day I spent at the university, first from my mother and then all over again from me. I knew I had to wrap it up when he started rolling his eyes skyward. But, I did that in much the same way I handle that task today. I may very well announce that I'm finishing something. But the actual, real conclusion can be minutes—or hours!—away.

My parents demonstrated early on that their three children would be raised in a manner that offered extreme permissiveness and tolerance. My father primarily deferred to my mother regarding decisions about family activities, not unlike fathers of many other young families during the Baby-Boom years following World War II. My father exercised total administrative control during the hours he put in at our family's well-established paint business. But it was this extraordinary freedom of expression at home, along with my parents' infinite encouragement bestowed on all three sons, that allowed my brothers and me to blossom so creatively early on. There simply were no barriers, no walls, never an instance when our artistic and social expressions were frowned upon. This was not the case with more traditional parenting, something I learned when comparing how our household operated with that of my friends. My parents elected to get out of our way, removing any and all obstructions.

There was also full, open freedom regarding all forms of speech in the Kahn household. This carte blanche attitude was employed by both my parents, non-stop, from early childhood through our adolescence. As a result, our house was a favorite place for our friends to congregate. I've heard many stories over the years, regarding how my father's home above the paint store, and even the store itself, had become a favorite gathering place for all the kids in his neighborhood during the 1920s and 1930s. Huge groups of neighborhood children would gather there after school. These concentrations of people arriving at one place became known as "The Gatherings." The paint store served as a hub of social activity for many of the youngsters in a severely congested area of South Philadelphia, populated by merchants intent on raising families there, right above their shops, which were the families' source of income. My mother, who grew up around the corner from the paint store, knew this local social aspect well. Her older brother Howard was my father's closest friend; they were inseparable until they both got married. This laissez-faire tradition carried over into my parents' home, providing an open stage on which their sons could perform. My parents were just so cool about this—all of the time. And we three boys knew we were being raised in a special environment, one that encouraged the development of our individual talents and abilities.

One year later in 1963, Evy Katz, a family friend, heard of auditions being held for summer-stock shows at Philadelphia's Playhouse in the Park. Her friend Shirley Goldberg was involved in kicking off a summer stock repertoire of shows there. The venue was one of several, popular tent-covered theaters-in-the-round that dotted the American landscape back then. "Audition" was all I needed to hear. I demanded an opportunity to try out for an acting part. My mother did not hesitate in enabling me to do this. I sensed she felt it would also provide a chance for her to vicariously experience some new acting challenges of her own—played out through me. A few days after my audition, the phone call came with news that I'd been selected to play parts in two shows that summer. This good fortune propelled me into a frenzy of joyous outbursts, spinning on the floor like Curly of The Three Stooges, laughing and screaming at the top of my lungs. I was about to experience my professional, on-stage acting debut! My maternal grand-mother Anne Weiss was visiting us from Mexico, where she lived at the time. Hearing all the commotion, she came run-ning into the living room thinking something was very wrong. In fact, something was very right.

This was the equivalent of hitting the Power Ball Lottery. I could not have been more excited, more ecstatic over the fact that I'd been chosen over a multitude of other youngsters who also auditioned for these parts. This could have sparked a bit of egocentric behavior, but my parents, BOTH of them, were quick to point out the fallout that comes from boasting. They taught me what it meant to be humble—and to be grateful that I'd been given a fabulous opportunity that many kids only dreamed about. I was going to be a real actor now—a profes-sional actor. This was pretty heady stuff for a ten-year-old kid.

My parts in two summer stock musicals geared to young audiences led to appearances on local television with other cast members. I was one of two child actors in our compa-ny. We were interviewed and asked to perform segments from our shows on Philadelphia's own "Gene London Show," aka "Cartoon Corners General Store." Gene was a terrific, multital-ented local personality who had created and hosted this dai-ly children's show that interspersed cartoons with live sketch performances from its regular cast—and visiting guest artists. This was still in the early years of television. Many times, our aired performances were live rather than from tapes recorded in advance. A local celebrity was in the making, I believed. And, you might well imagine how determined I was that it was going to be me.

Before the plethora of late-night television programs be-gan commanding the attention of night-owls, people "in the news" appeared on live TV programs broadcast in the early evening. In the early 1960s, late-night radio provided great op-portunities for celebrities to promote their new shows. It was a great way for authors to talk up books they'd written—and for local politicians to weigh in on current issues.

In Philadelphia, one such radio program scheduled during the bewitching hours on either side of midnight was "The Red

Benson Show." It was staged inside a Sun-Ray Drug store's coffee shop on the first floor of the stunning Art Déco-clad WPEN radio studio building on Walnut Street. Each evening, Red Benson, former host of the popular radio show "Name That Tune," interviewed local and well-known celebrities in front of a live audience. Benson's executive producer was Ted Reinhart, father of my absolutely best friend Fred, who lived just a few houses up the hill from us. (Fred Reinhart and I became real Blood Brothers back in a time when it was safe to do things like smear our blood together! Our friendship continues today; it has spanned 60 years.) The Reinharts quickly became my "adopted" parents. I was a frequent guest in their home, especially when I found myself needing a break from my family, which as I recall, was just about every day.

I visited Red Benson's show several times. I'd serve as my mother's midnight "date" while my father was sound asleep at home. Fred's mother Phyllis thought I'd make an interesting guest on the show, since I'd achieved local celebrity status as a child actor. I jumped at the chance to be interviewed on this program that normally had adults as the guests. As it turned out, the host was ill the night I was scheduled. Another well-known Philadelphia personality, politician Thacher Longstreth, filled in for Red. My parents were in the audience eating cheeseburgers, French fries and coffee milk shakes. Thatcher grilled me on how it felt to become a local celebrity at such a young age.

Red Benson's was one of the first radio shows to employ live audience interaction by telephone, and my appearance that night stimulated many listeners to call in. Some questions were from parents who believed their children had talent and wanted to know how to get their kids "into the business." I'm sure I had lots of interesting answers for them. Oh, how wish I had a recording of that show! I felt like such a big celebrity, being interviewed and queried by people of all backgrounds, wanting to hear what this precocious child had to say about life in the theater.

These certainly were heady days for me. My parents both reminded me constantly about never letting artistic success go to my head or boast too much around school. My friends, though, became my best Press Agents. I tried to keep my enthusiasm in check. This was easier said than done. I was an outspoken, talented boy who'd set his sights on much bigger and better things. My mother placed a silver-framed photo of me wearing a costume from one of my shows at Playhouse in the Park on the piano. It was taken the day before my 11th birthday, outside the theater. The frame was engraved: My Son, The Actor. That was the summer of 1963, when a number of comedians released comedy records targeted at the whole family. Alan Sherman's "My Son, The Folksinger" provided the inspiration for the words engraved on the picture frame, which still sits among my most treasured mementos in my Atlantic City home.

Dealing with adult actors who had many years of theater life under their belts provided me with experiences most children my age would never know. Drugs like hashish were openly shared around. I admit to having gotten high with the cast, some of whom were very much against allowing a young boy like me to partake. But several other cast members actually encouraged me to experience all that life has to offer. Hadn't that been my mother's philosophy, after all? She earnestly believed and often stated that she considered herself another version of Mame Dennis. Patrick Dennis' novel characterized his Auntie Mame as questing to "open a new window" or door, if for no other reason, than to just find out what wonders might await on the other side. I saw the sense and wisdom in such an attitude, and I knew my mother was right there with me. So I had no problem trying a substance I'd seen others around me inhale each day with total abandon. I had been warned by some cast members that smoking hashish was illegal, but it somehow didn't seem relevant in this situation.

Among my fellow cast members, I also witnessed high levels of ambition alongside frequent backstabbing. I encountered situations in which deep love and intense dislike existed side by side between the members of our acting companies. Open homosexuality was always on display, as was a lot of unabashed heterosexuality. I came to understand that this was just "life in the theater."

When I got home, I recounted my experiences to a mother who absorbed every last detail with wonder and glee. My father would listen for as long as he could before falling asleep on the couch in front of me.

It's no wonder that my mother and I would often escape at midnight to WPEN's coffee shop/radio studio and delight ourselves for a few hours, while satisfying other cravings by consuming cheeseburgers and milkshakes. I'm sure Phyllis Reinhart found it plenty odd whenever my mother would arrive, escorted by her young son, her own son Fred's best friend! We'd head back home around 2 am. Belmont Hills Elementary School expected me to show up six hours hence. Most of the time, I made it. Oh, how I loved the nightlife. I ate up every minute of it.

Following my summer shows, I got a small part in the drama "Galileo" by Bertolt Brecht. My fellow cast members were part of a new repertory acting company formed for a new venue called "Theatre of the Living Arts." The company's artistic director Samuel Rulon had produced the shows I performed in at Playhouse in the Park. This outstanding Brecht play was directed by Andre Gregory, who later would be both the star and center of discussion in an unusual movie about life in the acting world, "My Dinner with Andre." In our production of "Galileo," the title role of the astronomer/scientist was played by world-class actor David Hurst, well-known for his many dynamic portrayals in theatre, film and on television.

This was my first dramatic role as an actor. What made playing the part of Prince Cosmo di Medici so significant to my family, however, was the location of this new theatre. It was in an old stage and movie house that had been boarded up for decades—located just east of South Fourth Street on South Street. It was a totally renovated "new" performance space located only two blocks from our family business. Uncle Lloyd and my father had both frequented this theatre as teens. Even my grandfather seemed genuinely amazed that I'd be acting onstage at a theatre he knew well from his nearly 50 years on 4th Street. Another family coincidence? I doubt it. Our ties to this neighborhood had now reached into the next generation.

I gained enormous insights about life—and the characters who inhabit its various stages—at Theatre of the Living Arts.

And I learned a lot about my craft from the gifted actors who had been cast with me. Of course, I took most of my cues from the soon-to-be world-famous director Andre Gregory. Perhaps the most fun thing, though, was the name of the new company. It certainly seemed apropos that I would be a charter cast member of The Southwark Company—Philadelphia's newest repertory acting community. My father was particularly pleased by their moniker, since Southwark Paint Company was the name of our family business. As an actor with The Southwark Repertory Company, he figured I would feel at home. This time, however, the paint involved was of the grease variety.

I grew up really fast over the next few years—in the free, artistic environment at home and from hanging around Theatre People. I'd always found it easy to associate with people older than I was. Probably because of the many unusual experiences I had at a young age, I came across as being mature. In retrospect, I wouldn't change a thing that happened growing up. I believe my character predisposed me toward getting exactly the type of exposure and creative enlightenment I received. A precocious kid I was, that's for certain. Still, I am deeply grateful for all those associations I made with people who seemed to be comfortable with me exactly the way I was. They allowed me into their circles, much more than people who considered my world unrealistic or thought me pretentious. Whatever my world was, I was in it for keeps.

I've mellowed as I've aged. But the underlying feelings that go with being an artist, a musical performer, an actor, a lecturer—why, even a magician!—remain. I love to be the center of attention. But along with that comes a serious sense of responsibility. Talent, more often than not, exacts a tremendously heavy price. It can be a burden to those who don't know how to handle it. Examine the careers of legions of musicians, actors, sculptors, painters, and teachers who couldn't control themselves. Many took up inebriates to get themselves through the torture that the uncontrollable creativity in their brains doled out. Charlie Parker, arguably the greatest Jazz Tenor Saxophonist who ever lived, did anything but live. Though he died at the young age of 34, the coroner believed he was examining a 60-year-old man. Parker ravaged himself with drugs and alcohol. He felt it was the only way he could tame the creative demons that wouldn't stop screaming at him. No one played like him. No one ever will again. They will imitate him. But they likely won't ever reach the mantle of his creative genius. I'm glad I'm not a genius. Being a talented performer and esteemed teacher is more than satisfactory for me. I'd just like to be doing what I'm doing now for another 50 years. Is it possible, at age 66 to conjure such a notion? It remains to be seen just whether such an achievement is attainable.

THE PROFESSIONAL

During my early acting career, I started a business in our neighborhood. I was stimulated by my interest in all things mechanical and electrical. It all began with my grandfather's youngest brother Isadore Kahn. No one in my immediate family demonstrated any real ability for fixing things except me. Taking our washing machine apart, removing all the parts from the inside of a television and then reassembling these devices into working order again held an incessant fascination for me. There were many occasions when my father asked my mother why I felt compelled to take apart every appliance in the house. This was quickly followed by his inquiring about my ability to put them back together again. My mother's answers were that I was simply demonstrating my nature at being extraordinarily curious. Hoping to assuage his fears, she then assured him that my track record for reassembly was excellent.

Uncle Isadore was a particularly handy and clever man. All the Kahn families called on him when mechanical services were required in their houses. Often it was something as simple as replacing a light bulb in a ceiling fixture. Other times, a leaky faucet, a slow-running drain or an always-running toilet would be more than enough reason to send a distress signal in his direction.

This darling, exuberant man, my great uncle, noticed my interest in his talents when he came to our house to repair or install something (that had not been entrusted to me). His thick, black moustache would twitch up and down under his nose as he surveyed a technical problem requiring his expertise. His forehead, just below a shock of black hair combed straight back, would wrinkle and then relax; it resembled waves of a tide ebbing and flowing. I loved that Uncle Isadore was especially interested in my fascination with things mechanical and electrical.

Electronic devices were not his forte because he had grown up in an era right before such wireless wonders gained widespread use. So when I asked him about the purpose of a cluster of vacuum tubes in a television set or the inner workings of the station-selector components inside a radio, he would smile and give me his best on-the-spot explanation of how these parts functioned. I knew he didn't really know what he was talking about, but his joyful and buoyant personality, which long ago had won over every single member of our very large family, captivated me.

Uncle Isadore would sing and hum tunes while manipulating his tools—mostly folksongs from his Russian homeland. Then, he'd do his best to make it through some of the songs he'd heard in his adopted country of America. More important was that he taught me the basics of how to solder broken wires together and how to install lighting fixtures. My aptitude for this clearly came from the Kahn side of my family, albeit at least one generation removed.

My grandfather Abraham Kahn was one of seven brothers, Isadore being the youngest and therefore, destined to be the darling of his family. Another brother Nathan was a plumber by trade. So there was a thread of ingenuity and technical aptitude running selectively through the Kahns—who'd all come to America from their native Russia during the second decade of the twentieth century. Isadore was the one who received the utmost talents of that thread. I suspect they found their way to me in a fashion similar to the way they came to him.

I decided there had to be a need for electrical repairs in our neighborhood. And so I founded Roz-Core Electrical Services, named for the type of solder, rosin core, universally applied to secure electrical connections. I had business cards printed, which I circulated around our neighborhood, announcing my new business venture and targeting local residents. Before long, I was wiring speakers and installing hi-fi stereo systems in people's homes, fixing their lamps and repairing their vacuum cleaners. The homeowners were amazed at my abilities, but even more so at my chutzpah, without which I could never have pulled any of this off. I was eight at the time. One of my earliest clients was a young Philadelphia entertainment attorney Lloyd Remick, who hired me to hang strings of electrified party lanterns in his backyard, a little stretch up our street. There was no way of knowing then that he would become the lifelong legal representative for one of my future singing stars

Karen Young. And I didn't discover it until I was involved in the record business more than a decade and a half later.

I received a call from a young couple who had recently moved to Philadelphia from Israel. Could I hang a chandelier? "Of course," was my immediate response. The following day I arrived to complete the task. Enlisting the help of their amazed Jamaican housekeeper, I set about the task of installing a gigantic crystal chandelier in their dining room. When I arrived, the housekeeper was shocked to see who was standing at the door. Looking down at me, she was reluctant to let me in. I told her I was qualified to do the work and that she had no need to worry. Then I saw the magnitude of the task at hand. Oops.

My first instinct was to walk away from this one. Instead, I envisioned myself as Lucy Ricardo in the television series "I Love Lucy" in which nothing was beyond her capabilities, even though she knew up front she was in way over her head. And over my head (literally!) was I. Contemplating just how I would ever get this heavy and bulky lighting fixture wired into the small electrical box above their huge glass dining room table had me worried. I admit I could never have gotten it installed without the help of the housekeeper, who kept poking her head into the room, watching me warily from the kitchen the whole time I sat fiddling with the components on the floor. I asked if she would come in and help me by supporting the fixture from the bottom when I lifted it into place. First she helped me move the glass-top table to the side of the room, which, for a nine-year old boy, would have been a difficult task itself. Then she assisted me by carefully supporting the chandelier at its bottom section while I lifted it toward the ceiling — all the while standing on a rickety kitchen stepladder of theirs. I attempted, unsuccessfully several times, to get it threaded onto the metal post sticking out of the box above my head — a nefarious component that seemed to look down and dare me. When the threads finally took told, I became convinced I could tell this nervous, brave woman she could release her grasp on the chandelier. I told her to let go, but she was panicked, clearly afraid to take her hands away. She asked me over and over if I was sure about this. I assured her it was safe to move away and, with much trepidation, she cautiously let go, literally, one finger at a time. I still can hear her emitting a huge laugh, which was more a cry of relief, when that huge lighting fixture remained up there, attached to the ceiling and didn't come crashing down on top of this little boy who had insisted she could release her hold on it.

I then easily wired it into the ceiling electrical box, employing the Isadore Kahn method of insulating the leads with electrical tape in order to prevent any chance of the wires sparking a fire. After twisting the wire nuts to safely secure the connections, I placed the metal dome cover over the box, threaded it onto the shaft and the installation was complete.

If the homeowners had been there when I showed up to do this job, I suspect they never would have allowed a seemingly fearless kid to attempt the installation. They had received my business card in their mailbox and figured this local company could handle installing their antique chandelier, shipped from their previous home in Israel. All the arrangements were made over the telephone with their believing they were dealing with an established business staffed by adults. When these customers returned home, they were informed that a young boy, not an adult, had come to put up the fixture and was given the $15 they left to pay the installer. The husband called and asked to speak to me directly and then demanded to meet with me personally. Obliging him, I nervously walked to the bottom of our street and up the driveway to their front door. They were astonished to meet a young Jewish boy who installed a behemoth of a delicate chandelier. They were obviously impressed because they gave me a $5 tip for doing such a great job. This couple passed my name around to their family members in the area, some of whom periodically hired me to do repair and installation work in their homes. I learned early on that referrals are always the best advertisement a business could ever hope to get.

In addition to my interest in mechanical and electrical things, I developed a wild fascination toward the science of reporting and predicting the weather. Fred Reinhart, my trusted collaborator, and I convinced our parents to enroll us in a weekly Meteorology program at the Franklin Institute Science Museum. Dr. Francis Davis, a local TV news personality, not only reported the weather on Philadelphia's Channel 6 (the local ABC affiliate) but also conducted classes on Meteorology at the museum's impressive weather display installed there. Driven there by one of our mothers each week, Fred and I became well-versed in the science of weather prediction; we were often praised by the museum staff because we were only 11 and most of the other kids were older. Every other Saturday, Phyllis Reinhart dropped us off at the huge front steps of the Franklin Institute. On alternate Saturdays, without fail, my mother delivered us to those steps, always at least a half-hour late. True to her tardiness for any appointment anywhere, Fred and I waited, usually an hour or more for her to pick us up after class. My mother was infamous for her lateness. Phyllis Reinhart knew this and made sure that she was always available. I remember calling Fred's mother from the museum's payphone several times, requesting that she come and rescue us when it seemed we'd been completely abandoned by my mother. Sometimes, we actually had been.

I vowed I would never be late like my mother was, and I often expressed my chagrin about it to her vehemently. While I always intend to be on time now, I'm often distracted; scheduling myself too tightly tends to get me into trouble. I always run right down to the minute—or even a minute or two late—and even more sometimes. I'm certain I inherited this undignified behavior from my mother.

Meanwhile, my interest in meteorology grew immensely. I implored my parents to purchase some official United States Weather Service equipment. In what became my 5th grade, award-winning science project, I drew up detailed plans for the construction of a weather research lab in our backyard. Because I wanted to use the same type of professional equipment I became familiar with on the roof of the Franklin Institute, museum officials offered to help me directly contact a U.S. government agency in Washington, D.C. That office referred me to a distributor that manufactured and sold the same certified, professional weather-reporting equipment used in official outposts all across America. These locations were responsible for gathering critical weather data, which they in turn phoned in to the National Weather Bureau each day. Believing that

47

weather reporting on television might actually become my profession someday, my parents agreed to purchase a regulation U.S. Weather Service louvered-box called a Stephenson Screen. It stood 7-feet high and was mounted on wooden legs buried deep in the ground. A locking front panel door that was lowered on hinges at the bottom permitted access to the fragile equipment inside. Although the measuring devices remain protected from the sun and rain, air flows freely through the four louvered sides. This allows the instruments to react to changes in weather conditions. Four weeks after it was ordered, a huge motor-freight transport delivered the Stephenson Screen containment box to our house, where it was erected, facing north as required, shielding it from direct sunlight.

I was overcome with glee at having this strange-looking contraption in our backyard. Our neighbors on either side were bewildered by the sight of it. But by this time, they were accustomed to the odd and unusual happenings that occurred frequently at the Kahn home. I suppose they reconciled themselves to this new event being just another minor deviation from normalcy on our property. I admit it struck an imposing figure in the backyard, next to the rose bush garden my mother planted when we moved to this house a few years earlier. I ordered several thermometers, a psychrometer to measure relative humidity and a barometer to measure atmospheric pressure—available from another government-sanctioned manufacturer. These were all kept locked inside the Stephenson Screen.

I checked the weather instruments daily, carefully recording my measurements for my science project. I figured I'd be the envy of everyone I knew. I didn't realize that no one, except Fred Reinhart, understood what I was doing or the purpose of this outlandish, wooden structure. Just the same, I reported the weather dutifully to my class every day at school. And I took home First Prize for the science project! More important than winning, however, were the insights this project gave me into the world of meteorology.

Of course this was long before there were any computer models for predicting the weather. Consequently, in the 1960s, there was no such thing as predicting weather *accurately*. Today, we're still not able to do so reliably—even *with* all the new computer models and highly sophisticated apparatus. But that's a whole other discussion. Suffice it to say that with all my equipment and serious studying of the conditions that affected the weather, it sure looked like I knew what I was doing!

My friends and family remain astonished today at my knowledge of atmospheric conditions and cloud formations— what they mean and how they occur. My fascination with the weather and obsession with the cosmos—especially our nearest companion in the solar system—The Moon—remains very much intact. It influences me constantly and has even spilled over into my musical performances. Moon songs make me swoon—just as that stunning, round object orbiting our planet does.

During this time period, my brother Walter offered me the chance to become the young host of an audio program on an unlicensed—read that as "pirate"—AM radio station we set up at home. Walter and I built an AM radio transmitter from a kit ordered from Allied Electronics—a mail-order electronics dealer that was all the rage back then. Allied seemed to have its pulse on the changing world of electronics and the advent of that newest marvel—the Transistor. This tiny entity, which handily replaced electronic vacuum tubes, eventually evolved into the integrated circuit—the forerunner of the silicon chips installed in computers and just about every other piece of electronic gear in today's world.

By this point, I had assumed the professional name of Andy Stevens for everything. My radio program's format in-cluded show tunes and popular songs. Our broadcasts cov-ered a one-mile radius, sometimes more if the weather was clear. I must say that this was quite a thrill for a couple of am-bitious kids.

Someone informed us that there was a rival amateur ra-dio station about two miles away in Bala-Cynwyd. I was dis-patched by Walter to find out who was behind it and what this other local radio station was all about. A quick trip on my bicycle led me to a skeptical but interesting 9-year-old boy, Bruce Klauber—one of their station's three young "operators."

Discovering that the other participants who'd begun this broadcasting entity were also my age, I found it natural for me to join forces with Bruce Klauber and his "partners" Peter Green and Richard Cohen. They had managed to set up their radio studio in the display window of the Cynwyd Pharmacy, located on the corner of Bala and Montgomery Avenues. The space was given courtesy of the pharmacist Asher Kauffman, who saw this as a great advertising gimmick for his business—and an opportunity to help some neighborhood boys realize their dream to start a local radio station. I threw my experience from setting up the radio station in Penn Valley into the mix.

I immediately realized the potential this new station afforded because we had an opportunity to broadcast over loudspeakers we hoped to use, already installed up and down the two commercial blocks that lined Bala Avenue. When we said we would be mentioning businesses "on the air" at minimal cost to them, it didn't take long to sign up paying advertisers. At our price of One Dollar for an ad that would run a full minute, how could these shopkeepers lose? Such enterprising boys we were!

Convincing all these shopkeepers to allow me to climb onto their roofs in order to string up the wires necessary to carry our broadcasts over loudspeakers was another story. We promoted ourselves as knowing what we were doing, even though we had not yet reached ten years of age. More than a few people on the street were skeptical. Eventually, having gotten the majority of owners to give us the go-ahead, the rest fell in line—but not without their warning us that they simply didn't want to learn that one of us fell off their roof and onto the street below. My "partners" learned that I'd strung wires all over the roof of our house in Penn Valley. I'd told them that Halloween Trick-or-Treaters who came to 1220 Green Tree Lane were treated to a cacophony of spooky sounds from a tape recorder I had wired to several speakers on the roof of my house. This offered my new friends evidence of my fearlessness. I was elected to do all the overhead wiring.

The Bala-Cynwyd radio station project became local folklore. We were written up in area newspapers. We became instant local celebrities. What an amazing time it was! I looked forward to Saturdays, when we ran our radio station at the pharmacy all day. Situated in its corner display window, broadcasting in clear view of the cars and pedestrians who traveled up and down Bala Avenue, we thought we were stars.

Not long afterward, all of our radio stations had to be abandoned, however. We'd been discovered broadcasting "on the air" without permission or legal authority to use the public airwaves. The FCC doesn't look favorably on unlicensed broadcasting operations. One day, unannounced, they came around to my home to investigate. This would not be the first time my parents would find the limits of legality pushed in the field of electronic communication. The FCC "suggested" we cease using the public airwaves illegally, as these remained under strict control through licensing and were not available for our purposes. My parents took this in stride because they firmly believed that every life experience, no matter what it might be or how it ended up, was a good one. Their attitude toward our run-in with the Federal government was another example of how they nurtured us in the most lenient way, anticipating that we could always benefit or learn something from first-hand experience. They let us do just about anything—no holds barred! My friends often reminded me how "cool" my parents were about everything, allowing us to venture into escapades that their parents would have criticized, or worse, punished them for making the attempt.

One thing my parents did insist on, though, was that we save our money for personal things we wanted to acquire. The modest allowance given weekly to my brothers and me would never have been enough to acquire all the electronic apparatus I fancied owning. By the time I'd saved enough allowance money to purchase some piece of audio or electronic equipment I wanted, it would be out of fashion or obsolete, I cleverly complained. So my father offered me an opportunity to work at Southwark Paint on Saturdays in exchange for a "decent" wage. (The paint store was open on Saturdays until I took over—years later.)

Customers entered Southwark Paint through an old wooden door on the corner of 4th & Catharine Streets. It was outlined by classic, step-down wood framing. Eventually, when it rotted away rendering it useless, it was replaced with a modern aluminum and glass door. On the day the door was swapped out, customers began howling that they wanted the old door back! It was part of the charm of Southwark, they complained. "Next, you'll be adding computers in here!" which, of course, was prophetic—and inevitable. Just past the front door, an angled sweeping counter greeted everyone. It butted up against an adjacent counter, creating a slanted pathway that ran almost to the rear wall. Behind the counters were custom metal and wood shelves built by my grandfather and his brothers in 1920. The shelves were always stocked with gallons and quarts of paint. Sitting on the original wood-plank floor, it was not unusual to see parallel rows of five-gallon pails of paint stacked five-high. This created alleyways around which customers had to navigate when searching for their assorted paint accessories and sundries. To the left of the front door were two huge paint chip racks, loaded with samples. The thousands of colors Southwark sold were inserted into each rack.

We had an old National Cash Register—the kind with a crank you had to turn to complete an entry, complete with a bell that rang when the cash drawer opened! That register's largest denomination was $20. So if a sale was for $78.50, you had to manually press the $20 key three times, then the $10 key, and then the smaller denomination keys equal to the total cost of the sale! In 1984, we procured Southwark's first electronic cash register—considered by my Uncle Lloyd and my father to be a miracle—and also a pain in the ass for them to figure out. Next to the cash register was my grandfather's wood, antique roll-top desk. He once told me that the top never worked from the day he bought it! Screwed right into the side of the desk was an old-style black telephone, its rotary dial perched atop a small rectangular body. I remember my grandfather answering that phone, telling callers to "Hold the vire!" as he went to check the availability of an item or find my father to answer a question.

The huge plate glass windows that framed the corner of 4th & Catharine Streets were never decorated with displays or samples. Occasionally, signs were put in them, in hopes of attracting customers during a sale. These cavernous spaces were mainly used for storage of paint and supplies and housing the remains of hundreds of dead flies. After I took over the business, that changed Big Time.

The small office in the rear of the store was mainly closed off from view because of all of the cartons of paint and five-gallon pails stacked nearly to the ceiling. Strips of 8-foot-long fluorescent light fixtures with exposed bulbs lined the ceilings. They buzzed incessantly, adding to the old-world charm of the place. The hanging pendant glass fixtures that were there when my grandfather took over the two corner properties (which had once been a saloon) had long since vanished.

Merkin Paint Company of New York was one of the first paint lines my grandfather took in as a new independent paint dealer. Merkin was an innovator in the paint and coatings industry, among the first to offer an expanded line of bold colors mixed by an in-house tinting machine. My father took me to meet Michael Merkin in NYC when I was about eight years old. I hadn't been to New York before and had never seen a glamorous office perched way up in a high-rise building. During that impressionable visit to Merkin's corporate offices, I remember thinking I wanted to become successful so I could work in such an office, running my business empire.

When Merkin Paint Company was acquired by Baltimore Paint Company in 1962, Southwark's dedication to remain an independent paint dealer continued. The company began selling Baltimore Paint products exclusively, as it had done with the Merkin paint line. Baltimore Paint then purchased the world-famous line of Dutch Boy Paints. This led to the addition of the Dutch Boy paint line at Southwark. Having that well-recognized logo adorn the side of the building in the form of a large lighted sign gave Southwark unprecedented visibility. In 1980, a few years before I took control of Southwark Paint, Sherwin-Williams acquired Baltimore Paint. Sherwin's sights were set on integrating the hugely popular Dutch Boy line under their massive umbrella of paint coatings.

This precipitated Southwark having to face a major business decision. Sherwin-Williams began allowing Dutch Boy into emerging Big Box stores, something they promised would not happen when they acquired the line. We decided to abandon our almost 70-year history with a paint manufacturer's lineage dating back to the 1920s with Merkin Paint. We selected Bruning Paint Company, another Baltimore manufacture of architectural coatings. At the time we offered this new paint line for sale at Southwark, Bruning was virtually unknown in the Philadelphia area. Many longtime customers were skeptical about Bruning's products, which were all excellent in quality. Through our expertise, along with our well-honed and well-known customer service, we successfully changed their minds in short order.

When Bruning was later acquired by Insl-X Paint Company, we once again faced the daunting task of changing our main paint product line. Pratt & Lambert Paints, long-committed to independent paint retailers in America, became the next paint products sold at Southwark. This changed the entire look of the store again, as all of the various new labels took up positions on the dozens of shelves lining the store. Then, in 1995, Sherwin-Williams purchased Pratt & Lambert, claiming that it would keep that paint line autonomous from their other brands and that they would remain committed to serving the independents. Nice try. Pratt & Lambert Paint can now be found for sale in all Ace Hardware stores. Ah, the independent retailers in America....Where have you gone?

As a kid, I hated working at the paint store. It was dirty and lacked any kind of glamour. Selling paint to the rough-talking contractors who came in was not my speed at all. My paternal grandfather Abraham Kahn was still alive then. We'd pick him up at his apartment; he lived less than 10 minutes from our home in Penn Valley. He'd hang around the store and glare at everyone with a permanent frown plastered right where his mouth was located. If I went up to someone at the counter who had even the slightest appeal to me, my grandfather would stand over me with his arms folded (he was nearly 6 feet tall—the only member of our family to attain such stature). My grandfather would first stare at me, then the customer—the corners of his mouth always facing south. I thought I would just die every time, which occurred every Saturday that I chose to work at the paint store.

To alleviate this pain, I decided to bring along my reel-to-reel tape recorder, an amplifier and two speakers, which I set up on the counter. My grandfather protested, stating that he never had music playing when he was running the store so it made no sense that there should be music played there now. My father overrode him, coming to my defense. The real reason behind my dad's mutiny against his father, though, was the music I played. When he was there I played only Frank Sinatra, his favorite singer. If he left the store during the day, I'd switch over to Astrud Gilberto. So one thing was certain: Southwark Paint Company played the best music of any paint store in Philadelphia. Perhaps in the world.

A fellow named Ernest Evans lived right around the corner at 4th and Queen Streets. As a young boy, he worked for my father and grandfather filling glass gallon jugs with paint thinner, which was stored in a huge metal drum in a basement cove hollowed out under Catharine Street. Today, the city licensing officials and watchdog environmentalists would never allow such a dangerous health and safety hazard.

Each week Ernest would walk up South 4th street to Margolis' kosher wine store and get all the empty jugs that would otherwise have been thrown in the trash. He'd wash out the residual wine in Southwark's bathroom and remove all the labels. He'd then fill the jugs with mineral spirits delivered by a local solvent distributor who'd hook up their hose to the fill pipe out on Catharine Street. (This emptied into the steel drum in the basement for storage.) Ernest would then paste a Southwark Paint label onto the jugs and use a marker to write "Paint Thinner" on them.

This was gainful employment for Ernest Evans for a few years while he was a teenager. Not long afterward, though, he was discovered by the honchos at Cameo-Parkway Records, who recorded him doing a cover version of Hank Ballard's song "The Twist." Ernest Evans' musical hero was pianist and singer Fats Domino of the hit song "Blueberry Hill" fame. Inspired by Fats' full stage name, Ernest changed his name to Chubby Checker. Thus Southwark Paint Company was the breeding ground of a musical legend who changed the world with a dance record that set off a string of other dance crazes the likes of which the world had never experienced. "Chubby" had worked at Southwark for a few years before I started bringing in my Frank Sinatra recordings, and this was a little more than a decade before I'd reach one of my own musical destinies inside one of Southwark's paint warehouses, directly across the street. For years, whenever he came back to Philadelphia to see his family and visit the old neighborhood, Chubby Checker made it a point to stop by the paint store just to say hi.

When I managed to save up $250, I purchased the latest marvel from the burgeoning miniaturized-electronics industry. Sony had just introduced a four-inch portable black-and-white television. It weighed just two and a half pounds, and it could receive all the VHF channels. (UHF channels had not yet been assigned.) Proud owner of this unique electronic miracle, I brought it to the paint store the following Saturday. When I demonstrated it to my grandfather, a man with little interest in it, he interrupted me with the question "How much?" I stared at him, incredulous, knowing he didn't care about this tiny electronic miracle. I snapped back, "How much you think?" He thought about it for a moment. Realizing it probably cost much more than he thought it was possibly worth, he blurted out "A hundred dollars!" Knowing that telling him the real cost would have triggered an outburst of highly charged emotional negative responses and a tirade of opinions delivered in at least two languages I didn't understand, I replied "Good guess, Grandpop! Actually, I was able to bargain and get it for $10 less. It was only $90!" This made him happy, as it was less than his estimate. He beamed proudly, delighting in the thought that I'd actually absorbed some of his business acumen.

I had kept the peace with my grandfather through a diplomatic evaluation of how to answer his inquiry. This was probably my first business lesson—how to judge someone else's idea regarding the value of something. I admit I learned more than a few things from those people I admired. My grandfather Abraham Kahn was certainly one of my spirited teachers and heroes. I only wish he had smiled more.

SOUTH OF THE BORDER

In 1965 during my Bar Mitzvah celebration, uncle Stanley Weiss, my mother's younger brother, asked what I would like for a gift. He expected the usual answer: money or a material object. Instead, I told him I wanted to visit him in Mexico. My uncle was raising his young family in Mexico City, where he'd started a successful mineral business. Surprised and impressed with my request, he arranged for me to go to Mexico the following summer.

He and my Aunt Lisa lived in a stunning, modern house in an upscale residential section of this amazing city. I was given an extraordinary opportunity to experience another culture firsthand. Visiting Mexico City's marvelous museums and accompanying my uncle on two business trips way out in the Mexican countryside certainly opened my eyes. It was on one of those trips into the hills outside Mexico City that I was introduced to jalapeño peppers and home-brewed *cerveza*. I was astonished at the kick in those peppers, and it may have been my first taste of beer. The opportunity to speak in a tongue other than English ultimately led to my becoming somewhat fluent in Spanish. But perhaps the most significant aspect of this trip for me was experiencing a high style of living that seemed to have dropped right off the silver screen—one adopted by forward-thinking adults of substantial means. The jet-set lifestyle became very appealing to me. Of course, I had already demonstrated a penchant for glamour and fame in becoming a professional child actor. On a side-trip from Mexico City to Acapulco, we met an entourage of my uncle's attractive and alluring friends who made me yearn for experiencing more of their way of life.

While I was visiting Mexico, Aunt Flora Webber (my mother's younger sister) flew down from her home in California. My mother joined us for most of this extraordinary trip. I got to see new sides of her personality, ones she kept in check back in Philadelphia. It was clear that she also was intrigued by this way of life. In particular, she became smitten by one very handsome, well-built Italian fellow named Sergio. I never knew for sure if Sergio and my mother became intimate on any level, but I could sense the heat simmering between them, as my mother drooled over this fabulous-looking man.

So my first international trip educated me on many traditional levels, as it was meant to do. And I got to witness firsthand, at age 13, the "swinging" lifestyles of the rich and famous. The accoutrements enjoyed by those privileged people, which I absorbed during the time I spent with my uncle and aunt and their fascinating friends, ramped up my increasing appetite for sophisticated living. I knew this was how I wanted to live, and I saw my artistic talent as the way to get myself there. Of course, while in Mexico, I performed at the grand piano in my aunt and uncle's house for them and their friends, all of whom recognized that I was not just some ordinary kid visiting his relatives.

On my first night there, a place was set for me in the kitchen where I was expected to eat with my two young first cousins Lori and Anthony. My Aunt Lisa was reared in Europe, the only child of a well-to-do family. It was their custom for children to eat separately from their parents, at their own table in the kitchen but I was having none of this. I went to my mother and said, "I am not having dinner in the kitchen. I'll eat later or in my room, but I am not sitting at some kitchen table with Lori and Anthony." She took my appeal to Uncle Stanley, informing her brother that I got along famously with adults and that I was adamant about where I'd be dining while staying in his home. He, in turn, mentioned to my aunt that another place should be set at the dining room table because Andy preferred to eat with the adults. This was likely the first example (with more to come) of my uncle witnessing my strong and outspoken personality. I wanted to be with the adults, where I could interact with them on a level at which they could relate. I would not be relegated to being one of those children expected to be seen but not heard. Nope, not me.

With a live-in chauffeur, cook and maid at our disposal, everything was accessible all the time. I was introduced to new foods. It is there that I became familiar with artichokes. "What is this?" I asked when a whole artichoke was set before me. I'm certain Aunt Lisa was thinking at that moment I had no business being in the dining room with the adults. It was she, nevertheless, who showed me what to do. She plucked out one of the leaves and dipped the bottom into a small bowl of melted butter with a little lemon juice and salt. Using both upper-and lower-teeth clenched around the end of the leaf, she scraped the meaty fruit from the bottom and swallowed it. I was amazed that so little yield could be worth all this trouble! But I joined in and immediately became a believer. I requested an artichoke with every meal thereafter during my stay.

I learned about the sanitization practices regarding fruits and vegetables in Mexico. I love tomatoes. I always have. In fact, I don't think there is anything I eat that I love more voraciously than a red, ripe, juicy tomato—one that actually tastes like a tomato. Such tomatoes have evaporated from the grocery shelves during my lifetime, which I find particularly distasteful (in all aspects of the word). When I asked my aunt and uncle's cook Angela for a tomato with my salad, she became flustered and began speaking to me in her native tongue. I couldn't understand what she meant by "Tengo qui desinfectar," which she kept repeating over and over. Not one to be easily dissuaded, I persisted that she add a tomato to my salad. And she continued to balk at me, using the phrase that I did not understand. Finally, exasperated, Angela took me to my Aunt Lisa's bedroom, where she was taking a nap. Sheepishly, she knocked on the door, and we were invited in. Aunt Lisa explained to me why Angela wouldn't add the tomato, because it needed to be "disinfected" first, for a period of a few hours. The dietary health issues in Mexico were totally beyond my experience, but what a way to learn about such things! I should mention that Angela had tomatoes ready for me whenever I wanted them every day thereafter.

A three-day excursion to Acapulco further introduced me to the grand lifestyle of my relatives. The plush suites at The Pierre Marques Hotel were over-the-top. This is where I learned the delights of making a Caesar Salad from scratch. A group of my aunt and uncle's friends was gathered around a large table set up for us by the huge swimming pool. At one point, an animated, robust fellow in our midst named Mario stood up and announced he wanted to prepare a Caesar Salad for all of us. Uncle Stanley seemed a bit perturbed at one of his outgoing friends interrupting the peace and quiet of our lunch. Aunt Lisa patted him on the arm and said, "Oh, let him have his way. You know he will anyway." And so, Mario summoned the Maitre D', requesting that all the ingredients needed to prepare a Caesar Salad for eight be brought out immediately. I was hysterical over this whole unfolding escapade. In no time, a cart appeared with a huge wooden bowl, a dozen small glass bowls, seasonings, lemon juice, egg, anchovies, croutons, grated cheese and all the other ingredients. Mario orchestrated the preparation with flamboyant flourish and fabulous fanfare. It was, of course, delicious. We all loved it. Uncle Stanley acquiesced it was, after all, a very good idea to have let it happen. And I learned that theater can be tasty—not just entertaining.

My return to the former Idlewild Airport in New York (renamed John F. Kennedy International Airport in 1963 after JFK's death) was filled with melancholy. My mother stayed on a little while longer in Mexico, along with my Aunt Flora. I had just spent several weeks in a foreign country experiencing another culture, mingling with some of its poorest and richest people. I came away with a million memories that remain vivid to me to this day. My father picked me up at the terminal. You could always rely on Kenny Kahn to do this. If you were flying in or out of an airport within a hundred miles of Philadelphia, he was always eager and ready to offer his livery service. To anybody! That was just one of his many endearing qualities. He was always there for you. I believe I've acquired some of that quality in my own desire to "be there" when people are in need of something I can provide. The entire ride back to Philadelphia, I did not stop talking about things that happened while I was in Mexico. I know he tuned me out after the first ten minutes. But knowing this was something he usually did, I didn't really care that much. I just wanted him to hear how this trip had changed my life. Because, in fact, it had done exactly that.

JAZZ WAS BORN...
ALONG WITH OTHER
ENTERTAINMENT BUSINESS

When I got back to Philadelphia, I discovered that Bruce Klauber had already become an accomplished drummer. He *really* played drums—unlike any percussionist I'd ever heard. Bruce was influenced by Gene Krupa and Buddy Rich. He was also influenced by his older brother Joel who was a walking encyclopedia of jazz. Bruce was trying incessantly to get me to "swing" on the piano, and I was desperately trying to adapt my show-tune style of playing to his hard, driving swing jazz beat. Bruce drew a huge Number 4 on a piece of paper and placed it in front of me to keep me swinging in Four instead of the Two-beat feel usually associated with Broadway musicals. "Swing in Four, Pal, swing in FOUR!" I can still hear him shouting this out to me while I struggled to keep up with the swing beat. When we played together, Joel chimed in continuously, "Keep the SWING!" This kept us all on track.

Eventually, I got it. When you finally understand "the GROOVE," it never leaves you. It becomes part of your DNA. There's simply no losing it because, as the Duke Ellington song aptly warns, "It Don't Mean a Thing If It Ain't Got That Swing."

There will always be people who don't understand that clapping their hands or snapping their fingers to a song being played in 4/4 time on anything but beats 2 and 4 is just wrong. The "back beat," as it is called musically, is what gets people up to dance, to clap their hands and to move and sway, emanating from an infectious beat. In my case, it wasn't that I couldn't swing. It was merely that I didn't understand the feel attributed to the four distinct quarter notes in a measure of music. I was accustomed to the feel of two half notes or two quarter notes in a measure. The swing groove is based on a count of four. Counting measures in two is like the "oom-pah" effect one hears from a tuba player. The rhythm is there. But "it ain't got that swing." So, I got it. And when I did, it was a euphoric moment. It hugely delighted Bruce. He finally had a pianist to play with who could get into the groove he was creating on the drums. What a feeling! And it has never left me. Nor shall it. It doesn't go away. It stays with you forever. Amen.

Peter Green, whom I first met in 1961 when I was nine (on the same occasion I'd made Bruce Klauber's acquaintance), lived with his mother. He went to live with his father in 1966 who lived only a block away from me. Peter and I now went to the same school and were able to renew our friendship. We both became fascinated with Citizens Band Radio and, before long, we each owned five-watt "rigs." Our bedrooms became home base for reaching out over the public airwaves. This allowed us to make friends with people whom we otherwise would never have had the opportunity to engage. Getting on any one of the 23 local CB channels and putting out the "CQ" call for "any friends who might be listening for someone to shout out" was not unlike entering one of today's internet chat rooms.

We became members of local Citizen Band two-way radio clubs, meeting on the air dozens of people from Pennsylvania and our neighboring states of New Jersey, Delaware and Maryland. The roof of our house in Penn Valley was awash in antennae—spindly, amazingly tall metallic structures reaching toward the sky—their presence necessary in order to achieve any type of long-range communication. CB radio allowed me to hold over-the-air conversations late into the night. Long past my bedtime, outfitted with headphones and a hand-held microphone, the covers pulled way up over my head, I'd talk to my CB buddies about nothing at all. You may recall that my Uncle Lloyd, as a young boy, used to listen to his radio late at night. He'd pretend to be asleep when my grandfather checked in on him. CB radio was my version and it was so cool. Being cool was exactly my quest.

Kids, adults, men, women—you name it. Everyone was on their CBs, reaching out across the airwaves, making electronically-assisted acquaintances. I'd try to imagine what someone looked like whom I was talking to. Peter and I attended CB festivals providing local users an opportunity to meet in person. Not unlike people today "meeting" on the internet; they tell you what they look like and when you meet them, they look altogether different! Today, we can swap pictures first, although many of the pictures one receives are not their real or current likenesses. The disappointment felt when people finally meet after exchanging photos on the internet was not as acute back in the days of CB Radio. There was no scanning or uploading of images and transmitting them instantly to another person who can, in turn, download them seconds later. So, which is better? I think the former, actually. There's nothing like a little mystery experienced in the anticipation of meeting someone with whom you've just spent months communicating—then finally getting the chance to actually meet the person who contributed to that conversation.

Peter Green and I joined forces in another realm, starting a business venture called Grahnatronics International—a moniker formed using a combination of letters in our last names. We weren't sure what services we'd provide to the neighborhood but we were all juiced up and ready to take on the world—no matter what they might be. We were fascinated and in awe over the first home-oriented video-tape recorders and camera equipment that had just become available to consumers from Sony Corporation. We decided to pool our Bar Mitzvah money and purchase a Sony video reel-to-reel tape recording setup. Dealing with a local hi-fi stereo merchant in Bala-Cynwyd, we quickly learned the intricacies of haggling. John Schneller had a well-deserved reputation for being a tough cookie—and a colorful character, to boot. He apparently wasn't ready for two smart-ass kids like Peter and me to come in and upset his apple cart—something we did every weekend once we heard about this new audio and video gear.

After a great deal of pushing, pulling and begging with this extremely difficult man who pretended that he was not amused by us, we settled on a price for the equipment. Schneller then told us we'd have to wait two weeks for the stuff to come in. We called or visited his store every day, making pests of ourselves. One day he called and announced (with his infamous lisp that only served to make him an even more annoying individual), "Boyths, your Thony video-tape enthemble hath arrived!" I'm sure not more than ten minutes elapsed before my father was driving the two of us to Schneller's Radio Clinic, where the equipment we believed would dictate our future as entrepreneurs was waiting.

Our attempts to start a local-event video-recording service failed miserably. Unfortunately, this resulted in our having to sell all of the equipment we'd purchased together. We owned it equally. And we quarreled constantly about over whose house we'd keep it in. The only solution, finally decided by our parents and us, was to dispose of it. We advertised in the newspaper and within two days, a wealthy doctor who lived on Rittenhouse Square in Center City Philadelphia purchased all of our beloved video gear for about half of what we had paid for it. Crisis resolved. But our arguments persisted.

While my attempts at being a titan of industry (first, the radio station and then the video-production company) were short-lived, the experience I gained in dealing with a strong-minded business partner like Peter gave me insights that would prove very handy later on. The compromises I made in battles fought during my professional careers in both the entertainment business and retail commerce were influenced by my experience with Peter Green. He was stubborn, mean, vindictive and jealous. I had already learned a lot about those qualities through my relationship with my older brother Walter. But having to handle them with a guy who was not a member of my family, someone I could easily tell to go fuck himself (but learned not to), led to my ability for resolving many future episodes with frustrating people. In the meantime, I maintained my interest in being an actor—and those interests began to broaden.

Earlier, I mentioned my association with a new theater company associated with the Theatre of the Living Arts. As a charter member of the Southwark Repertory Company, I got to know Hollywood and television actor David Hurst, who offered me my first opportunity to work professionally with a real star. I'd only heard about the temperament of such people. I was given a chance to witness the real deal in action. It was here that I learned prima donnas are not restricted to being female! David was nice to me, however. I'm sure it was because I kept myself out of sight during rehearsals of scenes in which I was not involved. While he bullied his way around the rest of the cast and crew, I thought he was an amazing actor. If one was serious about learning from another professional, David Hurst could certainly be a model teacher.

I still cherish the Playbill with my name listed in the role of Prince Cosmo di Medici. I felt like a real prince through the entire run of "Galileo"—a dramatic stage event that ushered in a new era of live theater in Philadelphia. During rehearsals I entertained my fellow cast members by playing the piano. One of them, perhaps offering me an accurate assessment of my acting future, suggested I seriously consider pursuing a musical career of playing the piano instead. That suggestion turned out to be prophetic.

Toward the end of my acting pursuits, I frequently took the train to New York City to catch shows on Broadway. During one such trip with Peter Green, traveling with his new 35mm camera, I met Robert Preston. Here was the actor who introduced the world to the Broadway Musical character Professor Harold Hill in "The Music Man." We met backstage and the chemistry between us was instantaneous. I told him I played Professor Harold Hill in a young people's production and that I knew every word of the musical score. "Ah, The Music Man meets The Music 'Young Man'" were the words that Robert Preston uttered to me. He was starring in a new show at the 46th Street Theater with Mary Martin—the 1966 musical "I Do I Do!" This began a three-year friendship during which Bob invited me to attend future Broadway shows in which he was appearing. I held him in the highest regard as an actor. But he was so much more. He was a real man. And I admired him greatly for it. Here was a highly energetic actor who couldn't sing well, who spoke the lyrics of songs with barely a noticeable melody. He possessed a strong, dynamic masculine presence that oozed with infectious charm—which allowed him to put a song across in a way that was uniquely his. No one could ever have delivered "Ya Got Trouble" from "The Music Man" more convincingly than this extraordinarily gifted actor. Robert Preston was one of my heroes. He knew it, because I told him so. The fact is I truly loved him.

THE CHRISTMAS "EXPRESS"

Over the Christmas holiday in 1966, I took a train to Fort Lauderdale, Florida. I had been invited to visit cousins on my father's side whom I didn't know very well. I took my seat on the morning of December 24 next to a small, elderly woman named Viola. She and I became fast friends—and not just because we'd be spending the next 24 hours together. We were the only white people on the entire train. The trip turned into a traveling block party of incomprehensible proportions. While I took my meals and snacks in the club and dining cars, with Viola safely right by my side, the rest of the passengers came prepared for feasting in their seats and in the aisles. They shared a bountiful amount of fried chicken and other southern delights with everyone. Aromas permeating the coach cars of this train remain indelible to me to this day.

Viola and I witnessed an all-out picnic on this train, and we were clearly the outsiders—merely observers. But never one to shy away from an opportunity to be the center of attention, I proceeded to advise our fellow passengers that I was a budding stage performer. With that, some serious singing and dancing commenced in the aisles, kicking off what soon became a Show on Wheels. I made a lot of new friends on that train ride, amidst a huge amount of real talent—in our car, especially. The carrying-on was nonstop and in full force by the time we came to an unexpected halt in our southward movement. We suddenly found ourselves stuck outside of Richmond, Virginia. We were halted because of ice on the track, resulting in a partial derailment of the train just ahead of us. We were forced to sit motionless for about ten hours. When we stopped, a collective groan rose throughout the train, and people started to vocalize bitterly about the terrible timing of this unfortunate event. The major complaint, of course, was that they would not arrive in time to be with their families for planned holiday dinners and other events. Christmas was the following day, and we were stuck in Richmond—a long way from most passengers' destinations.

Just before finally getting underway again, the railroad staff brought cases filled with mountains of food onto the train, saying it was to be shared among all passengers. This was clearly designed to appease us for the inconvenience the delay had caused on the most important holiday of the year. Platters of turkey and ham popped up everywhere—all of it offered gratis. People were told they could eat in the dining car or in their seats. You never saw people who'd brought along countless bags of their own food get into line so fast for these holiday-inspired meals the train company delivered as a peace offering.

Everyone was very well fed. To top it off, some became a little drunk. Wine and liquor, gifts to their families the passengers were carrying, were consumed instead on the train. Apparently word had spread like wildfire that there was a young boy in one of the cars who was an actor and a musician. This intrigued a number of passengers. I'd quickly become the guy that everyone wanted to meet or had already met. We all began singing Christmas carols, Motown songs, Broadway standards, Be-Bop, Sinatra. You name it, we sang it! What a ride this was!

When the track was finally cleared for passage, everyone was told we'd be soon underway. There were still a few hours to go before reaching South Carolina, where a number of passengers were getting off. No one seemed to mind anymore. Free holiday food, lots of beer, wine and liquor coupled with sing-alongs and dancing in the aisles had lightened everyone's mood. This, of course, was way before mobile phones, so no one could call their friends and relatives. A few people had bravely gotten off the train, hoping to find pay-phones, but none were close enough to ensure they wouldn't miss the train. We collectively hoped that those meeting us at our final destinations would already know we'd be coming in a half-day later than expected. So we continued our unstoppable party. We were all celebrating Christmas together on a passenger train packed with black people and an elderly white woman— who might have been scared to death had it not been for the outgoing and fearless young white boy sitting next to her. If Viola didn't know what Soul Food and Soul Music were before she embarked on that train, she certainly had it down by the time she got off in Daytona Beach.

My cousins, who'd been calling the station regarding our progress, knew we had spent almost 12 hours in Virginia.

When I walked off the train in Fort Lauderdale, they asked me what the trip was like. All the while, dozens of black people kept coming up to kiss and hug me or shake my hand. While I barely knew these cousins on the Kahn side of my family, they were witnessing people coming off this train knowing my name and saying goodbye to me! I tried to explain all that happened on the trip but this was one of those "You had to be there" stories. I never saw any of the people from the train again, and I can't imagine what Viola told her family about the trip when they picked her up from the "Soul Train" she'd just been on. What I did know, though, was that this woman who initially felt very out of place ended up grateful to have had me by her side and, as a result, had a ball! After that wild train ride, my cousins decided that I'd do better flying back to Philadelphia on January 2.

I asked them to introduce me to all the places of interest in Fort Lauderdale and Miami. One trip to the Miracle Mile presented a shopping experience during which I was just dying to purchase a red brocade, formal smoking jacket with black satin lapels and a paisley ascot to match. I'd never seen such clothing in person before, only on movie stars in films. I begged my cousins to lend me the money, which I promised my father would repay them. I don't know if they got a kick out of me or just thought I was a weird kid—maybe both. What I did know was that I had become obsessed with owning that formal jacket. With the ascot, it still would have been a tame outfit for Liberace. But clearly, this was something no one in my family would have expected me to be wearing when I stepped off the plane in Philadelphia.

My parents watched their 14-year-old son walk down the steps from the aircraft (this was before enclosed jetways) wearing my new formal duds and a pair of very dark sunglasses. My father had told my mother early on that he recognized I was very different from his other two sons. It was probably never more obvious to him than at that moment he saw me in the doorway of the plane wearing the ascot. I caught a glimpse of my parents in the window of the airport's waiting area and started waving at them. Or maybe I imagined myself waving to an adoring crowd waiting to get a look at this young movie star emerging from the jet. I paused for a moment or two on each step, clearly showing off my jazzy new wardrobe for everyone to see. You think maybe I was cut out to be a performer?

I LOVE A PIANO

I was about to make my first major entertainment career move. When I turned 15, my father, always the family Enabler, managed to land me my first professional gig playing solo piano at a hip Italian restaurant called The Saloon in South Philadelphia. This place is still thriving today. Just three blocks from our family's paint store, he took me there for lunch. He knew the owner Bobby Santore, who'd also become a customer of ours. My father told him that I played the piano. While I was kicking him under the table for embarrassing me in front of someone I'd just met, Bobby suggested I play a few tunes—something that no one ever had to ask me to do twice. Bobby said he'd been thinking about adding live music on Monday and Tuesday nights. A well-seasoned Italian musician named Ted DeFiore did the honors Wednesday through Saturday. "What do you usually do on Monday and Tuesday nights?" he asked me. My father jumped in replying "He's supposed to be doing his homework." We struck a deal. Bobby would pay me $15 a night and feed me dinner two nights each week. I was to begin performing the following Monday night. I had my first real gig! Because I wasn't old enough to drive, my father offered to bring me in and come back four hours later to pick me up. What a guy! "Of course I did my homework," I lied to him each Monday and Tuesday night before he'd take me down to The Saloon.

Playing there was all that mattered to me at the time. I was getting paid and eating some of the freshest and most delicious Italian food in town. Chef Nino Bari said he would teach me to make his outrageous Linguine Pescatore in exchange for my playing his favorite Italian song "Ana Mae Core," all of which I was more than happy to do.

The Saloon was always humming with activity at the bar. There were lots of well-dressed mature men who saddled up to fine-looking younger women. It didn't take me long to discover why none of these men wore wedding rings. From my vantage point at the piano in the middle of the room, I saw one slick guy wiggle the ring off his finger and slip it into his pocket. Supposedly, no one who hung out at the bar was "married";

they all were single and available! My liberal education got a huge boost during my nights playing piano at The Saloon. And so did my wallet.

One night the owner of the Eagles football franchise at that time, Leonard Tose, placed a $20 bill in my tip jar—without even asking me to play a tune for him! This was certainly the Big Time for a 15-year-old kid.

Sometime after that, my father, always my biggest fan, arranged for me to sit-in with a trio at The Host Farms Resort in Lancaster, where we were vacationing there for a long week-end. That was my first time ever playing with other musicians. A bass and a set of drums changed my whole outlook on playing the piano, producing a fever in me. I decided to search for some young guys with whom I could form a musical group. It was time to form a band!

Bruce Klauber: *When I started playing the drums with Andy Kahn in 1963, after our radio station days were just about over—we were both 11 years old—it sounded like a musical mix of oil and water. All I knew about jazz back then, by way of my few years of drum lessons, was from listening to the 1937-1938 Benny Goodman band with Gene Krupa on the drums. Though my ears were untrained—my brother, as Andy has said, was much more musically astute than we were—Krupa and the band had a sound that was electrifying. These guys were on fire. This must be, I figured, swing. Andy came out of the theatrical tradition where everything is sung and played "as written" with a two-beat feel—and swinging is close to being illegal. Whatever the beat, this boy knew tunes. All of them. In terms of jazz, my thought was, if I played the bass drum loud enough "in four" and in Andy's ear, he would ultimately start swinging. It didn't take long. Andy had ears. And heart. And plenty of guts. Though we must have sounded awful, I can tell you this: we were swinging.*

BELLS ARE RINGING

During my quest to form a band, my interest in electronics found me involved with a couple of neighborhood boys who, like me, had developed a fascination for modern telephone equipment. We'd often cut school and spend the day hanging out with repair technicians dispatched by Bell Telephone of Pennsylvania. My interest in telephone technology was so great that I would skip school for days in exchange for the exciting experience of accompanying those telephone guys on their service calls. When I was in my doctor's office one day with a cold, I "borrowed" a pad of prescriptions. I used them to forge absence notes required by my high school. I got really good at offering up medical explanations for not attending classes for long periods of time. One of them, as I recall, had the following words: *"Please excuse Andrew Kahn for the entire week of March 1, Monday, March 8 and Tuesday, March 9 of the following week as he was suffering from a severe asthma attack and was under my care during that time. Sincerely, J.W., M.D."* How I never got caught doing this repeatedly is something I will never know.

In exchange for our help running telephone-company cables between walls in offices and also providing coffee and snacks to the telephone service professionals, hordes of equipment seemed to mysteriously "fall" off their trucks periodically, ending up in our possession. Before long, my family had a three-line telephone network setup throughout our house. Sophisticated, office-style phone sets were wired in every room—often two or three of them, paired with speakerphones and intercom-paging systems. Most businesses would have loved to have had a phone system like ours. And if my mother wanted to change the color of her Princess phone, I simply went into my "stock," producing one in the color of her choice. My bedroom had become a storeroom for phones of every style and color available at the time. My "telephone" friends installed similar systems in their houses.

Of course, more is never enough. One of my comrades boasted to the wrong person about our escapades, and word spread from there. Sure enough, one day the doorbell rang, and two detectives from the Lower Merion Police Department appeared in the doorway. They wanted to know all about our telephone equipment and wanted to see what had been installed throughout the house. This was the second time that my antics, promoted by my incessant curiosity, aptitude and ambition, brought me to the attention of the legal authorities. (The first was my involvement with those two illegal radio broadcasting stations.)

This time, my friends and I were arrested as minors. We had long ago made a pact among us that we wouldn't give up our sources of the equipment. Refusing to "rat" on the telephone company employees who were our "suppliers," we landed in Montgomery County Juvenile Court. The judge seemed to be both overwhelmed and intrigued by our abilities and craftiness. He was amazed at the engineering knowledge we had amassed and the sophisticated use we made of the equipment. I was asked to define in detail the communications system I'd set up at home. And he asked me more than once if I really was only 16 years old. His obvious amusement led to his offering leniency for the three of us. He imposed a small fine for each offender, set a short probation period and insisted that we promise to stay away from The Telephone Company! Because we would all still be under the age of 18 at the end of our probation, he offered to have our records expunged if our probation was completed without further incident. He then smiled warmly and offered some genuine praise to us. He informed the three of us that our entrepreneurial spirit is precisely what made America great, adding that without such boldness, we'd all still be drinking English tea and paying our taxes to the Crown!

The inquisitiveness I'd always shown about things technical, especially electronics, has never left me. I continue to wire, re-wire, string together and construct communications networks, audio components and lighting, though all of it is legal now. My love for connecting devices is steadfastly a part of my life on a multitude of levels. If it has to do with electronics, count me in. Thank you, Uncle Isadore. This is in my blood, and I simply love any challenge having to do with interfacing equipment.

PLANET JANICE

It should be obvious that I had not one, but two very unusual parents. I don't believe it was ever a conscious decision of my mother and father to raise their sons with the huge amount of freedom they provided the three of us. It occurred naturally with my father. Here was a man intent on playing golf on Thursdays and Sundays, and the rest of the week, instead of doing parental duties in Penn Valley, he escaped to his familiar life at the paint store. At some point, he became the man in charge of the family business.

Because my mother was permitted to express herself by an adoring husband who felt she could simply do no wrong, she found it easy to give her sons that same opportunity. She was not expected to work or contribute to the family income. That would have been unheard of, based on traditional family values instilled in both my parents by their parents. So my mother tended to the house—with the help of a housekeeper who came several days a week. She saw that her sons got up each day, made it to school and provided something that resembled dinner for her four "men" every night. The rest of the time, she tried to keep herself amused. This was, after all, The American Dream.

Artistic by nature, my mother sought out friends who liked to go to theater, art galleries and museums. She joined organizations in which she'd encounter women living similar lives, wives with husbands who earned good livings and let the women handle the household during the day. My mother enjoyed her freedom but she became disenchanted early on with the repetitiveness of her daily routines. She'd been a school teacher before marrying my father, something she said she enjoyed, something at which she'd been successful. She gave up teaching when she became pregnant with my brother Walter. Here was a woman who would have loved becoming a professional actress. But real life ruled, and the family came first. Or did it?

Although I was agile and had demonstrated highly developed acrobatic skills before my teenage years, I became disinclined toward athletic activities. My father participated in ritual front yard ballgames with other boys in the neighbor-hood—one of them, my pal Fred Reinhart. I opted instead to play the piano or listen to music inside. Perhaps this attitude was derived from more than a few of Walter's criticisms of my true athletic prowess, which he preferred to denigrate.

When I was eight, Walter and I were on opposing Color War teams at Camp Green Lane, an overnight summer camp located about an hour outside of Philadelphia. I won an important track race for my team, having been far and away the fastest member on my team. Walter came up to me immediately after the race and called me "a little prick," adding "You HAD to win that race, didn't you?" This would not be the first time I achieved something that I hoped would produce my older brother's approval. Instead, I got ridiculed for my success and shot down with insults and profanity.

So I took great solace in my artistic pursuits, many of which my mother related to. Of her three sons, she identified most with me, living out many of her creative dreams vicariously through my activities. This created a bond that I recognized and cherished at an early age. It was easy for me to get and maintain her approval; our similar interests served as my personal insurance policy. We had a unique relationship, very different from the one she had with Walter and my younger brother Billy. My mother had taken years of music lessons as a child, becoming proficient at reading music and playing the piano. She even dreamed of becoming an actress, having performed in plays during her years in grade school and later in dramatic and musical theater groups while in college. When she watched me perform onstage, as either an actor or a musician, I could see that glimmer of her own yearnings whenever I'd catch her eye. I could tell she felt like she was onstage with me. And she knew that I knew this to be true.

Her frustration at not having fulfilled her artistic dreams was ameliorated at museums and lecture halls, where she encountered people with similar interests. Most of the time, they were women. Occasionally, they were men. One thing my mother wasn't, was shy. If someone intrigued her, she expressed her feelings openly no matter where she might be or with whom. In restaurants, she would strike up conversations with perfect strangers at neighboring tables. I know my father found this very odd at the beginning of their marriage. But soon he realized this was the way it simply was going to be and found himself more amused by it than annoyed. He came to expect it no matter where in the world they happened to travel.

My parents toured extensively, and the stories about whom my mother chose to engage with were family legend. In dozens of envelopes, there are hundreds of photographs showing my parents all over the world, with full plates of food, next to strangers my mother had befriended. The look on my father's face in all of them is one of placid resignation. He admitted to me years later, he spent his entire married life in disbelief over her ability to bring strangers into their lives at any turn. As The Great Enabler, though, he rarely, if ever, tried to dissuade her or express his displeasure over this. He was with his Janice. That was good enough for him. It was not, however, good enough for my mother.

When I was 15 years old, my mother came into my bedroom, as she had on those many nights five years earlier when we'd set off to have some "extraordinary fun" by sneaking out together. That was the term we used when we went to the Red Benson radio show for a midnight snack and to hobnob with the celebrities. Sometimes we shot over to the Fairfield Inn, a late-night eatery at the nearby Marriott Hotel located on City Avenue, only about ten minutes away. We'd sit and talk over hamburgers and milkshakes. All during this time, my father was fast asleep—his snoring keeping him company.

This night was different, however. She told me she was frustrated. I didn't understand and asked her to explain what she meant. There was a peculiar look on her face and she hesitated. I said, "C'mon, mom. You always tell me everything!" She fumbled her way through some statements that began with her disappointments regarding my father, something I'd heard from her plenty of times through the years, especially related to his not sharing her artistic interests. She then mentioned her need for him to stay awake with her at night, to which he usually responded by falling asleep while she was talking to him. She told me that she needed a man to share her thoughts and interests with and to be able to communicate with on a level that my father was incapable of offering her. She explained that she desired a man who was exciting and who was "on her wavelength!"

I was beginning to understand, recalling how stimulated she was when we were together in Mexico two summers earlier. There had been many "attractive" people in my uncle's circle of friends. I'd seen how she flirted with a couple of them. And I witnessed other married couples doing that there. So at the time, it didn't seem taboo to me. She was having a great time and clearly enjoying the open social atmosphere during those Swinging 60s, which my aunt and uncle's lifestyle provided. It was then that she told me she'd met a man in an art gallery who was interested in the same pieces she'd been studying. That day they had lunch together, something she said they'd done a few times. Relating how attractive he was to her, both physically and mentally, she danced around the conversation until she admitted they had an afternoon sexual liaison. She added that she hoped I could understand.

I was finally shocked by something my mother said and had done. It took this very powerful subject to awaken me to the fact that my mother was capable of doing such things. I can't imagine any therapist suggesting that it was a terrific idea for a mother to tell her teenage child this story. But a therapist would likely not understand the connection I had with my mother. We were very close on a spiritual level. And I, like her, found my father a frustrating man to be around. He never attempted to understand my creative and technical aptitudes. Those were too far beyond his mental grasp. While he was amazed by them, he paid me very little attention even when I tried to share the details with him. So it wasn't difficult for me to relate to my mother when she said he couldn't satisfy her. I was too young to interpret the full meaning that the word "satisfy" held for her. But I was old enough to sense that she'd found it necessary to step out of the widely accepted social boundaries in order to be satisfied. Even though I told her I understood, I remained a bit bewildered. Here was my mother telling me that she had been unfaithful to my father, and I'm actually feeling sympathy for HER, not him—knowing how much she longed for certain things he was unable to give her.

She insisted she still loved him dearly, but that he just couldn't provide for all of her needs. After 21 years of marriage to her darling Kenny, Janice needed to spread her wings to fly. And fly, she did.

It wasn't much later that she began taking off on her own to catch some shows in New York City. She'd drive herself, take a room at the Piccadilly Hotel in the theatre district and stay there for a few days during the week. She'd go to galleries, museums, Broadway plays and musicals, day and night, until she got it out of her system. Sometimes my father would hop a train and join her there on the weekend, and they'd drive home together. She went mainly for the culture and the arts New York City has to offer. But if she made the acquaintance of someone along the way, my mother had no trouble justifying her time spent with that person on any level, all in the interest of enjoying what they shared in common.

It would be inconceivable to consider the whole character of my mother without mentioning one of her most famous attributes. Her lateness was storied. We're not talking a few hours late. She could, and sometimes would, be a day or more late for an event or occasion. During the almost 50 years I knew my mother, she was never able to leave the house on time to catch a plane or train, be in her seat as a curtain went up in a theatre, arrive at the start of a meeting or conference or appear when expected for mundane appointments like getting her hair done. Her friends tried in vain to find humor in it, though most admitted it was more a nuisance than entertainment. The legend carried through on every level in her interactions with humanity, and it cost her several close friendships. It also interfered with her relationships with her doctors and other professionals. Had she not been so affable and charming, qualities she mastered early in life, no one would have ever counted on her for anything. She was that undependable.

Even when it didn't involve her directly, my mother could cause a person to be late themselves. It was tough getting my mother somewhere on time. But once she was situated there, it was even more difficult to get her to leave at the expected time. I was to fly home alone from Mexico City in the summer of 1966 because my mother chose to stay on. She managed to stall my departure from my uncle's home, however. I arrived at the airport late enough that my flight to New York on Aeronaves de Mexico had already left the gate. Through some fast talking by my mother and my uncle's driver, and perhaps because of influence my Uncle Stanley's name wielded with the Mexican authorities, I was suddenly escorted to a jeep and driven out to the Boeing 707, which had been ordered to stop on its way across the tarmac. A set of steps was then wheeled into position and the door of the jet opened. I was led up the steps by an airline staff member and ushered to my seat in the rear of the aircraft. You can't imagine the looks on passengers' faces when I walked onto the plane. Such a thing could not possibly occur today, aviation regulations being what they are. I still can't figure out how what occurred at the airport actually happened. It must have been the power of Janice!

My parents were invited to my Uncle Stanley and Aunt Lisa's daughter Lori's wedding in Switzerland, a weekend-long affair that began without a trace of my parents. They'd been scheduled to arrive on Thursday night in Gstaad—expected to attend a dinner for close family members only. My mother's siblings knew all about my mother's lateness, so two days without my parents being there was really nothing too surprising to them. On Saturday night, moments before the wedding ceremony was about to begin high up in the Swiss Alps, my parents arrived. Legions of guests from all over the world witnessed them hop out of a car dressed in the same clothing worn on their flight from New York—my mother, still in her pink sweatsuit and my father still in his grey one. They joined the celebration amidst all the guests dressed in formal apparel and exquisite jewelry—an indelible visual for those witnessing it. True to form, my mother caused their arrival to be two whole days late, performing on a new level the role she always played so extremely well.

One day, my mother discovered a lump in one of her breasts. She chose to remain silent about it, knowing we all would insist she see a doctor right away. When the lump didn't go away, she finally brought it up to her physician. Because she had waited so long, she had to undergo immediate radiation therapy. Alternative treatments might have been available to her had she not delayed. The therapy was successful and all traces of the lump were removed, but her heart began to show signs of weakening. A pacemaker was installed, which required another hospital visit.

My mother viewed her hospitalizations as if they were hotel stays. With a 24-hour staff to attend to her every need, bringing her food and paying her unlimited attention, she was content being an in-patient for an extended amount of time. On the morning she was released, she asked if she could stay through lunch before vacating her bed. And they agreed. Only my mother would choose to linger in a hospital after a lengthy stay simply to get one more tray of lousy food delivered to her bedside.

Following her recuperation, a month-long trip to California was planned—to celebrate the first birthday of my brother Walter's first son Avery. In preparation for this trip, my mother began to show signs of coming undone—emotionally. On January 24, 2001, while I was on a business trip in Florida, I spoke to her on the phone. She was distraught and clearly upset about having to get herself together for the trip. She said she really wanted to go to Florida instead, and alone, because she needed time away for herself. I did my best to console her during a typically long conversation. At the end of the call, she seemed calmer and told me she appreciated the time I spent trying to build up her confidence. She said she'd go to California after all, because she really did want to be part of her only grandson's birthday celebration. This was a tough phone call for me, filled with emotion and struggle for both of us. Because the flight to Los Angeles was in two days, I hoped she would spend the following day packing—a chore she always found torturous and nearly impossible.

At 2 am on January 26, while asleep in my Orlando hotel room, the phone rang. It was my father babbling something about going to bed around 10 pm while my mother was still packing, which was not unusual for her. He warned her before getting into bed that their flight was at noon and that they had to leave before 10 am. He woke up for his ritual mid-sleep trip to the bathroom in their bedroom suite. When he went to see what she was doing, he discovered her sitting on the toilet in the hall bathroom, slumped toward the wall. She wasn't moving. He shook her a little and found her unresponsive. Panicking, he called 911. The ambulance came right away and took her to the hospital. All he kept repeating to me was "She left." When I asked what he meant, he said, "I think your mother's gone!" I still wasn't sure if he meant she had decided to flee before taking the trip to California. So I asked him to explain what he was saying. He thought the paramedics said she was dead, but he just wasn't sure. So disturbed over preparing for a month-long trip to California, the stress was too much for my mother. She passed away quietly, without fanfare, perhaps so she didn't have to deal with packing any longer.

My mother's death officially made her the Late Janice Kahn. People at her funeral said that ironically this time she reached her destination way in advance. The sentiment was that she arrived someplace early for the first time in her life. To this day, people who attended my mother's funeral in January, 2001, reflect on how much they "enjoyed" her service that day. One had to be there to know what was meant by such a peculiar attitude regarding what should normally have been a somber occasion.

My mother did not do many things that people considered normal during her lifetime. So it was really no surprise that following the praise delivered in several eulogies about my mother's colorful, storied life, her Jewish funeral turned into a Holy-Rollers Baptist revival meeting. Near the end of the service, a voice bellowed from the rear of the chapel, inquiring "May I speak?" Everyone in the crowded room turned to see Mary Wilson, our former black housekeeper who'd been one of my mother's most trusted confidantes during her many years of service to our family, hobbling down the aisle on a cane. This elderly woman, whose face eerily reminded me of James Brown, was dressed in full, white Easter regalia—from her multi-faceted, ribboned hat down to her shoes. "May I speak?" she demanded again as she approached the front rows of seated guests who were astonished by what they were witnessing. I immediately rushed to Mary's side, helping her up onto the platform, where she took her place behind the podium and began silently nodding as she surveyed the hundreds of people assembled to pay their respects to my mother. Pastor Mary Wilson, a title she achieved after forming her own church in West Philadelphia, had plenty to say about "Missus Kahns." She spoke not a single derogatory phrase about my mother, offering only words of pure praise.

Mary said that Janice was an individual, unique in her thinking, a woman who sought happiness in her own way, always searching for enlightenment. The words "Praise Jesus" and "Praise God" punctuated the end of most of her sentences. She went on and on about my mother's special qualities. The room was silent. I believe some people actually gasped and held their breath when Mary took the podium, and they didn't exhale until she stepped down.

As I held Mary's hand to steady her while moving off the stage, some people began to applaud. A black female pastor preaching at a Jewish funeral service in a Jewish funeral home is something you don't hear about too often. Joe Levine, the funeral director, took me aside afterward and said, "We've had Philadelphia mummers strutting through here, musicians playing and groups of people in colorful costumes sometimes, all lending a unique atmosphere to these emotional services. But this, THIS!! A black female pastor coming from a Baptist church in West Philadelphia demanding to be heard? In all my years working in this family business, I've never witnessed such a thing. This is surely one for the Jewish history books." No matter what the circumstance, my mother insisted on making history. Because she was always different in some way, it would have been impossible for her to have a normal funeral. I wouldn't be surprised if my mother told Mary Wilson that, should she predecease her, Mary should speak at the funeral. Well, it was a beautiful funeral and, yes, very entertaining. My mother would not have tolerated anything less. She used her one last chance to show everyone who knew her that she was, indeed, a superstar.

THE BIRTH OF A BAND

A few years earlier, I decided it was time to start my own musical group. I recruited Paul Cooper, a school friend who played the bass. Paul said he knew a drummer our age he would ask to join us. That drummer just happened to be my old friend Bruce Klauber. Destiny brought us together once again. And so the Paul Stevens Trio was born. (The group used this name so as not to favor any one member.) We began to look for people who would pay us to perform, and we found them. Though Paul was a spirited and dedicated musician (today very much on the music scene as a solo Blues guitarist and singer), Bruce and I changed bass players a few times over the next three years. Because we were determined to set our local nightlife on fire, we hit the Philadelphia music scene hard.

At times, it seemed we might set the Kahn home on fire. One weekend, my jazz group was rehearsing in the basement, my younger brother Billy's rock group was fiercely attempting to play on the first floor and Walter was playing soul music on the second floor—at maximum volume. Add in three dogs, three cats, four parakeets, two guinea pigs, assorted fish in two tanks and for a short while—I kid you not—a stump-tailed macaque monkey that was Walter's college fraternity mascot visiting during semester break. Our home on Green Tree Lane was truly a zoo. Rather than try to quiet the cacophony of dissonant, clashing musical styles and animal sounds, my parents moved out for the weekend. They took a hotel room a few miles away allowing us to make all the noise we wanted, and they could do what married couples do. They were permissive to such a degree that we Kahn Boys were the envy of all our friends who made it clear that our house was the place to be. And my darling parents gave us their blessing. All of the time.

With demand for our jazz trio building, Bruce Klauber and I became brazen. In our minds, no restaurant or club was off limits. We hadn't yet learned you can't play real jazz at a restaurant filled with affluent suburbanites who want to dance between meal courses. Playing a Thelonious Monk song like "Hackensack" (adapted from George Gershwin's "Lady Be Good") didn't go over well at a swanky supper club. I barked back at the bald-headed man who kept complaining as he tried dancing with his wife and didn't recognize the song. "This song is based on the harmony and chords of a George Gershwin standard!" He had no idea what I was talking about. We were booted out of that joint in nothing flat. But many times, the owners truly loved us. Other times we were told that our music was too avant-garde for their patrons. I recalled my parents politely warning me when I was five, during a somber occasion, not to play the piano after my grandmother died. But this was something very different. This was Jazz!

We continued to do our best at imposing sophisticated jazz compositions onto audiences who were less than friendly to us; this happened more than a few times. Before our arrogance got us into real trouble, though, we were smart enough to engage a professional booking agent. A relative newcomer to the business, Gerry Glasgow began promoting our group. He landed us an amazing, high-paying job at a spot called The Rathskellar, which had just opened up in Philadelphia's downtown Sheraton Hotel. We were slated to back up a supposedly sexy female singer named Barbara Noel, several years our senior. Having this "chick" up there shaking her breasts for the customers provided us a lot of leeway to sneak in some jazz during our sets. There's nothing like a pair of knockers to divert the attention of onlookers!

In no time, we became fixtures in the vibrant nightlife of Philadelphia's downtown nightclubs. Though only 19 and not yet of legal age to purchase liquor, we still managed to imbibe many a drink and hobnob with pub-crawlers who came regularly to hear us—often showing their gratitude by sending drinks our way. Bruce Klauber and I preferred to tap the ever-present hidden flasks of Jack Daniels we kept on hand, pouring whiskey into club sodas on nights when the patrons weren't feeling particularly generous.

Bruce Klauber: *The gig with the breast-shaking singer was really something. It happened to be located in the underground concourse adjacent to the bustling Suburban Station commuter train terminal. This engagement likely stands as one of the only times jazz was played nightly in a public underground train station. There was no budget for a bassist, so it was piano and* drums only. The money at that time was incredible. We were booked to play during a 5:00-to-7:00 happy hour. We then had two hours off, performing again from 9:00 into the wee hours. The hotel provided us with a luxury room in which to change, rest and lounge. I recall that we appeared only Monday through Friday in that there was very little commuter traffic on the weekend. Back then, most establishments booking live music had to deal with the Philadelphia Musician's Union. Philadelphia's Local #77 maintained that the band's billable hours MUST include a two-hour break. This meant our gig required payment for nine hours!

Musically? The singer thought she was Barbra Streisand, who she was not. And we thought we were Oscar Peterson and Buddy Rich, who we were not. We didn't get along well with this woman. She didn't swing, and she didn't want to either. She looked her nose down at us, continually addressing Andy and me as kids—which we hated. She claimed to have appeared on The Tonight Show starring Johnny Carson. We tried unsuccessfully to have it written into our contract that she was forbidden to speak to us when we were off the stage! I imagine we thought we were pretty hot stuff back then.

To put it in perspective, though, the pianist/composer Erroll Garner ("Misty") was in the room one night to hear us play. Wisely, he kept to himself and said nothing to any of us.

IF I CAN MAKE IT THERE

The following year Bruce Klauber and I left Philadelphia for college. He went to Rider College in Trenton, New Jersey. I was enrolled at New York's Hofstra University. It had just launched a new music program, one that promised young musicians a more contemporary curriculum than those normally offered by traditional music institutions. I met other young jazz players who, recognizing my ability to improvise, offered me chances to join their jam sessions held regularly in the music department's rehearsal rooms. My interest wore thin very quickly, as most of them played in the John Coltrane-oriented modal school that influenced the majority of young jazz students back then. I never wanted to be a modal player, preferring to improvise on a song's originally-written harmony, extending into be-bop style jazz chord inversions. The modal approach made everyone sound alike. As a player, that was the last thing I wanted.

As a pianist, I was required to take at least one classical piano subject. Professor Marconi opened my eyes to how little I knew about sight-reading music. Recognizing that I was an "ear" player who was mostly self-taught, he demanded a lot of discipline from me. But, as with my first piano teachers in Philadelphia, I again had trouble concentrating and adhering to the structural demands of learning how to read the music. Marconi became impatient with me each time I arrived at our private session, demonstrating that I hadn't practiced much since our previous one. While his glare of disapproval was intense, sometimes I just felt sorry for him. After all, I still believed I knew more than everyone else. And feeling sorry for Professor Marconi was simply not enough to get me to change my ways.

Acquiescing to the fact that I only wanted to play jazz, Marconi made a last ditch attempt to bring me into his program. If this didn't work, he planned to kick me out of his course. He introduced me to George Gershwin's Etudes for piano and Frederic Chopin's piano Preludes. These works incorporate more contemporary harmony than the pieces he originally wanted me to learn. It dawned on him that forcing me to study Bach, Beethoven and Mozart would further alienate me from learning to play Classical music. The maestro's hope was that the style of more modern composers would finally inspire me to practice. He was correct. The Gershwin and Chopin pieces opened my eyes—providing me with fresh insight into what makes Classical music so awe-inspiring. Marconi clapped his two palms together, then looked toward the ceiling and audibly—in Italian—thanked God for helping me to finally see the light.

I wanted to play jazz. And that was the real reason I went to college in New York, not to receive a college degree from Hofstra per se. While enrolled at the university, I nailed down weekend solo piano gigs up and down Long Island, booked through an agent with an overinflated ego who handled most of the area's clubs. No one ever actually saw King Broder. One only spoke to him on the telephone. He reminded me of the Wizard of Oz.

One place he booked me was in Roslyn, not far from Hempstead where Hofstra was located. It was called The Tomahawk Room, set within a small motel. I was booked to play in their piano bar. The tip jar was a brandy snifter that seemed as large as the top of the piano. In no time, it was filled with singles and fives. When I gained the confidence of the married couple who owned and ran the place, I suggested they bring in a drummer to liven up the joint. These two characters were old-time jazz fans, and they agreed that my pal Bruce Klauber could join me the following weekend.

This couple had a Dalmatian named Mojo who lay most of the night right by my feet, sometimes interfering with the piano's pedals. I figured this animal was a jazz lover with good taste. I took it that the patrons of The Tomahawk had equally good taste because we began to pack them in every weekend. Bruce and I played jazz late into the night—again without a bass player. Together, we sowed more than a few oats, on and offstage. Ah, the people we met and hung out with! What an education for two young guys who just couldn't get enough of everything!

Every Friday, I hopped into my two-seater Fiat convertible and drove down to Rider College. We'd strap Bruce's bass drum onto the side of my blue sports car, pack the rest of the drums inside and haul ourselves off to Long Island for the weekend. Imagine trying to get away with that on the New Jersey Turnpike today! Bruce would stay over in my dorm room, which I shared with two other students. He'd sleep on the floor, wake up and prepare himself an Alka-Seltzer breakfast, and we'd pal around all day Saturday. We'd buy records. We'd go into Manhattan. After grabbing some dinner at a local pub, we'd head off to our gig in Roslyn—and do it all over again that night.

Bruce booked our trio for a concert at Rider. We were still billing ourselves as The Paul Stevens Trio, though this time, Bruce's high school pal David Myers was playing upright bass for us. We didn't go on at our designated performance time because we were waiting impatiently for David to show up—which he never did. As the crowd got rowdy, the emcee took the microphone onstage. An audience member who saw Bruce and me pacing the floor asked him why we weren't playing yet. The emcee made a spontaneous decision, announcing we'd be playing as a duo rather than a trio. Bruce and I couldn't believe what we heard. When the audience expressed their disapproval, he added "You think that's weird? The Paul Stevens Trio doesn't even have anyone in it named Paul or Steven!" The die was cast. Bruce and I went on—piano and drums yet again—and, of course, we knocked them out. The standing ovation we received was all we needed as confirmation that we still knew how to play—and that we could pull off miracles whenever it became necessary.

On Sundays, following our weekend Tomahawk Club gig, we'd drive back into Manhattan and visit the Greenwich Village clubs. We witnessed the remaining true masters of jazz piano performing live. The Village Gate and The Village Vanguard lured us back repeatedly. This was truly "where it was at" for me. We were two "hot shot" jazz musicians all right. And for us these were life-changing experiences. We were hanging out in the lounges, playing our music for sophisticated audiences— thrown in among older, seasoned jazz fans and veteran players alike. We were both in heaven. This was New York, and we had arrived!

COMING HOME

Even with all the excitement that seemed to come very quickly for me, I didn't stay in New York for more than six months. I wasn't setting New York on fire. It was more like New York had set me on fire. There seemed to be more opportunity for "real" recognition back home in Philadelphia. The Saloon hired me again to play solo piano in their new upper-floor lounge. I was recognized each night as a young man blessed with great talent. It was a thrill for me to get dressed up, drive into town and sit behind the piano, playing in their stunning new bar to a clientele of wealthy suburbanites and various center-city types. And, of course, there were those sharply dressed women, looking for dinner and a ride "home"—wherever that meant on any given night. Leonard Tose, still the owner of The Philadelphia Eagles, again walked by my tip jar one night, and he dropped a $100 bill into it. I guess that's what they mean by inflation. My ego got an inflated boost right then.

I was feeling pretty good about myself, having "seen" New York, survived it and left it—still intact. And I continued to garner experiences that most 18-year-olds could only dream of having so early in life. But, all along, I reminded myself to keep my ego in check, hearing my parents' warnings from years earlier. Nobody wants to listen to someone boast about his accomplishments. They'll admire someone's achievements just the same without being told about them via a first-person narrative. In fact, I learned early on that instead of admiration, feelings of detest and jealousy can breed in some people who aspire to the level that others have surmounted. I've seen it happen over and over in the music industry. And I've witnessed it in lots of people engaged in the other arts and sciences. Being aware of this, I adopted personal checks and balances, paying specific attention to not making everything about me. My father was always gregarious and interested in the health, careers, families and accomplishments of his customers and other acquaintances. I am the same way. Perhaps I learned this, or maybe it's just a part of my personality I inherited from him. I have no doubt it has helped me disarm certain individuals who otherwise might have thought of me as a cocky, confident and overly-fortunate guy. I'll sign onto those last two attributes. But I never want to come across as being a snob. That really puts most people off. I know this because it really puts me off. When I'm around people who can't see past their own personal world, I run for the hills. I know how to take credit and accept praise, believe me. But I'll eagerly dish it out in equal or greater amounts whenever and wherever it's deserved.

I enrolled at Villanova University, thinking maybe I should follow my maternal grandfather Walter Weiss' footsteps and become a lawyer. My grandfather was well-liked by everyone, and he was a genuinely intelligent thinker. More than carving out a solid living to support his family, he preferred to focus on doing good within the local community. He gave legal advice to his neighbors, rich and poor, at no charge. He was pretty laid back with little aspiration for being financially successful. He was widely recognized as a leader; his professional peers seriously considered him for a run as the Republican candidate for the Pennsylvania State Senate. He lacked the personal drive for that, however. I'm glad he didn't pass that character trait onto me. If there is one thing I do not lack, it's drive.

I considered myself intelligent enough to become an attorney, and I certainly believed I had the guts and personality to make a living in the field of Law. But Villanova was a terribly dreary place. This had nothing to do with the religious aspect evident at this Catholic institution; it just seemed so unwelcoming. Further, I couldn't wrap my head around the subjects I was required to delve into if I were to remain a student there — and eventually go to Law School. In short order, I saw that I wouldn't last long in their archaic, highly-disciplined environment. One semester was all it took to realize this was not the place for me. I was in search of fame and fortune. I continued to see that in the crosshairs of my future as a professional, performing artist. The road to becoming a lawyer seemed way too long and arduous. And that profession was one I wasn't certain about pursuing anyway. My desire to be successful right then was clear. The entertainment field squarely held my attention. I decided to keep my focus there — in order to achieve the goals that really seemed to define both my personality and my desires.

HIGH SCHOOL MUSICAL

S till having a toe or two dipped in the waters of musical theater dreams, I visited Harriton High School in Rosemont, PA, where I'd graduated in 1970—the year before. I proposed allowing me to direct and produce a musical, one that was different from those annually presented there. They never employed anything larger than a piano trio to perform the scores of Broadway shows. I wanted to present a musical using a full orchestra! Knowing the school would require a faculty member to sponsor and "oversee" such a project, I approached one of my former teachers, their longtime choir director Mr. Ronald Teare. I knew he thought of me as one of his favorite pupils. I promoted myself as an alumnus who'd gotten his feet wet playing piano professionally in New York. It's amazing how those two words "New" and "York" impress people anywhere in the world. Although the school's administration was shocked by what I wanted to do, I was given the green light to produce an "alternate" musical with a full orchestra to play the score. I assured them a unique and positive result.

We contracted for the script and score of "The Apple Tree," a semi-successful Broadway musical written by the same writers who'd penned "Fiddler on the Roof" a few years earlier. My production would include Harriton students in roles both on and off the stage. Recruiting musicians from the ranks of the 10th, 11th and 12th grade who promised to take my rehearsal schedule seriously provided many obstacles. Rehearsals were to be held at my home on weekends. Getting all the students to actually show up with their instruments was a logistical nightmare. With much effort, cajoling and constantly following up, the sound of live music returned to my family's basement. This time though, it was a full orchestra of 31 teenaged student musicians along with one teacher, Mr. Teare, on acoustic bass—and returning alumnus Andy Kahn as conductor. This was my first attempt ever at conducting—or even reading an orchestral score. Mr. Teare's coaching was invaluable. His participation served as an indispensable insurance policy I relied on for getting the orchestra to a level where they'd actually be able to play together under my baton. The experience was particularly useful for me in the next few years, when I was arranging and conducting dozens of orchestral sections in a recording studio environment. More about that later.

"The Apple Tree" was a success. Parents and students alike had never witnessed a musical staged at Harriton with a full orchestra in the pit. On December 3 and 4, 1971, the efforts of more than 50 people paid off. I'd built all the scenery with the help of three volunteer students who were also actors in the production. I directed a talented cast, all of whom adapted marvelously onstage to their alter-egos. I'd made no plans to play piano this time around. Instead, I conducted the orchestra from the pit—directing the 31 musicians I managed to hold together to play the show's full score. It turned into one glorious production—setting the stage for my career in arranging and producing, upon which I was about to embark. It was a highlight, an *A-ha!* moment for me. And, if the thrill of having pulled this feat off wasn't enough, a cheering, on-their-feet audience of proud parents and students, along with the cast and the teacher who sponsored the event called me up onto the stage. There, they presented me with a dozen roses! Talk about Show-Biz!

I got a thrill from this endeavor, beginning the day Harriton High School's administration gave me the thumbs-up. That thrill I felt then has remained with me. Whether it's playing in a small combo, conducting whole string and horn sections playing my arrangements in a recording studio or standing in front of a swinging band performing music, these occasions always make me beam like the beacon in an old-fashioned lighthouse. The brilliance I feel when connecting with other musicians, whether as the leader, a sideman, a conductor or the arranger of the music being performed has never diminished. If anything, it continues to shine for me. It compels me to continue being a creator of music. And, THAT really is Show Business!

FINALLY A STUDENT

At the prodding of Philadelphia's outstanding trumpeter/arranger Evan Solot, a key jazz educator at what was then The Philadelphia Musical Academy (now The University of the Arts), I enlisted myself as a student in jazz improvisation and harmony with Jimmy Amadie. Jimmy was a superb pianist who'd played with Woody Herman and worked with Mel Tormé. He had tons of experience leading house trios and small groups in the last true jazz clubs—before Rock and Roll took over the music scene. When acute tendonitis caused him to have to stop playing, he took up teaching. From his home in Philadelphia, Jimmy provided students with a solid foundation in jazz harmony, rhythm, chord construction and improvisation. It was the first time I felt comfortable signing on to a strict, enforced regimen with a music instructor. Before Jimmy, I rejected an army of piano teachers whom my parents paid for lessons—all of them trying in vain to structure my learning about the rudiments of music theory.

Before going to Jimmy, I believed that I knew more than my teachers and, in fact, many times I did. At the age of nine, participating in a recital with other students, one of my piano teachers was expecting me to perform a short, well-known passage from Tchaikovsky's "Pathetique" Symphony Number Six—which she had me learn. I liked the music, but only in the full symphonic versions I had heard on recordings. This simple, watered-down version for piano beginners just didn't make it for me. When it was my time to perform, I did something I thought about while the other kids were playing their recital pieces. I didn't tell anyone what was swirling around in my mind. After taking my seat on the bench, I thought, "Okay, Andy. You can do it. DO IT!" And so, I launched into a medley of tunes from "My Fair Lady" instead. As I was finishing "On the Street Where You Live," I was watching my teacher's face go from shock to mortification, then total melt-down. I stood up at the end and took a bow to what seemed like an enthralled audience of parents and students. I received my first-ever standing ovation. Of course, Mrs. Deimler informed my parents, who were naturally beaming over my accomplishment at the recital, that I wouldn't be coming back to her for piano lessons. No kidding?!

No such antics would ever be tolerated by Jimmy Amadie. He was the real deal. And I knew it. Why? Because he insisted on informing all of his students at every session of that very fact! Still, I was really impressed by him—enough to take his lessons seriously and actually practice and study in between our weekly sessions. I finally discovered someone from whom I had much more to learn. Studying with Jimmy Amadie was a defining and humbling experience. I would study with this brilliant and charismatic man at three different points during my lifetime. The third one lasted the longest—eight years. And it was during this extended period that our relationship went up in flames—as was well-known to have happened with a number of Jimmy's other students. He had a very short-temper. He was also tremendously frustrated because of the severe physical problems he suffered with his hands, stifling his performing career early on and hindering his continuing as a pianist and arranger. He was often domineering, and a great many of his students couldn't handle that.

Because he couldn't use his hands to protect himself in times of danger, Jimmy kept a small, loaded revolver in his sock. He claimed he carried it for protection. He was also not afraid to pull it out and wave it around saying, "Do I have to use this to make my point?" I found it difficult to deal with Jimmy during the first two periods I studied with him. His overbearing personality eventually caused me twice to stop taking lessons from him. Our third time around occurred when our paths crossed again, and Jimmy invited me to his home in Bala-Cynwyd. What was supposed to be just a friendly get-together for old times' sake turned into an extended period of studying with this master musician. I was in my 40s, having enjoyed a successful career in the recording industry, something I chose not to discuss with Jimmy. I was running my family's paint and decorating business then. He figured that's what I'd been doing all along.

I wasn't performing anywhere in public at the time, having taken a long hiatus from music in order to administrate the family business with my partner Bruce. I never told Jimmy about my music business endeavors; they really didn't relate to anything in our sessions. Those were centered on my becoming a better pianist. Jimmy was insanely jealous of other people's success in the music industry, however. So when he finally learned of my many achievements, he was astonished, and he freaked out. He accused me of being an actor rather than a serious musician. He warned me that as a result, the jazz community would never accept me as an accredited member, and they would harbor ill feelings toward me—thinking me as someone who'd sold out. This type of talk continued for a while, finally managing to torpedo our relationship. I could never bring myself to inform Jimmy Amadie that the greatest jazz musician of all, Louis Armstrong, on his later-year tax returns, listed "Actor" as his occupation. Nevertheless, what I learned from Jimmy Amadie remains the central solid foundation of my approach to playing piano to this day.

Another influential person in my life was David Kay, a close friend of Bruce Klauber. David greatly advanced my appreciation of Jazz. Our relationship developed through many hours of listening to music together. Whenever I visited David, jazz was either playing in the background or we would study an artist's performance. Pianist Art Tatum held a particular fascination for him; Art was always spinning on his turntable. David had every one of Tatum's known recorded performances. From the rare to the more commonplace selections, the music of Art Tatum defined the mood during the majority of time I spent in David's apartment. David also helped me appreciate the music of pianist Lennie Tristano, whom at first I found difficult to grasp and understand. Listening carefully to his work repeatedly, though, brought me around. It wasn't long before Tristano began to influence my own approach to solo jazz piano improvisation. David had a broad knowledge of jazz, stimulated by his mother, Carol Stevens. She was a noted jazz vocalist on the New York City scene in the 1950s. David taught me a lot. He was moody and supremely intelligent and possessed a dark, yet intoxicating, sense of humor. He left an indelible impression on me, providing many years that were full of opportunities to absorb everything about jazz. I developed an intimate and deep appreciation of my cherished friend who left this world way too soon after becoming ill in the early 1980s. I'll always remember him as someone who had an enormous and profound influence on me—and on my performance as a pianist.

Bruce Klauber transferred to Temple University, bringing him back to Philadelphia. We continued to play gigs together, grabbing every opportunity to be seen at events where local jazz players were performing. We entered an audition tape for a performance competition at the Villanova Jazz Festival—the world-famous event held annually at the university. We were accepted as contestants in this event featuring more than a dozen groups, hosted and judged that year by legendary bandleader Stan Kenton. Dave Myers actually showed up this time to play bass. True to his fashion, he arrived late, forcing Bruce and me onto the stage without him. We looked at each other incredulously as we took up our positions as an all-too-familiar piano and drums duo once again! Three minutes into our playing Thelonious Monk's "Straight, No Chaser," Dave appeared out of nowhere. He walked onstage with his upright bass and began to play along. He remained onstage for our second and final number, flashing a wide grin at us as if nothing was wrong. I will say that we all played our asses off. Despite Dave's late arrival, we managed to win second place in this revered competition. Dave, we learned later on, was late because he needed to rearrange his attitude out in the parking lot, using a substance he insisted helped him play better. Perhaps he was right. Our trio, including one of its rotating bass players, had scored Big-Time in the jazz-playing field once again.

RESCUING A JAZZ GENIUS

Around this time, I was given an unusual opportunity to be a hero to a few incredibly talented musicians. Whenever the extraordinarily gifted keyboard virtuoso, French-born pianist Bernard Peiffer, performed in public, the incredibly talented upright bassist Al Stauffer played with him. Peiffer's career took a severe reverse jolt when he became gravely ill just as his star was ascending on the international jazz scene. By the time he was well enough to perform again, jazz had fallen from grace. Bernard was living in Philadelphia, where he taught and performed occasionally. Scheduled to do a concert at the Loveladies Art Center on New Jersey's Long Beach Island, Bernard would be playing a grand piano on loan from a local resident's home. In transit, the movers badly damaged the piano's trap work—the extension containing the pedals beneath the instrument. This rendered the piano, in Bernard's word "unplayable." By the time Bruce Klauber and I arrived (with our bassist-of-the-moment Lenny Chase, a student of Al's), the house was packed. The genius pianist was hanging his head drearily over the keys. He kept somberly repeating over and over, "I cannot play. I cannot play!" Al Stauffer spotted us and came over with a long face. He said, "Binard's not gonna play tonight. The piano's broke."

Bruce, brightening immediately, told Al that his pal Andy Kahn should be given an opportunity to fix the piano. Al looked at me and said, "Hey, Andy, whaddya think?" I must point out that Bernard Peiffer was not even slightly a fan of mine. He was known to refer to me as "a little smart-ass with a sports car and nice clothes," "not much of a player" and more of a "showman" than anything else. I suggested that Al politely ask Bernard if I might take a look under the piano to see if I was able to do anything. I watched carefully as Al thrust his hands deep into his pockets and sauntered sheepishly over to Bernard to take the artist's temperature on this last-ditch idea. Bernard threw his hands up in the air, almost shouting "I don't care, Ahl. Let heem do what he wants. I cannot play. I cannot play thees piano as eet eez now!"

So, under the grand piano I went. I discovered a broken wooden armature, the one that lifts the felt dampers off of the strings—a critical motion required to function properly for any pianist, let alone one of Bernard Peiffer's caliber. I crawled out from under the instrument. Not a seat in the auditorium was empty. On this Saturday evening, any hopes of the audience hearing some good jazz from a master pianist and his trio suddenly hinged on my fixing the piano.

I asked if the building's superintendent was around, and they found him. I requested he locate some wood planks or shims, some nails, a hammer and some sheet metal. Amazingly, all these items were produced in short order. I asked the woman who owned the piano whether she would allow me to hammer some nails into the under-structure. I promised it would not damage any visible part and was simply a temporary repair so that Bernard Peiffer could perform. She gushed, "Whatever you need to do! Please!"

The famed pianist sipped coffee off in a corner with his two trio partners, watching me warily. There was a fair amount of my banging wood and nails together—and a lot of praying. I tried everything I could think of to stabilize the broken parts. By a stroke of luck, I was able to jury-rig the trap in such a fashion that the moving parts would hold in place; its pedals were once again fully functional. I hoped they'd stay that way for this one concert performance by the master pianist.

After I softly played a few notes to test the instrument's functionality, Bernard came over, coffee in hand. He motioned me out of the way and forcefully played a number of cascading chord sequences to check it out for himself. He then smiled broadly. He put his arm around me, saying he was grateful that I'd come there that night. He then thumped the keyboard loudly to get the audience's attention and announced that his trio would be playing after all. To much applause, he then asked them to demonstrate their sincere appreciation for "the efforts of thees young man who feexed thees piano for me."

The Bernard Peiffer Trio did indeed play a fantastic jazz concert that night. The by-product: Bernard and I became friends. And when Al Stauffer played bass with us, Bernard occasionally came to listen and even sat-in with our group, now called The All-Star Jazz Trio. My technical skills had really come in handy at Bernard's gig that night. They allowed me to demonstrate to this gifted and amazing pianist, who otherwise would have continued to dismiss me as irrelevant, that I had some real credentials. To Bernard Peiffer, I was just fine now, even if it was only as an emergency piano technician. Being handy with tools does have its advantages. That would be revealed to me often during the years ahead. Having dexterity with my hands and an understanding of the instrument I play has endeared me to more than a few individuals who otherwise would likely have paid me no mind.

THE BEST JAZZ IN TOWN

When we played at the Rathskellar with our female vocalist a year and a half earlier, a Philadelphia booking agent came around after hearing the buzz about us. This mystery woman with a hoarse voice pursued me to become her client. Lee Rendi was widely regarded on the Philadelphia restaurant and pub scene as entertainment royalty—the ultimate booking agent.

Lee wore long blond wigs and a mountain of war-paint on her face. She dressed fashionably, outfitting herself in dazzling jewelry and carried an aura that commanded respect from acts she booked as well as the owners and managers of the places she solicited to hire her talent. Lee booked me to play a solo gig at a new place called Skewers on Rittenhouse Square. This quickly grew into a trio gig. I told the owner I worked with a great drummer and that having him on this gig would really energize the place. So Bruce Klauber was included, and we were a Piano and Drums act once again! Our duo soon evolved into a trio with the addition of bassist Lenny Chase. The son of Charlie Chase, a Philadelphia-born swing guitarist of some notoriety, Lenny was several years our senior. He lived in an apartment in the same building as Skewers. An insatiable womanizer with an uncanny ability to pick up any female he desired, he came to hear us every night. Having informed us about his musical prowess, one night he showed up with his upright bass and started playing. When the owners of Skewers saw how well our "trio" was going over with the guests in their restaurant/club, Lenny became a permanent member of the band.

Believing she might have hit pay-dirt with the next "big" act in Philadelphia, Lee Rendi went out on a limb. Acting on our behalf, not only as booking agent, but now also as our "manager," she took us into a men's high-fashion clothier on Walnut Street. At Sidney Arnold for Men, Lee selected some new clothes for our performances—not matching outfits, but well-coordinated. Our salesman Irv Mamet was a downtown Philadelphia nightlife legend in his own time. Hearing that we were jazz musicians, he tried to impress us with his first-hand knowledge of jazz. When Lee Rendi paid for our new outfits, she told us that this was a first for any act she'd ever booked. Our fans at Skewers encountered the trio proudly wearing our new duds the very next night. Even Lenny got a new leisure suit courtesy of Lee Rendi!

Irv Mamet was also a self-styled scat singer who began coming to Skewers regularly. He drank himself into oblivion while we performed, but not before grabbing the microphone to deliver his spirited Be-Bop and jazz scat vocals to an adoring crowd—ad-libbing to jazz and American standards, often tossing in the names of people at the bar during his rant. Irv would also bring his tenor saxophone and blow jazz riffs in between vocalizing. The place went wild each time he got up to perform with us. They ate it up! At this time, Bruce and I were only 20 years old. We were forbidden to drink at the club; the owners insisted on following the legal age for alcohol consumption. All the while, we were surrounded by high-class hookers, married men on the prowl and an array of Center City characters who could have fallen right out of a Damon Runyon novel. We couldn't drink, but what a liberal education we were getting!

Our trio was now squarely in the spotlight of Philadelphia's jazz scene. We were playing no small part in rejuvenating live jazz in Philadelphia; jazz started being offered in other downtown nightspots. Only behind NYC, Philadelphia, at one time, claimed the best jazz clubs and musicians on the East Coast. Bruce Klauber and I started a resurgence in a city that had seen its hot jazz scene all but dry up.

Our stint at Skewers continued for well over a year. In the meantime, a large two-level nightclub called Just Jazz opened up in a cavernous warehouse on Arch Street. Just Jazz presented name jazz artists every week on two floors, both outfitted with stages and small tables for listening and drinking. You could see and hear the biggest names in jazz there. It became an instant hit in our town.

One night, pianist Gene Harris was scheduled to perform with his trio "The Three Sounds." Gene became ill a few hours before showtime. Rather than cancel the gig, the owners of Just Jazz decided on trying to find another pianist. They called me, asking if I'd be willing to sub for this well-known artist and play with his bassist and drummer. Here I was just 21 years old, and they were asking me to fill in for Gene Harris! Given this once-in-a-lifetime experience, I wouldn't have said no in exchange for a sack of gold and diamonds. Talk about learning on the job! Traditional schooling can never teach what I learned from those two cats up on the main stage of Just Jazz that night I was seated at the keyboard of the club's grand piano. It was such a thrill! I will never forget the warm reception I received from Gene's sidemen. It was an honor to play with them. They both told me it was *their* honor to play with me! My head was reeling over this opportunity that had come my way. The club owners could have called any number of fine, seasoned pianists in Philadelphia. But they chose me. For that, I was, and remain truly grateful—especially over their confidence that I could pull it off. That night certainly represents a true highlight in my career as a performing musician!

It was time for the Trio to hire a press agent. Sam Bushman, a local public relations expert who specialized in getting blurbs into local newspapers' gossip columns, was the man for the job. Sam made it his point to visit all the watering holes around town to see who was doing what, with whom and where it was being done. He'd write up juicy tidbits and submit them to the newspapers the following day. Bushman developed a reputation for having his finger on the pulse of Philadelphia's late-night entertainment scene. For a mere $25 a week, Sam saw that our Trio got mentioned frequently in the social columns. He would embellish the tiniest details regarding some musician who sat-in with us, reports about our recording plans, if we made a personnel change—even what we thought about the price of eggs! From the power of being written up often in newspapers, our Trio began attracting individuals from world-famous jazz ensembles who came to sit-in with us, blowing their nonstop solos into the wee small hours at Skewers.

How ironic that I'd be playing piano each night in this historically certified building formerly known as The Chateau Crillon, the first modern high-rise on trés chic Rittenhouse Square. The tower was erected in 1928 by Louis H. Cahan, my future life-partner Bruce Cahan's grandfather. It was a landmark hotel and apartment residence. Bruce's father grew up living in the penthouse. More ironic was that his father celebrated his 16th birthday at a huge party held in the same space as Skewers. But perhaps the most ironic thing was Bruce's connection to Sam Bushman. Sam was a very close friend of my future partner's mother Jayne, long-since divorced from Bruce's father. He frequently squired her all over town during his routine visits to the clubs each night. I'm sure Jayne was at the bar at Skewers with Sam on some of those nights we performed. I have come to learn that there really are no coincidences in life.

Two jazz-playing members of The Philadelphia Orchestra jammed with us regularly—often right after performing their evening classical concerts at Philadelphia's famed Academy of Music. Ronald Reuben, their world-renowned bass clarinetist and Glenn Dodson, the orchestra's first trombonist, brought their horns to Skewers where they would wail with us. We became a pretty big deal in Philadelphia—by now a major part of its busy nightclub music scene. Truly believing we'd become true big shots, Bruce and I renamed ourselves "The All-Star Jazz Trio" that year, 1972.

About eight months into the gig at Skewers, Lenny Chase left the group suddenly. He announced he was relocating and hopped a bus for Las Vegas—never to be heard from again. We were fortunate to replace him with Al Stauffer—a genius on his instrument and an outstanding music educator. At this critical period of our performing careers, what we learned about jazz could only have occurred by having a player of his gigantic musical stature and superb technique on stage with us every night. One of the true jazz greats of all time, Al was a musical icon. And—he was playing with us!

I was now renting a 33rd-floor penthouse apartment in the South Building of Society Hill Towers. One of three modern high-rise buildings designed by world-famous architect I. M. Pei, the Society Hill Towers are situated along the Delaware River. This is where I became a full-time resident of Center City Philadelphia. The social experiences occurring on our floor were continuously entertaining, fitting very nicely into my lifestyle at the time. A professional madam ran her business from her apartment, directly next door to mine. Down the hall lived a prominent gay attorney and his partner. Across from their unit lived a local, bon vivant merchant hailing from a well-known South Philadelphia family. He threw many lavish, over-the-top parties, often hiring dozens of Philadelphia Mummers in full feathered regalia. Strumming banjos and playing saxophones in our hallway, they entertained his guests—and the rest of us living on that floor.

It seemed like a college dormitory most of the time. Our doors remained open all the time, and none of us thought twice about visiting each other's apartments at any hour of the day or night. I threw a fabulous bash along with S. Lee Rosenberg, a good friend who also lived in the building. We served tons of catered Chinese food, telling our guests that we cooked all the food earlier that day. They believed us! Live entertainment was provided by Bernard Peiffer on my grand piano with Al Stauffer, of course, on upright bass.

Al came to my apartment once a week, as I'd begun studying jazz harmony with him—coinciding with the time he was performing with our trio. Positioned high up in the sky with spectacular—I mean knock-out views of the city below—I was living the high life, indeed. And learning...Oh boy, was I learning!

In 1973, the trio (Bruce Klauber, Al Stauffer and I) embarked on a never-to-be-forgotten road trip to Washington, D.C.—to play a one-nighter. It was booked by Mitch Goldfarb, one of the last authentic hippies who befriended me while we were in high school. (Several interactions occurring with Mitch during my recording career are mentioned later.) Mitch wanted us to do a jazz concert at American University where he was a student. He had the responsibility of running their coffee house and booked its live musical entertainment. So, we piled into Al's station wagon and were off to Washington.

As luck would have it, the first American oil embargo by the Arabian OPEC oil ministers was imposed that month. Getting gasoline required much patience and ingenuity. Stations were offering fuel in increments of $2.00—the maximum per visit. The lines were 20 cars or more in every lane at each stop along the highway. We would travel 30 miles and then get in line to pump a little more gas—all the way down I-95 to D.C.

A normal two-and-a-half hour trip became a five-hour journey requiring a sense of humor and some serious musical dedication. We made it to D.C., albeit more than an hour later than the starting time for our gig. We put on an amazing show, however, and received standing ovations from the appreciative students who came out on that frigid night to hear some real jazz. The event was a huge success—in no small measure because Al had lots of experience being on the road. Al's disarming personality and the fact that we were these two "young lions" eager to play on stage with our master upright-bassist in front of a music-oriented audience (for a change) didn't hurt one bit.

After the concert, we went out for the requisite greasy-spoon food that follows every such event. We then repeated the $2-maximum stop-and-gas-up routine in reverse back to Philadelphia. Another five hours on the road—that was one brutal out-of-town gig. But Bruce and I were in heaven. We discovered what it was like to really be "on the road"—something we'd only heard about from other weary musicians. The guys who did it for years said that while it made for great experiences, they never wanted to do it again! Al was an old hand at it, having played for comedian Lenny Bruce, with jazz pianist Bud Powell and a host of larger-than-life jazz legends throughout his career. During our trip to D.C., Bruce and I heard hundreds of Al's stories, the kind that remain with us as jazz folklore. I'm certain that many of Al's musical disciples and students continue to regard his colorful stories the same way.

I have never met anyone like Al Stauffer. And I truly believe there will never be anyone like him again. That man was a total giant. Physically. Musically. Personally. They just don't come any greater. Al Stauffer died in 1991, a tragic loss to performers, educators and audiences of the jazz world. Bruce Klauber attended Al's funeral. I was pretty much out of the music business by then. I used that as my excuse for not personally paying my respects to this jazz icon. It was a poor one, for which my dear musical colleague has never totally let me off the hook. In retrospect, there were more than enough reasons for me to be there to see Al Stauffer off—just as much as any one of the legions of fans and students who did attend. Still, something held me back. Was it because I'd been away from the music scene for so many years? Was it that I didn't want to acknowledge how truly important Al Stauffer was in my life? I'll probably never understand my reticence to personally say goodbye to this man who figured so hugely in my musical upbringing. He left an indelible impression on me as a human being—truly one of my most incredible influences as an authentic musical mentor. I look back and shake my head in disbelief that I wasn't there to honor him. Through these words I've written here about him, I hope to set a piece of the record straight, giving this incredible individual his just due. Al Stauffer: You were the most extraordinary teacher, an icon in the music world, an inspiration to me and to countless other people. You were one of my most treasured colleagues. And you were my friend. You'll remain in the hearts of those with whom you came in contact—musically, personally, professionally—and more than anything else, humanly.

TIME OUT

While the trio was engaged to play five nights a week, most of my two nights off were spent in Royal Oak, Maryland, near the St. Michaels waterfront. I was invited weekly to the private home of the retired chairman of a Fortune 500 pharmaceutical company. He had a huge estate on Maryland's Eastern Shore on the Tred Avon River; it was simply breathtaking in every aspect. I schlepped my portable Wurlitzer electric piano to practice and to entertain my hosts, their family, friends and an assortment of their high-profile acquaintances. Sometimes I'd play outside, admiring the landscaped view on the river. Other times I'd be in their gorgeous wood-paneled study. I also spent hours writing new songs and arrangements there. I was privileged to have the opportunity to relax in a spacious, magnificent environment that few people might get to experience. A former girlfriend of mine introduced me to this family when they were still living in a stunning home in Rosemont, PA. When they moved to Maryland, I was invited there.

The first time I drove up the seemingly endless driveway toward the breathtaking house built on the river, my jaw dropped as the expanse of the property unveiled itself. Never before had I seen anything like this. I was shown to "my room"—a comfortable old-world space placed at my disposal on weekends for a good number of years that followed.

I learned to catch my own food there. I had never been introduced to crabbing, much less off a private dock, or shooting geese from a duck blind—or dressing every evening for semi-formal dinners that often consisted of main courses we'd caught earlier in the day. I honored the family's request to cook Linguine Pescatore, the dish I learned from Chef Nino Bari at The Saloon a few years earlier.

Dinner was always served in the huge dining room of this grand old mansion. I couldn't comprehend how the cook and maid showed up at precisely the right time during dinner each night. When the concealed foot-switch under the carpet where the lady of the house sat was pointed out to me, I became even more fascinated by this family's lifestyle. It was all being played out in this special enclave so far away from the clamor of the rest of the world. I dreamed of a day when I might enjoy a setup of my own like theirs.

The background of this family was vastly different from mine. Theirs was pure White Anglo-Saxon, Main Line Philadelphia, with ties to American history, spanning centuries. Mine was a totally "New American," Jewish-immigrant Russian heritage, following the many traditions of those who fled to America at the turn of the twentieth century. Despite our differences in upbringing, we all got along famously. I brought "color" to their conservative, refined lifestyle on the weekends—not to mention the addition of live music to their household. I met diplomats, dignitaries, politicians and high-ranking executives of well-known American corporations. I got to know some of them on a first-name basis.

Each weekend, I looked forward to my 3-½ hour drive down to the Eastern Shore where I would spend free time at this idyllic place where one could totally unwind. Those two days away from the intense energy that pumped the heart of Philadelphia's Center City lifestyle were heavenly.

Back in Philadelphia, a much more decadent and revved-up pace captivated me all over again. This flip-flop routine provided some well-deserved sanity away from the insane schedule I maintained. Of course, I thrived on this. I lived for the nightlife in which I was totally engaged. (Some people suggested I was one of its engines!) I'd carved out a special niche for myself and was lucky enough to have gained some notoriety in the jazz world—a musical realm that had gone unnoticed for years. Bruce Klauber and I were "on the scene," making waves, getting reviewed, attracting a following of downtown characters who belonged on the storyboard of a cartoon sketch. I continued to work hard at keeping my ego in check, fully aware that at any moment, it could all go up in a puff of smoke. But, in fact, my life dream had become my life reality.

Skewers closed down for a few days over the July 4th holiday in 1972, giving the trio our first five-day break in a long time. I decided to get out of Philadelphia, opting for a long drive north in search of cooler weather. Never having been to

New England, the state of Maine was in the crosshairs as my target destination. Immediately following our last set, off I went in my blue, two-seater Fiat convertible. My co-pilot was Bonnie Moore, the girl I'd won in a contest between Bruce Klauber and David Kay. You wouldn't think this possible in 1972, but they'd actually set up a contest for themselves. They each made a list of Pros and Cons. Whoever had the most Pros would be the victor. It was the most ridiculous thing imaginable. They were putting down stuff like: who had a better hairstyle, who had a better record collection and who had longer toenails! If the tally ended in a draw, Andy Kahn would be the de facto winner. They never expected I would consider collecting my prize. They were both unfamiliar with the adage "Be careful what you wish for; you might just get it." Anyway, their contest tally ended in a draw, so Bonnie was mine. Oddly, she and I became a solid romantic couple, together for more than a year.

We drove through the night, pulling into a rest stop only once for about an hour to catch a little sleep. We finally crossed the bridge at Kittery, Maine, leaving the coast of New Hampshire behind us. At the Tourist Information Center a little farther up Interstate 95, I inquired where people go when visiting Maine. They suggested Bar Harbor, Acadia National Park and the beaches of Wells, Ogunquit and Kennebunkport. These all sounded way too familiar and promised hordes of people on summer vacation. I asked, "How about a place in Maine that most people haven't heard of?" It was suggested I head to the lake region in the north-central section of the state—specifically Moosehead Lake. This sounded great: seeing the state's largest lake way up in the mountains, far from the summer crowds.

The little town of Greenville at the southern tip of Moosehead Lake became our destination. We were not told, however, how far away Greenville and Moosehead Lake were. And we also hadn't mentioned our long drive through the night. Off we went in search of an exciting adventure in Maine's lake region. This just happened to be another 200 miles and 4 hours away! We'd already covered 350 miles over about 8 hours. Heading toward Greenville, we were facing half the length of our trip all over again. Had they told me this at the Tourist Bureau, I don't think we would have opted for Moosehead after all. Of course, they'd simply retort, in typical Maine fashion, "Well, you didn't ask!"

It seemed to Bonnie and me as though we would never get there. We were exhausted and ready to collapse long before our arrival. Finally, a sign appeared announcing: Greenville 26 miles. Those last 30 minutes on that winding mountain roadway seemed like an eternity. But they dissolved into euphoria when we finally reached the crest of a heavy slope and advanced onto the other side of that high point in the road. There, two unbelieving pairs of eyes encountered the most pristine sight either of us had ever seen. A huge lake with 280 miles of shoreline covering nearly 1300 square miles appeared without warning. We both gasped audibly in delight.

The southern tip of the lake caressed the bottom of the hill leading down to the small village of Greenville. From our high vantage point, we were dazzled as the lake fanned out gracefully over a huge vista, stretching its fingers off toward the horizon. Its rippling surface glistened like diamonds in the gleaming sunlight. We were mesmerized, and I was forced to pull over. We sat there and stared at this image for several minutes. When we recovered, I nosed my car toward the sleepy little town waiting just below us. Close by, on the left-hand side was the Indian Hill Motel. We decided to stop there. The thought was to catch some much-needed sleep and then venture out, refreshed from our very, very long 14-hour journey.

As we were leaving the hotel to go exploring, I noticed an appealing offer on a pamphlet at the front desk. "Come check out the land deals for sale and receive Dinner for Two at the historic Greenville Inn." Bonnie thought this was a silly idea. I was beginning to think that she was a silly idea. It was my car and my vacation, so I prevailed.

We signed up for a tour of the area that would be conducted by a representative of the J. M. Huber Corporation, Maine's largest landholder. Scott Paper's holdings, though vast, still placed them at #2. This nice young guy came to the hotel, and we hopped into his Jeep. He took us around the village pointing out Greenville's historic sites. He described events that occurred in Greenville during prohibition—events that affected our whole country. It seems that bootleggers, industrialists, mobsters in organized crime and town locals had created a thriving network smuggling alcohol in from Canada—only about an hour away by car. Automobiles drove in caravans to Greenville, picked up cases of precious liquid booty and hauled them to Boston, New York, Philadelphia, Atlantic City, Baltimore, Washington and points in between. There was also a freight train that ran between Canada and Nova Scotia, stopping at only two stations in the U.S.—the first one being Greenville Junction. These trains brought the hooch to cars lined up in the middle of the night under black skies dotted with endless arrays of stars. The coveted bottles were then hauled off to depots that stored the illegal contents before distribution to speakeasies. They in turn served thirsty imbibers eager to pay dearly for high-quality liquor, still illegal in America. We were fascinated that this little hamlet of Greenville, Maine, played a pivotal role in keeping America's East Coast residents supplied with great Canadian whiskey. Good spirits? You bet!

Then it was off to Beaver Cove. This development had about 50 lots for sale by J. M. Huber Corporation. They planned to build a marina on the lake, a community recreation center, a refreshment and retail concession and even a dock where you could hop onto a sea plane for an aerial tour of the lake. All of the developer's ambitious plans came to pass in the years that followed my first visit to Greenville.

We were shown a variety of wooded lots near the Beaver Cove town center. They were populated with gorgeous white birch trees, spruce trees, evergreens and huge boulders that lent an aura of mystery and character to each lot. We stopped at a 1.58-acre lot—Lot 220. It was at the end of a strip with six other "For Sale" properties, its rear borders touching 55 acres of greenbelt forest. That greenbelt area was under contract with the state. It was to remain undeveloped for 99 years. I interpreted this to mean that a total of 56.58 acres would be accessible to the lucky person who bought this lot—someone who would be able to wander through and to get lost in it, before reaching another property on the other side of the greenbelt. While it was absolutely beautiful, I wasn't buying anything. After all, I just wanted to get a free dinner for two at the Greenville Inn after enduring the sales spiel, which I hoped was going to end soon.

At the far edge of the lot was a stream of sparkling, clear water, a magical "babbling brook," trickling its way over to the lot's border, a few hundred feet away. The salesperson remarked that this was fresh Maine spring water, from snow melting into a mountain run-off. He said this water could be consumed directly from the stream. Being a city-dweller with 20 years on our planet, I found this absolutely beyond any realm of possibility. He bent down, cupped his hands, drew some water up from the stream and sipped it. On this very hot day up in the mountains of Maine, he seemed instantly refreshed.

I waited for him to die. He didn't. On the contrary, he looked better than before consuming the water he scooped up from this fresh mountain source. He let out a long "Ahhhhhh!" as the cold water refreshed him. Okay. I figured I'd also survive this, so I mimicked his actions. Sold! All it took was that drink of water from a fresh mountain spring that fed into a brook running through this little slice of heaven. My focus was now on this lot at the intersection of Spruce Lane and North Ridge Road in Beaver Cove adjacent to Lily Bay State Park on the eastern shore of Moosehead Lake, just 4 miles north of the village of Greenville, Maine. I came from a big metropolitan city. The thought of drinking water from a source other than what is supplied by a water utility through a set of old municipal pipes was inconceivable to me. Suddenly, I wanted to be a part of this more than anything I'd ever desired.

Lot #220 was offered for sale at $5500. Whoa! Where was I going to get that kind of money to buy a piece of land in Maine? I knew I'd never be able to convince my parents this was a good idea. "No worries, Andy," I was told by the agent at J. M. Huber Corporation. They were offering new buyers a seven-year mortgage with an attractive interest rate. I was allowed to buy the property with only a small down payment. How small, I asked? Five percent ($275) would be sufficient. Knowing I had a few personal checks in my wallet, I asked if they'd take one for the deposit. "Of course," was their reply.

Back at the town office, I filled out a ton of papers before I realized that I'd just bought my first piece of real estate! Never mind that I had no plans for it and that I would probably never come back to visit it and, even more likely, I'd never improve it by putting up a structure. When I inquired if I could pitch a tent on my land, I was told this was forbidden. Instantly intoxicating thoughts of moving up to Maine began to tantalize me. And this feeling and desire has not abated in the least—46 years later.

Before getting ready for our dinner courtesy of J. M. Huber Corporation, I entered a metal phone booth, the kind with bi-fold doors, just outside the hotel office. I dialed my father (yes, dialed on a rotary payphone) using my Bell of Pennsylvania phone charge card. I told my father I was thinking of buying a piece of property in Maine, informing him first that I actually was in Maine! There was silence on the other end of the line. His reply: "You're thinking of doing what, Andy?" Repeating my "idea" to him, I could sense that he was rolling his eyes toward the ceiling, thinking that his impetuous son was just being himself again. My father didn't have a clue about what would make me want to do what I was suggesting to him. His intuition, from years of experience with me, however, took hold. He finally said, "Look Andy, knowing you, ya probably already bought it." (Yep, he knew me pretty well!) "I think you ought to get off the phone right now so you can start saving the money you'll need to begin paying for it." I laughed, telling him he was right, that I had actually already signed the mortgage papers and that I was glad I did. "What the Hell are you going to do with a piece of property out in the sticks of Maine, Andy? Are you crazy?" "Yep," I answered, and we ended our conversation on that note.

It was time to collect the dinner we'd been promised for agreeing to hear the sales pitch that turned into a sale for the company—and the realization of another dream for Andy Kahn. How little I knew how close to that dream I really was, how relevant this purchase of land in Maine would be for me in the years to follow. For now, though, it felt good just knowing that I had become the owner of a tiny magical speck of Terra Firma—a unique spot where I could drink the water running over its surface just by cupping my hands, reaching down and bringing it up to my lips. Heaven on Earth: I had found it.

Someone told me that the train I'd been hearing in the middle of the night ran from St. Johns, New Brunswick, to Montreal passed through Greenville Junction. Furthermore, one could actually halt the train at the junction by literally flagging it down. What? Impossible, I thought. That night I went to the station at 2 am, around the time I usually heard the train's whistle. Under a black sky peppered with a million stars, I thought, "No way this fucking train is going to stop for little me waving a small white flag attached to an even smaller wooden pole." When that huge locomotive appeared in the distance with its beacon illuminating the track, my heart began to pound rapidly. Believe it or not, this behemoth slowed down, came to a full stop and allowed me to board. No one approached me for hours. It wasn't until daybreak, when the train began taking on commuters that a conductor asked my destination and collected the fare from me. I spent a fun-filled day shopping in Montreal, spending nearly $1200. Catching the train back to Greenville was a lot less daunting.

When we arrived at the Jackman, Maine entry point to the United States, an officer boarded the train and inquired where I'd been and what the purpose of my visit to Canada was. He noticed the many packages occupying the seat next to me and asked if they were mine. Answering proudly in the affirmative, he asked me for the customs form, assuming I'd already filled it out. Form? Customs? Duty? Are you kidding? It never entered my mind. He was shocked that I didn't have a clue, which was true. He whipped out a Customs Itemization Form, wrote "Duty Waived" across it and told me to have a nice day. This worked out perfectly because I only had about $20 in my pocket, and the duty would have been nearly $80.

I held onto that parcel of land on Moosehead Lake for 21 years. I paid off the mortgage in 1979, having never missed a single payment. I appeared at the County Seat office in Dover-Foxcroft, Maine, where the original deed had been recorded and filed. I had a companion with me on this trip also. But this was no ordinary companion. This was the person with whom I'd be spending the rest of my life.

It was a beautiful day when we walked out of the registry office. I was amazed as I held the certified deed in my hand.

This had started as a split-second whim based on a cool taste of fresh, mountain-stream water. Now Lot #220 was officially mine. Yes, Dad, I was crazy…crazy enough to stick with it and follow through—ensuring that one more dream of mine would absolutely, positively, unequivocally come true.

THE SCENE CHANGES

The Trio's relationship with booking agent Lee Rendi went south right after the job at Skewers came to a close. She couldn't provide us with steady employment at a high enough income to justify both our needs and her commission. I phoned her saying she needed to find other ways to achieve more dependable employment for us. She got pissed-off and insulted that I'd question her ability to find suitable clubs where we could perform regularly. She spontaneously terminated our relationship in an astonishing telegram I received the next day. Her pride was wounded. I was the spokesman for our group. I took the fall, as I usually did. I didn't think I was being rude to her, just honest. Such is life.

Following 14 months of playing jazz and gaining fame at Skewers, I managed to book us into H. A. Winston & Co. by directly approaching owner Herb Spivak. This was a hip, new restaurant and lounge in the up-and-coming, tony Society Hill section of Philadelphia. Herb was one of three brothers. With partner Larry Magid, they created Electric Factory Concerts, the Philadelphia-based entertainment goliath. Herb was aware of our success across town. He offered to take a shot with the trio, arranging for us to appear onstage in the upstairs Riverside lounge—a terrific room facing the Delaware River. We played there for a year and a half during which time the Philadelphia jazz fad began to show signs of waning. All the while, though, I was honing my skills as a jazz pianist and as an accompanist for all those great horn players who would come regularly to blow with The All-Star Jazz Trio.

During our stint at H. A. Winston, I kept studying with Al Stauffer once a week. He'd come to my apartment at Society Hill Towers, lugging his huge double bass with him across the parking lot, through the lobby and up the elevator to the 32nd floor. Al and I would play together for more than an hour, during which time I learned intricate and brilliant harmonic concepts. At age 22, my life was going well—musically and personally. My apartment's southwest corner view provided a breathtaking backdrop. When I wasn't working during the day at Queen Village Recording Studios, a mere seven blocks away, or playing with the Trio at night, I could always be found way up in the clouds. It felt like I was in heaven.

Herb Spivak came over to me one night at the beginning of the week and asked me to sit down with him. Here was a guy who'd taken a long shot with The All-Star Jazz Trio. Before bringing us onboard, he hadn't booked anything other than a solo pianist in his upstairs lounge. I'd been able to muscle our way in—mostly because of the great press we'd been getting for more than a year. Initially, he told us he'd give us a few weeks to see if we could make this worthwhile. Those few weeks turned into 18 months! Now, sadly, it was over. Herb put his arm around me and in a fatherly way told me he thought we were all great and that we'd made a positive difference in his restaurant, helping tremendously with its exposure. But it was time to call it quits. Dejected? Of course I was. But we had all witnessed the declining attendance.

I broke the news to Bruce and Al who, like me, were disappointed. I must point out that Herb was truly a gentleman. He offered to pay us for the whole week even though that Tuesday night would be our last performance. This would allow us the opportunity to seek another performance venue right away. Severance pay in the live entertainment business is virtually unknown. Once in a while, you meet someone who really gets it, someone who truly is a mensch. Such a man was Herb Spivak, and he remains one to this day. Our paths cross regularly. When they do, Herb warmly reminisces about those marvelous old days at H. A. Winston & Co. They were extraordinary days—make no mistake about it.

Bruce Klauber: *Andy Kahn, like many pianists and other instrumentalists past and present, was mesmerized by the playing of Oscar Peterson. Who wouldn't be? On one occasion, we discovered a record store on Long Island that just happened to stock every record Peterson ever made for Verve Records. Andy bought all of them and as he says today, "I even bought some that weren't made!" But as much as he listened to Oscar Peterson—and he surely did listen—he never copied the man. To this day, Andy plays no one else's licks or clichés, although* *when asked, he can sound exactly like Lennie Tristano or Erroll Garner. Peterson, I think, taught him just how joyous and easy swing could be at various tempos and how pianistic technique could be applied logically and intelligently. He got the same thing, plus essential harmonic and rhythmic knowledge, from his studies with pianist/educator Jimmy Amadie.*

We built up a huge rep as The All-Star Jazz Trio because we were the only game in town then and were an entertaining— and yes, often quite cooking—group of excitable youngsters. It was only when we fell under the spell of our bassist and guru Al Stauffer, and were encouraged by world-renowned jazz saxophonists like Pepper Adams and Jerry Dodgian sitting in with us, that we moved on musically. It was about time. Al helped bring us into the modern age—literally forcing us to listen to, study and analyze the music of Bill Evans, McCoy Tyner, Denny Zeitlen, Miles Davis, Bernard Peiffer and other modernists—as well as their bassists and drummers. To these ears, when Andy started getting into Bill Evans, he found his true voice. He developed sensitivity, lyricism and learned just how to get into a tune.   It's no surprise that Bill Evans was heavily influenced by another of Andy's heroes—Lennie Tristano.

Here is an example, told to the best of my recollection, of the rarified company we kept back then:

NORMAN MAILER MEETS THE ALL-STARS

Philadelphia jazz fans had nowhere to go after the demise of clubs like Peps, the Showboat, the Aqua Lounge and New Jersey's Red Hill Inn. Word got out that a couple of rambunctious 20-year-olds were playing. Reed players from the Thad Jones/ Mel Lewis Jazz Orchestra, the Woody Herman Orchestra, the great trombonist Al Grey and other jazz performers started coming by to sit in with our trio. Early on, the owner of Skewers gave us a piece of advice: "You gotta please the people." That became our goal.

Supporting us through the years in our musical endeavors was our dear friend David Kay. Kay was not a jazz musician, though he should have been. He was a devoted fan and an as-

tute listener who was exposed to the real stuff in New York City at a young age. His mother was jazz singer Carol Stevens who recorded several impressive projects for Atlantic Records— backed by the likes of Herbie Mann. Stevens had been living at that time with Norman Mailer, the literary giant with a larger-than-life personality.

Mailer decided to throw himself a 50th birthday bash in February of 1973. It was held at the Four Seasons in New York City. In true Mailer style, each of the 550 people invited had to pay $30 (then a hefty fee) to attend. The guest list in-cluded such names as Shirley MacLaine, Muhammad Ali and then-Senator Jacob Javits. Some lesser names on the guest list, courtesy of David Kay and his mother: Andy Kahn and Bruce Klauber. We didn't have to pay the $30. People were jammed in everywhere, with big stars at every turn. The crowd at this incredible event was buzzing in anticipation of the re-marks Mailer planned to deliver later in the evening. He had something of major consequence to say. Long-time Mailer crit-ic Gore Vidal once commented that everything Norman ever said in public was supposed to be of major consequence.

Andy and I were greeted by David Kay, Carol Stevens and the Man of the Hour. Mailer was very gracious. He said that he'd heard how we were doing as young jazz musicians and that he understood us to be "very talented." Then the music began. This was music of the certifiable, all-star variety. The players included baritone saxophonist Pepper Adams, who'd been very supportive of Andy and me when he played with us in Philadel-phia, composer/multi-instrumentalist David Amram, jazz bassist and composer Charles Mingus. I felt I was in way over my head that night. Andy Kahn, however, was not in over his head. He was in his element and was seemingly born to be there.

Guests were invited to select whatever they wanted, from appetizers to entrees to desserts, directly from The Four Sea-sons' open kitchen—and even eat in the kitchen if they so desired. None other than Charles Mingus saw to it that Andy and I ("You two young jazzers from Philadelphia") were escort-ed properly into the kitchen. He suggested we all dine on ap-ple pie, which he deemed "the best in the world." It was. The Charles Mingus who was said to be among the most volatile of personalities in the music world was not on view that evening. The partying, eating and drinking continued long into the night. When I was ready to leave, of course, Andy, bless his heart, wanted to stay until morning. Norman Mailer and Carol Stevens were evidently taken with Andy, and not too long after this event, he was invited to spend a long weekend with David Kay, Carol and Norman at his compound in Stockbridge, Massachusetts.

I have no memory as to when we got back to Philadelphia or even how we got there. What I do know was that we shared a once-in-a-lifetime experience that defined jazz and exemplified New York City for us. Our press agent certainly worked overtime. An item appeared in the entertainment column of the Philadelphia Inquirer that read in part, "Andy Kahn and Bruce Klauber of The All-Star Jazz Trio, now playing at Skewers, were the Philadelphia representatives and invited guests at Norman Mailer's 50th birthday party held at New York City's Four Seasons Hotel."

And it's true. I still have the press clipping. Andy and I were, indeed, there.

2004 with
Bruce Klauber
Ocean Club
Atlantic City

1972 Andy Kahn
and Bruce Klauber
Promo

1995 with Kenny Kahn at Southwark Paint

1961 as Professor Harold Hill in "The Music Man" at Beth David Synagogue

June 12, 1965 with Kenny and Janice Kahn at Bar Mitzvah

July 22, 1963 Playhouse in The Park

June 12, 1965 on day of Bar Mitzvah

122

1971 conducting orchestra for "The Apple Tree" at Harriton High

1975 Promo for Marty Portnoy Orchestras

1990 ActionAIDS award presented at benefit concert

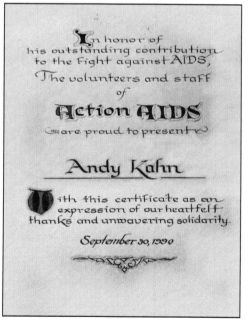

In honor of his outstanding contribution to the fight against AIDS,

The volunteers and staff

of

Action AIDS

are proud to present

Andy Kahn

With this certificate as an expression of our heartfelt thanks and unwavering solidarity.

September 30, 1990

1990 Promo Head Shot for Real Music concert Mandell Theater Philadelphia

1972 at Skewers on Rittenhouse Square in Philadelphia

August 1991 with Janice and Kenny Kahn

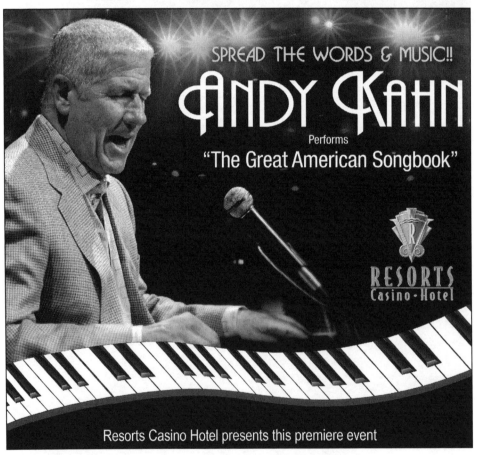

2011 Promo for Resorts Casino Hotel Starlight Room

1952 7-1/2 months old at piano

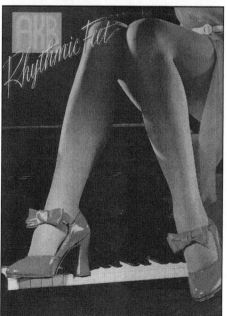

1979 front and back covers AKB "Rhythmic Feet" LP on RSO

2015 The All-Star Jazz Trio

2015 Promo at Steinway Recital Hall Jacobs Music Philadelphia

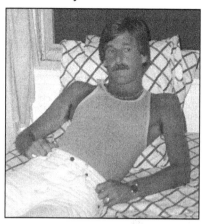

1978 Bruce H. Cahan
Atlantic City

1994 with
Bruce H. Cahan

With Bruce H. Cahan —
November 15, 2015
wedding reception

1976 with Princess Grace of Monaco at Queen Village Recording Studios Philadelphia

1963 with Bernie Evans at rehearsal for "A Thousand Clowns"

2007 performing with Connie Crothers in Rangeley, Maine

1972 Skewers on Rittenhouse Square. New trio with bassist Lenny Chase

2015 Bassist Bruce Kaminsky

1973 Stevie Wonder at Queen Village Recording Studios

2015 Drummer Bruce Klauber

Al Stauffer, Bassist

1978 "Hot Shot" LP,
front and rear covers

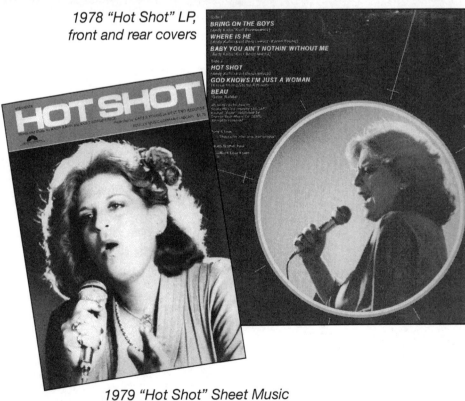

1979 "Hot Shot" Sheet Music

Thirst for Jazz? Try Skewers

It is a time when a lot of people around town are talking about a jazz revival, while aficionados keep searching for the evidence.

And, for the most part, facts supporting the claim are rather hard to come by. We did have the recent Philadelphia Jazz Festival which wqas hardly a smashing commercial success, and there is an occasional concert at the Academy or jazz booking at a spot such as the Bijou Cafe.

But jazz in Philadelphia is sporadic; the famos center city jazz rooms that once abounded are a thing of the past.

AT LAST, though, there is hope, and while Rittenhouse Square might seem to be an unlikely setting for salvation, jazz buffs are heading in increasing numbers to a spot on the square's west side called Skewers.

They are being lured by three young musicians who call themselves collectively the All-Star Jazz Trio. Check out the names — Andy Kahn, piano; Len Chase, bass, and Bob Bruce, drums — and try to pinpoint their association with the established combos you've encountered in the past. You'll come up empty-handed.

So where do these guys get off calling themselves the All-Star Jazz Trio. One's first reaction is to figure Kahm, Chase anyd Bruce are somewhat premature in their self-evaluation. But the trio's following will tell you that the name is prophetic.

THEY PLAY up-front jazz. You don't require a textbook on electronic to follow the music. The sound is solid jazz. Crisp and clear. The innovations are subtle rather than spaced out. And they haven't overlooked the fact that most people figure melody is a vital ingredient in music.

Local jazz fans are not the only ones getting the message these days. Many of the area's top musicians are finding time to drop into Skewers to observe a time-honored practice in jazz circles — the jam.

On a given night, for · instance, you might find Ronald Reuben sitting in with the All-Star Trio. Reuben's steady job is playing bass clarinet with the Philadelphia Orchestra, but he periodically airs out his tenor sax with the All-Stars.

On another night, maybe you'll find someone like John Boni sitting in on sax. Boni used to play with Woody Herman.

That's the kind of reputation being established by the All-Star Jazz Trio. Tangible evidence, at last, that the jazz revival may be more than wishful thinking.

JACK LLOYD

1972 The All-Star Jazz Trio article by Jack Lloyd Philadelphia Inquirer

1973 The All-Star Jazz Trio print ad

1972 The All-Star Jazz Trio blurb by Joe Sharkey Philadelphia Inquirer

On the Go With Joe Sharkey

... AT SKEWER'S, one of the brightest jazz spots in the area, Woody Herman's Herd's entire rhythm section sat in with the All-Star Jazz Trio. That's on Rittenhouse Square.

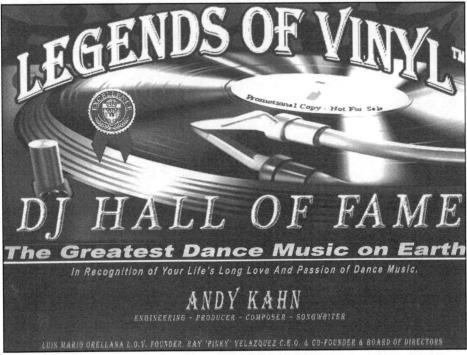

Legends of Vinyl Award

1972 Ad for The All-Star Jazz Trio at Skewers on Rittenhouse Square in Philadelphia

The Philadelphia Inquirer

entertainment/art

By JOHN CORR

On the
town

*He doesn't sing
for his supper*

The best-dressed saloon singer in town doesn't dream of the big time — concert halls, recording sessions, fan mail. He dreams of debentures, commodities and municipal bonds.

As a matter of fact, **Andy Kahn** plays piano and sings the songs of Cole Porter and George Gershwin every evening at the **Brasserie** in the Warwick Hotel principally for therapeutic reasons.

"It certainly is a relaxing change of pace after a day of dealing with lawyers and accountants and brokers."

Yes, the handsome young man who sings romantic songs between 5 and 8 p.m. spends the daylight hours "managing my investments."

"Are you telling me," I asked, "that the secret life of Andy Kahn, the entertainer in the $500 suit, is, well . . . boring?"

"Yes, it is a bit of grind," he said, "but I am considering taking over management of my father's paint-supply business. That should be pretty exciting. It's the sort of operation that . . ."

"Never mind, Andy. Just sing something."

*Jan 16, 1983 Blurb by John Carr
in Philadelphia Inquirer*

ANDY KAHN: LOCAL "HOT SHOT"

by Carol Diggs

For Andy Kahn, today is more than just another foul wet Monday in Philadelphia. Last night was a celebration for his hottest client, disco singer Karen Young, another Philadelphian. That party kept Andy dancing until well after dawn. Tonight he will put the finishing touches, the final vocal track, on the next single from Karen Young's soon-to-be-released first album. But today also happens to be the day that 'Hot Shot'—the record that started Karen Young and Andy Kahn in the disco world—hit Number One on Billboard's disco chart.

"We knew it was going to happen," explains co-producer Kahn, who is also half-owner of Queen Village Recording Studios where the record was made. "We knew last Wednesday that we had finally hit it. But it's still such a thrill — I can't believe it, I'm really choked up." And he is, sheepishly wiping his eyes, still bleary from last night's carousing. Perhaps this gesture from the hardened executive in a cutthroat business can be excused — after all, it was only a few days ago that Andy Kahn turned 26.

For most of his 26 years the curly-haired blue-eyed kid from Penn Valley has been involved in "entertainment — please don't call it show business, that's such a cliche. And please don't call me Mr. Kahn." He began his acting career at age 10, in summer productions of children's theatre at Playhouse in the Park. Within two years he was playing his first role at the Theatre of the Living Arts downtown (now the TLA Cinema), as The Prince in Bertold Brecht's Galileo. "It was a dramatic role, even if I only had a few lines. I had to look and act serious, and play a character. It was very different. That was okay. But I met a lot of loony people who weren't my cup of tea. They bugged me and they bored me. I didn't lose my interest in legitimate theatre, I just stopped wanting to be an actor."

Acting had only been an offshoot, however, of his original interest — music. He had been playing the piano since age five — "popular music, Broadway show tunes — I would play and sing along, all by ear. I was aware of rock music, but I wasn't really interested. Yeah, I was a weird kid."

By his early teens Andy was addicted to another kind of music, still a little unusual for a 14-year-old Frank Sinatra. "By 15 I was what I considered the definitive authority on Sinatra. I would go to New York to buy records that I didn't have. I wanted the complete discography." With his Sinatra addiction went a devotion to Astrud Gilberto, a Penn Valley neighbor who also happened to be 'The Girl from Ipanema'. "I have every single album she ever made — 11 of them. Why the world has never hailed her as the one who bought bossa nova and Latin rhythm into American music, and really started disco, I'll never know — it really disgusts me. Really, 'The Girl from Ipanema' started it all. Anyone who wants to argue with me, I'll sit down for a day or two and play them songs and they'll lose.

"So there I was, listening to Sinatra and Gilberto. From Sinatra I learned how to arrange and how to orchestrate. From Astrud Gilberto I learned about the sensitivity in a lyric. Any song that I write now that has any

sensual, sensitive meaning is due to her. I wrote a song for her, 'Strangers When We Wake Up', that I offered to her and she loved it. I was just her little friend, she had no idea that I was in the record business and wrote songs . . . But I'm ahead of myself.

"By this time I was 16 and playing piano in a small restaurant downtown called The Saloon. But meanwhile I have two friends who are really into jazz and bebop. Bruce Klauber, who's the drummer in the band I have now, has been my close friend since I was nine. When I was playing Broadway show tunes, he was listening to Count Basie and Buddy Rich. He still says the first time we played together he was doing 'One O'Clock Jump' and I was playing 'You Are Sixteen, Going On Seventeen'.

"The other friend who's really influenced me is David Kay. His mother is Carol Stevens, Norman Mailer's fifth wife and a jazz singer in New York. Fifteen years ago David was growing up in the middle of the New York jazz-bebop-recording-ersatz-drug scene. David grew up very worldly, but he knows so much about jazz. And his mother is a brilliant woman, brilliant. So I introduced David to Bruce, and there we were, the Three Musketeers of Music. They introduced me to jazz and to creative, improvised music. Bruce and I formed a jazz band when I was 16. That's when I realized that I wanted to be a pianist and songwriter."

Andy dropped out of Villanova to form a jazz trio with his friend Bruce on drums. Their band opened a club called Skewers on Rittenhouse Square and was part of a jazz resurgence in Philadelphia. Soon they moved from Skewers to Winston's at Front and Chestnut. And then the jazz resurgence started to fade.

"Skewers closed a month after we left," Andy recalls. "And then we were let go from Winston's. There I was, with a brand new apartment in Society Hill Towers, and I'm out of a job. So that's when my brother Walter and I started the recording studio. He

had been a disc jockey, and had learned a tremendous amount about editing and production. We were heavily financed, and we just kept hustling business doing commercials for ad agencies, and jingles; stuff like that. That was when I started writing music commercially. I was also the studio piano player — we did Gino's and the United Fund and God knows how many auto stores and candy bars."

Trial and error in the jingle business taught Andy and Walter about independent production, hiring studio musicians, and dealing with national companies. Soon they branched into independent production of records by local artists for national distribution. "We've had 15 artists," explains the piano player-turned-businessman, "And of them we've had 5 signed to record deals, and only one of them has gone anywhere. She's our first success story."

That artist is Karen Young of 'Hot Shot' fame. Queen Village had used the young singer as background vocals on other records, and when Andy rewrote his song 'Stop Sign' as 'Hot Shot', he knew the song was meant for Karen Young. So did his new collaborator, disco spinner Kurt Borusiewicz — and that's another story.

"Two years ago I came very close to tossing in everything. I was disgusted, and for nine months I was non-productive. Our disco records weren't making it, so I decided to go out and really listen and hear what disco was all about. People told me that the best disco spinner in the world was Kurt at the DCA. When I saw what he did to people, how he did it, how the music worked, I went up to him and said 'You and I have to get into a recording studio together.' The coincidences are amazing — he used to live on the same street in the Village as I did when I lived in New York, and all the time I lived in Society Hill Towers, he lived above me — same place one floor up, right over my head, and we never met. He used to listen to me playing my piano and kept meaning to come down.

"When I first played 'Hot Shot' for him, Kurt said he had the perfect singer in mind for it, and I said so do I, but she's in Fort Lauderdale now. And he said, 'So's mine', and of course it turned out we were both thinking of Karen. It's a freaky thing between me and Kurt. And Karen — she's the only singer I know who can scream like a disco mama and scat like Ella Fitzgerald. And the rest is history." Andy's jazz background and Kurt's intimate knowledge of disco had fused with Karen's powerhouse voice to produce a record that in test runs at the DCA "had them screaming and pounding the walls and yelling 'More! More!'"

In the midst of his new success, though, the level-headed musician is far from carried away. Schedules at the recording studio go on as usual. And once a week, every Wednesday night, Andy and acoustic bassist Vincent Fay play their own kind of music — the creative, improvised, sophisticated modern jazz that they love best — at the Borgia Cafe in Head House Square. For the last two years Andy has played every week, without pay. "That's what I do for myself," he says, "to keep myself sane."

Aug 17, 1978 article in Main Line Jewish Expression

Andy Kahn, 11, of 1220 Green Tree lane, Narberth, portrayed a herald who writes the familiar nursery rhyme, "Sing a Song of Sixpence," in the last production. Earlier this season he played the younger brother of the Wild West queen in "Annie Oakley." A student at Belmont Hills Elementary School, he has been seen on the Gene London program over WCAU-TV. In addition to his work at the Children's Theatre, he is taking a science course at the Franklin Institute.

Andy Kahn

1963 Philadelphia Jewish Times

*1967 with Robert Preston
in NYC at "I Do I Do"*

PLAYBILL
the magazine for theatregoers

The Theatre of the Living Arts WA 2-3101

inaugural season

Galileo
BERTOLT BRECHT

Who's Who In The Cast

The Southwark Company

Andre Gregory, Artistic Director

Kevin Allen	Morgan Gopnik	Paul B. Price
Anatole	Marcia Haufrecht	Anne Ramsey
Peter Blaxill	David Hurst	Logan Ramsey
Tom Brannum	Andrew Kahn	Paul Rodger-Reid
Marc Brown	Edward Kovens	Frank Savino
Jerome Dempsey	Ralph Lee	Audrey Shaw
Dan Dietrich	Ron Leibman	Lois Smith
Frank Freda	David Matson	David Swenson
Adam Gopnik	John O'Shaughnessy	David Tress
Alison Gopnik	Miriam Phillips	M. Emmet Walsh
Hilary Gopnik	Wendell K. Phillips, Sr.	Hilda Young

The actors you see tonight have come from many cities and many backgrounds to form a new professional company, resident here at the Theatre of the Living Arts. Most have enjoyed extensive and successful careers — many in starring roles — on Broadway, "off-Broadway," in films and television. Nevertheless, it is their decision to forego the usual "program biographies in favor of being thought of as an acting ensemble without "stars."

Southwark was the designation given in Colonial times to this section of the city. It was here that America's first theatrical performances were presented, in a converted warehouse on Water Street below Pine. It was on South Street just above 4th that America's first permanent theatre, "The New Theatre in Southwark," was built in 1766. Here was presented on April 24, 1767, Thomas Godfrey's "The Prince of Parthia," the first play written by an American for production on an American stage by a professional company.

With these historical facts in mind, our actors and staff together wish to be known as The Southwark Company.

*1964 Playbill "Galileo", front and back cover —
Southwark Repertory Company*

1987 Jayne

1979 with Kurt Borusiewicz Promo
for AKB "Rhythmic Feet" LP

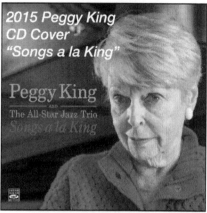

2015 Peggy King
CD Cover
"Songs a la King"

April 11, 1979 with Kurt Borusiewicz
on Green Tree Lane Penn Valley

2015 Peggy King and
The All-Star Jazz Trio
CD Insert

TEMPLE UNIVERSITY
PHILADELPHIA 22, PA.

DEPARTMENT OF PSYCHOLOGY

July 27, 1962

CLINICS

PSYCHOLOGICAL CLINIC

READING CLINIC

VOCATIONAL AND EDUCATIONAL GUIDANCE CLINIC

UNITS

PSYCHOLOGY LABORATORY

TESTING BUREAU

READING CLINIC LABORATORY SCHOOL

Mr. Andy Kahn
1220 Greentree Lane
Narberth, Pennsylvania

Dear Andy:

All members of our class hope that you did not miss too much of your special trip to Valley Forge. Everyone has expressed the hope that you were there in time for lunch.

May we thank you for your attendance at class on Wednesday of this week. Certainly, the opportunity of listening to you tell of your ideas concerning the career that you wish for yourself as well as your reaction to school work gave us a better understanding of how a young man like yourself reacts in a new and different situation.

As you well know, you took an individual intelligence test in front of the class which had a number of questions on information, comprehension, arithmetic, and vocabulary. You did very well on most of these tests, and we should like to have you tell your mother that you do belong as a member of the gifted group according to the results of this test. Andy, the fact that you are bright means that you will have to do the excellent kind of academic work that you did during the past year at school. We know that should you continue this you will be quite successful in the science area of electronics.

It is our hope that some time in the future you may find the opportunity to visit with us once again because we so much enjoyed having you this time.

Sincerely yours,

Harold C. Reppert

Harold C. Reppert, Ph.D.
Professor of Psychology

Joyce Parkinson
Helen Howells
John A. Cann
Judy Rebone
Wm. J. Schultz
Saul Katz
Dolores J. Loveck
Genevieve J. Collett
Patricia Craven
Beatrice Eckles
Jack O. Hyle
Jimmie Nabors

Rosemary Dunn

Lorry Finkel
Avra Bershad
Irene Oxlick
Marie Hogg
Carol Fisher

1962 Letter from Temple University "Psychology of the Gifted Child" program

PART TWO

On the Record

THE OUTSIDE

lthough opportunities to perform jazz were diminishing, I remained firmly entrenched in Philadelphia's music scene during the early 1970s. Marty Portnoy, a well-known Philadelphia band leader thought I should begin leading my own society orchestra on the weekends. (This would include Bruce Klauber on the drums.) Marty was always looking to recruit new players and groups for his busy booking and management office. To get me acclimated to this type of performing, he mentioned that orchestra leader Paul Willig needing a new pianist. Paul lived in Overbrook Park, a few blocks from where I'd lived until I was 5. I called Paul to discuss playing with his "Outside" band. Playing the Outside was a phrase familiar mostly to Philadelphia musicians. These players had day jobs unrelated to the music industry. On weekends, they'd perform at social engagements with their own or another leader's band. I had always referred to these ensembles as Wedding and Bar Mitzvah Bands. In short order I understood what it meant when a musician said he played The Outside.

I went to visit Paul. His house reminded me of the one we'd lived in on nearby Drexel Road, which was almost visible from his. All of these row houses looked the same. Only the wallpaper and furniture allowed one to tell one residence from another! Paul and I took to each other immediately. He asked me if I'd play at a country club engagement that weekend. I mentioned this would be a far departure from jazz. Paul said, "Jazz? Are you kidding, kid? I got the greatest jazz musicians playin' in my band! These guys are veterans who can swing their asses off! My drummer's a killer! My tenor sax man, you won't believe how he can play! You're gonna love playing with my guys!"

Paul's enthusiasm about his players was infectious. With the local Philadelphia jazz scene in decline, coupled with my need to earn enough money for rent, I agreed to give it a go with Paul Willig and his Orchestra. He promised me I was "gonna have a blast!" Paul asked if I owned a tux. I told him I did, but added I'd have to buy a new pair of black shoes. He jumped up from the dining room table. Paul asked me what size shoe I wore. When I responded "8-1/2," he ran upstairs. He came down with a brand new pair of gleaming, black patent leather slip-ons in Size 9. "Here, kid, wear these. Save your money!" I said I couldn't take his shoes. He yelled out to his wife, "Ethel, this kid won't wear my shoes!" Ethel Willig came in from the kitchen (which looked exactly like ours had) and gave me a look that only a Jewish mother is capable of giving to a reluctant son, no matter whose son it is. So, I took Paul's shoes. Never mind that I had to stuff the back of each one with black socks so they wouldn't fall off my feet. I knew that I'd better show up at his gig wearing those shoes—and that Paul would be looking for them. If they weren't the shoes he gave me, I'd certainly expect an earful from Ethel.

The first musician in Paul's band I met that Saturday night was Barry Smith, a handsome, cool guy, several years older than I was. Barry was carrying in his drums while I was unloading my electric Wurlitzer keyboard—the piano that would be my instrument at that gig and hundreds of such gigs to come. Barry, as Paul had insisted, knew how to swing. He drove all seven band members hard that night, starting with the first number. I liked Barry from the moment I sat down with him when we left the bandstand for our first break. He smoked cigarettes and drank black coffee. A jazzman, indeed!

Paul's bassist John Troutman was a decent Fender bass player—a musician with whom I'd come into contact while playing local jazz clubs. His horn section guys were all accomplished musicians, capable of playing every current Top 40 pop hit, Adult Contemporary tunes, Jewish Horas, Irish, Polish and Italian classics and real jazz, to boot. But it was Paul's tenor sax man Jerry Brody who really blew me away!

Jerry joined Barry and me during a break while the party guests were eating their salads. He was almost 20 years my senior and one of the nicest musician's I'd ever met. Because he dug the way I played, he immediately began encouraging me to become Paul's permanent keyboardist. He said that Paul also loved the way I played and had enlisted Jerry to coerce me into joining the band. I saw that I was actually going to have fun, even while playing "Tie a Yellow Ribbon" and "Proud Mary" at these affairs. Although I don't care for these songs, they never fail to get people on their feet and out onto a dance floor while the caterers clear tables for the next course. It also didn't hurt that I took a puff or two of a joint offered by one of the band members in the parking lot.

We played a number of country clubs including White Manor, Foxwood, Blue Bell and Meadowlands. And swing, we did, just as Paul had said we would! I had a ball performing with Paul's band every weekend, sometimes playing a "double" (Saturday and Sunday), and I was making some great dough. The party guests loved "Mr. Personality" Paul Willig. He was a natural showman. His impeccable timing helped him know exactly what tunes to call and when. After the final number each night, many guests would crowd around him to gush over how much they loved the music his band played. They'd ask him for his card and tell him they'd never danced so much at an affair. I was totally impressed. I learned important lessons about marrying real musical talent with pure stage theatrics. By pairing me up with this exuberant and popular bandleader, Marty Portnoy knew exactly what he was doing—and whom he was grooming.

Not even a year had passed when Jerry Brody called me to say that Paul suddenly dropped dead from a heart attack, the second one he'd suffered in his young life. With a number of gigs already booked, our Outside band was instantly orphaned. Ethel and Jerry discussed my "taking over" Paul's dates. I was unsure that I could pull off what Paul accomplished easily in front of the band. I knew I could lead, but I wasn't at ease with the idea that I'd suddenly be "running the show." I'd have to coordinate the band's music with the banquet maitre d's and take on the huge responsibility of producing a smooth affair for the guests. It was easy following Paul's lead while sitting behind my piano at these social affairs. He knew every angle, had heard every kind of special request and dealt with any possible demand from a bride, groom and their parents. He lived for getting in front of an audience each weekend to put on his "show."

I didn't have any experience being an Outside leader. Fronting a jazz group, playing in clubs and on stage, my personality at this point had been handily delivered through my piano-playing. While spirited and inspired, I had not yet had the opportunity to be the one focused on setting the mood for hundreds of party guests, providing them with a social experience they'd carry as a future memento of a family event meant to be an "affair to remember" throughout their lives. But I also was not the type to shy away from a challenge. It was Jerry who convinced me I could do it. He reminded me how much fun we had playing together. It became clear that I should pick up Paul's remaining dates and become an Outside leader.

Ethel and I worked out a fair financial arrangement. She would get almost all of Paul's share because he had been the group's leader and its lure. Barry Smith informed me that he was done, though. While he thought highly of me, Barry said the only reason he continued making the trip each weekend from his home in Annapolis, Maryland, was Paul. He didn't want to play for anyone else. No longer having Paul Willig as his inspiration to be an Outside musician, he was ready to put away his drum sticks.

It wasn't hard for me to convince Bruce Klauber to take up Barry's position as the drummer in this swinging band. Without a large roster of upcoming "Willig" gigs left to play, the problem I faced was how to keep the rest of his group together and get new work for the band. I consulted with Marty Portnoy again. Paul Willig had worked for Marty, who was then a partner in Music Associates, Philadelphia's premiere organization that booked live musicians and bands at social engagements held at hotels, catering houses, country clubs and the like. Music Associates was a business owned by all the best Jewish band leaders in town, men who fronted their own popular groups while parceling out the overflow work to "secondary" leaders. They also paired local musicians with their huge stable of working, in-demand orchestras.

Paul had struck out on his own a number of years earlier, independently booking his own event dates. Marty felt that I was not entirely ready to lead my own society orchestra. He suggested arranging for me to play with other leaders' bands under the Music Associates umbrella. I felt I'd become a Leader—and told him so. Not long afterward, Marty left Music Associates to open his own office, which would continue booking his own very popular band. He now needed to recruit other leaders and musicians to join him.

Ronnie Lewis, a bandleader who immediately left Music Associates to join Marty's office, called me to meet with Marty and him. They wanted to discuss developing "Andy Kahn and his Orchestra" into a budding band on the Outside circuit. They promised they would promote me as an up-and-coming entertainer fronting a great band, a leader who could handle any social event.

Marty had secured a contract with Merion Caterers, a large banquet complex in Cinnaminson, New Jersey, which became his lead account. "The Merion" was an extremely popular venue—with multiple weddings, anniversaries, Bar/Bat Mitzvahs and/or office parties booked every weekend. Marty's priority remained the stellar high-paying private gigs at country clubs and hotels. Ronnie Lewis' band was first choice for any event Marty couldn't play. As more events were booked, they positioned me right behind Ronnie.

Marty Portnoy Orchestras arranged for me to have professional head shots taken and high-quality business cards printed. A résumé of my musical talents and abilities was prepared. They took out impressive ads in The Jewish Exponent—Philadelphia's widely-circulated ethnic publication that many Jews read religiously each week. My face was prominently displayed in these ads for weeks at a time.

Marty advised me to get rid of my beloved Italian sports car. "Immediately," he said. "You can't pull up to a country club in that. You need a Cadillac or something very close to one." He insisted that if I wanted to be a successful bandleader, I needed to look like one when I showed up at a gig. So—I traded in my two-seater, convertible Fiat 128 Spider for a 1975 Oldsmobile Toronado, a behemoth of a vehicle—I think it was longer than a city block! At Crisconi Oldsmobile on South Broad Street in Philadelphia, I met Sonny Crisconi. Sonny would marry my future partner Bruce Cahan's first cousin Sallie and thus become my cousin. Some things are just meant to be!

I'd already been a recognized band leader around town. But it was at The Merion that I tossed off my training wheels and developed into a true society bandleader. I learned all the moves including how to coordinate our music with the banquet managers and maitre d's needs; this provided me with a deep appreciation and understanding of what I'd seen Paul Willig do so effortlessly just a year earlier. Jerry Brody signed on as a permanent member of my new orchestra, permitting one very special flavor of Paul Willig's group to be preserved. Jerry encouraged me from the start, saying that I could be a successful society bandleader with a band that would be in demand. How right he was!

Jerry Brody played his tenor sax at every event "Andy Kahn and his Orchestra" performed over the next four years. He faithfully delivered that huge wall of alluring sound that he alone produced so distinctly on his instrument. And Jerry knew every Jewish "Freilach"—a term I'd never heard before playing with him. I'd always referred to these songs as "Horas." There wasn't one that Jerry didn't know, and he taught me all of them, right up there on the bandstand. What an education I got playing with this man, whom I grew to love like a member of my own family.

I'd gathered together an amazing bunch of truly swinging, schooled players: Bruce Klauber on drums, Jerry Brody on Tenor Sax, Richard SanFilippo on bass and me. What a solid quartet! As gigs required more players, we brought in more horns and transformed our small group into an orchestra—effortlessly. Playing all the current hits and interspersing a fair amount of real jazz, we immediately became popular at country clubs and catering houses. It was while the partiers were eating chicken or roast beef that we snuck in our jazz tunes. We also played fire halls where the guests might be eating sausages and drinking beer. No matter where we were, our group swung like hell. There were always a few guests who would come up to the bandstand and inform us they knew exactly what we were playing—and that they dug it! That always made us feel great. Somehow we managed to inject some "real" music into each gig. And we were booked every weekend. The money coming in was nothing less than terrific.

Through a mean twist of fate in 1976, I was given the opportunity to again play with bassist Al Stauffer. I had maintained an engagement every Tuesday night where I played solo jazz piano at a small, crowded, underground bistro, The Borgia Café—in the Society Hill section of Philadelphia. The outstanding pianist Bernard Peiffer had played there every Wednesday night with Al until Bernard's deteriorating health took his life. Edward Bottone, the owner of The Borgia Café, asked me to take Bernard's place by also playing on Wednesdays with Al. "Let's be frank," I told him. "NO ONE could ever take the place of Bernard Peiffer." That extraordinary pianist possessed creative genius and technical prowess on par with Art Tatum. Don't take my word for it. Check out his recordings for yourself. There was only one Bernard Peiffer. Period. I had already learned a great deal from Al during our private studies together, but this was something altogether different. I humbly and graciously accepted. Each night that I played with Al at The Borgia—on their great Mason and Hamlin grand piano— was like being in graduate school. By this time, I'd become the most eager of students! How cool to be studying jazz and getting paid for playing it at the same time!

MY KICKOFF IN RECORDING STUDIO MUSIC PRODUCTION

Pre-Sound of Philadelphia:
A glance in the Rear-View Mirror

Cameo-Parkway Records was the pre-eminent record label in Philadelphia during the glory days of rock and roll. Their recording studio was at 309 South Broad Street. A technician named Joe Tarsia was hired as Cameo's full-time engineer. I learned from Bernie Lowe, Cameo's founder, that Joe had worked for Philco Radio, the one-time Philadelphia-based electronics giant located on Wissahickon Ave. Bernie and his partner Kal Mann, a songwriter extraordinaire, offered Joe a position at Cameo to set up and run their in-house recording facility. Apparently this had been a simple operation. As Bernie put it, "We came in, set up a microphone, turned on the tape recorder, recorded the 'hit' with some live group and put it out the next day."

Huge hit songs like "Bristol Stomp" by The Dovells were recorded exactly in this fashion. Bernie told me that one weekend Kal went to a record hop in Bristol, PA, just outside of Philadelphia. He'd heard that kids had just developed a new dance out there. Following Cameo's successes with Chubby Checker's "The Twist," "The Hully Gully," "The Swim," "The Fish" and "The Mashed Potato," they were always looking for something that would become the next dance craze. Something new called The Stomp was about to take the world by storm. Kal called the studio from the dance hall and sang the tune to the group of musicians and singers Bernie had assembled there. Bernie knocked out the tune on the piano, the group picked up on it and they recorded "Bristol Stomp" in one or two takes. It was mastered, pressed onto acetate and released to the radio stations the very next day—another hit song that would take its rightful place on the mantle of record business history. This is the way it was done then, but not for much longer.

Joe Tarsia believed in using the most advanced technology for Cameo-Parkway's studio—whatever was the state-of-the-art at the time. Dozens of their recordings had become hits, and demands for their studio's technical capabilities increased. Joe planned on building his own studio someday, but that wouldn't happen until Cameo had one-Hell-of-a-run. From its inception in 1956 until it was sold to ABKCO Records in 1967, Cameo-Parkway had a line-up of pure hit-makers. These included Chubby Checker, Charlie Gracie, Bobby Rydell, The Orlons, The Rays and The Dovells. Cameo even tried their hands at recording jazz from time to time; one memorable opus they did was by a big band led by trumpeter Maynard Ferguson.

In the midst of a lot of local independent record label commotion, Cameo-Parkway employed a man named Kenny Gamble. He and his piano-playing pal Leon Huff hoped they might both get a break there as songwriters. When Cameo vanished from the industry's landscape, Kenny Gamble was poised to create his own studio productions. He began with a group called The Intruders and followed them with dozens of other acts singing his songs. This made Kenny Gamble a natural client for Joe Tarsia's brand new Sigma Sound Studios, which had opened at 212 N. 12th Street. The recording environment and its needs in Philadelphia around then (1970) catapulted Sigma Sound to success. In fact, it became a historic recording venue thanks to its built-in clients, Gamble and Huff, and another stellar songwriter named Thom Bell. Their two production companies spawned a plethora of terrific musical talent. Many of these gifted people started their own production companies. But everyone clamored for recording time at Joe Tarsia's facilities. They knew that his place might just be the only studio capable of delivering the sound necessary to make their project into a hit. In no time, Sigma Sound Studios had produced dozens of hit records.

Thus began a nonstop musical enterprise made up of innovators sitting at the top of the heap in what would become a run-up in the music business' most glorious days. They later found themselves smack in the middle of the industry's ultimate fall, triggered by a disgraceful and nasty bloodbath. This was followed by the media's overhyped bashing of disco music—a sound that these men pioneered almost single-handedly. They, and many others who were working in this lucrative part of the music industry, were forced to witness the aftermath in anguish. It is one that continues to beleaguer the record industry today.

TAKING THE GAMBLE

My brother Walter was itching to get involved with Kenny Gamble. Our family's accountant Earl Morgenstern believed that Walter could provide Gamble and Huff's productions with some "blue-eyed soul" to round out their artist roster. Walter took a group of white guys he discovered named "Faustus" into Sigma Sound and used Gamble's spec dollars to create their demo. I was asked to come in and lay down a piano track; at the age of 17, this was my first professional recording experience. This project never reaped much for my brother or the group, though. Nonetheless, Morgenstern, who did the books for Southwark Paint and Queen Village Recording Studios—and coincidentally served as Gamble's financial planner—continually promoted my brother's value to Gamble and Huff. Kenny, however, preferred farming out all their extracurricular recording projects to his "family." He didn't follow Morgenstern's advice to expand his company's dimension and scope by allowing my brother to run a special division. And knowing my brother as I do, I understand that this might never have been a marriage made in heaven. Because Walter was very aggressive, it's likely that Kenny Gamble felt uncomfortable with him from the start. In any case, theirs was not a musical union to be.

Sigma's records were all over the charts. Gamble and Huff and Thom Bell quickly became industry legends; they had established their musical style, which became known as "The Sound of Philadelphia." It became the city's musical signature. Recordings produced at Sigma Sound always headed straight to the top of the charts.

Another small downtown studio, Baker Sound, was handling almost all of Philadelphia's advertising voiceover work. Still, my brother and I believed there just had to be enough demand in both the music and advertising platforms around town to allow room for another recording studio to flourish.

TEST! TEST! THIS IS A TEST! WE'RE RECORDING!

While gaining fame and having life-changing experiences at the forefront of Philadelphia's late-night music scene, I spent my days working with Walter to build our recording studio. He had been eyeing one of Southwark Paint's buildings on 4th Street. My father stored paint on the first floor and housed low-rent tenants on its upper floors. Walter deemed it ideal for a brand new recording studio. When we told my father what we wanted to do, he (always The Enabler) demonstrated his unwavering dedication to his sons by offering us this fully-occupied building. Queen Village Recording Studios was born in 1970.

When talking about the recording industry, Philadelphia was too often referred to as a one-horse town. Walter was convinced it could support another recording studio. I signed onto this idea because it was right up my alley. Despite protests from my parents, I dropped out of college and devoted all my time to building the studio and running the business with Walter. Having our own studio gave us the opportunity to produce, compose, arrange and publish our own songs—and also to manage local talent.

The Philadelphia area has always been a breeding ground for stars of radio and movies, stage actors, singers, dancers and musicians. Many talented people who hailed from this fertile city felt like they'd been blessed with an entertainment "birthright." We set about building our recording mecca into a multi-faceted in-house production facility where burgeoning talent could feel at home on every level.

We began by closing up the first floor windows to create a fortress-like interior that would house a home-made console and several tape machines capable of two- and four-track recording. We constructed Queen Village Recording Studios from almost nothing. This involved my hammering nails into wooden studs, building walls, soldering thousands of hard-wire connections onto terminals, running endless lengths of shielded cables between rooms and learning how to operate the new recording console and all of the reel-to-reel tape machines that would serve our operation. Upon finishing it, we hit the ground running. We decided to be Philadelphia's "bridge" recording facility, handling both advertising and music under one roof. We sought out new business from advertising agencies, explaining we could record their voiceovers and also write and produce musical jingles for them. The equipment we installed could be used for both commercials and musical demos. We were right on the money with this business venture.

While I continued my full-time performing schedule, our recording studio was operational. We were booking music sessions regularly, and I had the opportunity to learn techniques in producing; arranging orchestrations for strings, horns and percussion; and editing and composing original songs. I also became a studio session player. I played the keyboard on all of my productions and on countless other projects recorded at Queen Village Recording Studios. It was a decade of nonstop musical immersion for me. All day. All night. With little time allotted for sleep, I wanted to spend all of my waking hours creating original sounds and effects, performing at the piano, writing new songs and composing string and horn arrangements for orchestral projects. For me, this was another of my dreams that came true.

The voiceover talent ad agencies brought in constantly praised QVRS for both our engineering expertise and our creativity—both behind the console and in the live studio space. They let their colleagues know about us, and word spread quickly that there was a new game in town. The same held true with lots of musical talent floating around; bands hoping to be discovered came to record musical demos using their own dollars. Sometimes we elected to "sign" them—becoming their managers/producers with the intention of hawking these artists to record companies in order to obtain a recording contract for them. Queen Village Recording Studios proved itself as an alternate destination to do voiceovers for ads, make a musical demo, get signed to a record production deal in hopes of landing a major label recording contract and/or just learn all about "the biz" by being a part of our multi-faceted studio environment.

Bruce Klauber: *When the studio was just about finished, Andy and I used to steal in there in the dead of night to record ourselves singing and playing. (I pray that none of the tapes with my vocalizing and playing alto saxophone survived.) When things got serious at QVRS, I was asked to play drums on some demo sessions, and one of the singles from those dates was released on the major record label RCA. The song was a remake of "Bobby's Girl" featuring a local singer named Jill Baby Love. This was an early coup for QVRS. Whether Andy Kahn was playing piano on a recording date or was behind the recording console, he never ever told me how to play. His brother Walter did, however. When it got to the point where Walter regularly came into the drum booth, took hold of my hands and placed my sticks—which I was holding—on that cymbal or this drum and demonstrated what the "proper beat" was, I realized that being a session drummer wasn't for me. The recording process, for all involved, requires an infinite amount of patience and attention to detail, which Andy and Walter had. Truth be told, I was generally pretty lousy, which is a shame because, by that time, big bass drum sounds were back in!*

ENTER...THE LEGENDS

I t didn't take long for Queen Village Recording Studios to out-grow its original four-track analog tape equipment and its main input console. Our quest was to expand into a true, multitrack recording facility. The studio had jumped that im-possible hurdle, providing another "horse" for musical talent and advertising agencies of Philadelphia to ride on. Never mind that the public transportation electric trolley still rode the rails that remained embedded in the paved-over cobblestone streets lining the front and side of our corner studio building. It caused a significant rumble, and the tremors shook the floors and walls during recording sessions. But we were committed, sometimes I believed destined, no matter what, to become the second busiest recording facility in the city—trolleys or not. We succeeded in overcoming obstacles that would have derailed lesser men.

Bernie Lowe called me one day. That would be THE Ber-nie Lowe. The same Bernie Lowe who wrote all those hit songs, who owned Cameo-Parkway Records and made a gazillion dollars in the process—becoming one of the recording in-dustry's first true business moguls. Bernie had retired by this point, and he had serious health issues. He said he'd heard good things about me and the studio—and that he wanted to get back in the biz, claiming he really missed it. I think his wife Roz just wanted him out of the house.

Bernie's arrival at QVRS was a very big deal for me. Here was the equivalent of a modern-day Clive Davis sitting in the waiting room of our office, wearing dark sunglasses and a trench coat. His one expressed purpose for being there: To talk to ME! I was deeply honored. And I told Bernie so.

We hit it off right away, and our meeting went extremely well. Bernie had recently attempted making a demo at Sigma using some of their musicians, but it didn't work out. Together, we tackled finishing up writing this song "I Just Got to Find Someone to Love Me." Co-authored by Bernie and me, this became my first published song with ASCAP (American So-ciety of Composers, Authors and Publishers). Sung by Philadelphian Jill "Baby Love" Cohen, a member of Queen Village Recording Studios' stable of backup singers, it was produced by Walter and me. Bernie Lowe was listed as executive producer. This full-scale production ballad, complemented by strings and horns that I arranged, was signed to RCA Records in 1975. I still get royalties from that beautiful song, mostly from Europe where they have a deeper appreciation for such romantic and lush productions.

"I Just Got to Find Someone to Love Me" provided my first opportunity to take an artist on tour. With Jill in my car, we hit all the radio stations in Pennsylvania, New Jersey, Delaware, Maryland and New York. This was the age-old, traditional method of promoting an artist and new song product — going to meet the Program Directors of secondary-market radio stations. We'd just show up and introduce ourselves at these little nondescript radio station buildings that dotted the country and hillsides of rural and only slightly more cosmopolitan towns. For decades, this practice was the proven way to get songs played on the air and develop a wider audience.

When she floated into their studios, Jill was flamboyant enough to wow the disk jockeys. She was accompanied by me and the local promoter employed by RCA who showed us in. Here I was, at age 23, getting my feet wet in a part of the music profession not traditionally known for being entirely honorable. Jill ate it up, though. Literally. If nothing else, she chomped down more than a few big steaks and plates of gnocchi (her favorite) while on the road, all courtesy of the record label.

Record companies set aside large sums of money for their promotion departments. Sometimes it was used for meals. Sometimes it would be allocated to provide drugs as favors to radio jocks. Other times, it came in handy for procuring sex for the radio station's program director. It didn't matter then, to the record company executives, exactly how a recording managed to get added to a radio station's playlist — just so it did. "Hush money" or "payola," as this type of pay-for-play was referred to in the music industry, ran rampant. This practice continues to this day, though the "steaks" are much higher. As for the "gnocchi," well, I'll leave that to the reader's imagination...

We did well with Jill's first RCA release. So well, in fact, that RCA picked up her contract's option for a second record—a remake of the rock and roll classic hit "Bobby's Girl." Two records with RCA, and that was the end of Jill Baby Love's professional association with that label. The label decided against releasing an LP, even with a number of new songs already completed. But we had fun. And the experience I had working with Jill as a featured artist set the stage for many future recording artists and productions to come out of QVRS and the other studios in which I worked on record projects.

Following the lead of the Kahn brothers, several new recording facilities began popping up. The record business was on an ascent to heights never before imagined. The technology boom was just getting underway, and the equipment coming out was leaps and bounds ahead of each predecessor. This was the 1970s, and there was no end in sight.

Sigma decided it was time to unload its 16-track Scully two-inch tape behemoth. This machine recorded tons of hits for Gamble and Huff—and many other musical organizations. When they upgraded to 3M's sleek 24-track newcomer to our industry, QVRS bought Sigma's hit-making tape machine. Our control room door had to be enlarged, made wider and taller, in order to get this monster situated inside; it commandeered a whole corner. Its history literally dared the producer and engineer sitting beside it to make another hit on its fabled mechanical transport and magnetic tape heads.

We bought a new audio console, and the arduous task of rewiring the studio for 16 tracks began. The studio had to be shut down to all recording activity. Only rehearsals took place in the studio's main sound room. We worked around the clock for an entire week to turn QVRS into a major multitrack facility. Two-inch magnetic tape, true multitrack recording filled my dreams—that is, whenever I allowed myself to get some sleep, which was mostly never.

The stage was being set for famous musical projects to be recorded at our growing facility. They would include Karen Young's #1 hit "Hot Shot," The Dixie Hummingbirds' Grammy-award winning "Loves Me Like a Rock," "Stand Up Sit

Down" by AKB, the first studio recordings ever made by The Gipsy Kings, overdub sessions with Stevie Wonder and new recordings by Astrud Gilberto and Bobby Rydell. In 1976, Princess Grace of Monaco—the former actress Grace Kelly of Philadelphia—paid us a day-long visit. She recorded her narration for a full-length documentary film celebrating Philadelphia's Bicentennial.

The day before Princess Grace's arrival, we received a call from the Monaco Embassy with detailed instructions on how their monarch was to be addressed by everyone. They also gave us a list of her favorite things and suggested we have them on hand. Among them, yellow roses. When Her Serene Highness arrived the next day in a limousine bearing two flags of Monaco, the studio was decorated with several vases—each containing a dozen yellow American Beauties. She appeared not to notice and never mentioned them. Who cared? We had a real-life princess, true royalty, right there in our facility. That was magical enough to cause our feet to hover above the floor. She was there to record and to share her beneficence with us. My father was in awe: Princess Grace of Monaco at his sons' recording studio, housed in his old paint warehouse across the street from his paint store. I know he was proud of us, but it was not just that. Having such a famous person, an authentic royal, in this former run-down building that used to house 5-gallon paint cans made him beam with total pride. And why not?

My high-school friend Mitch Goldfarb had been to QVRS a couple of times: to sit in on a number of sessions, watch me conduct my arrangements for string and horn sections, listen to us create rhythm tracks for new songs we were producing and take in our whole recording-studio environment. He was so impressed, he decided to open his own studio. At Mitch's request, I offered him some advice and gave him access to suppliers—a concept my brother Walter never understood. (This was not unlike the disdain he showed me when we were kids, when I befriended Bruce Klauber and Peter Green with their rival radio station.) While allowing a potential competitor to enter the scene might not have helped increase our business, this is what friends do for each other. I also knew that

Mitch would have found a way to do it without any help. My assisting him, however, ensured that he and his partners got off to a running start.

Kajem Recording Studios was born in a small carriage house in the Wynnefield section outside of Philadelphia. Committed to providing its clients with a comfortable and musician-friendly atmosphere in which to record, their studio soon outgrew its first digs. They made an ambitious move to a large warehouse—a long-abandoned old stone mill in nearby Gladwyne. There, in the woods, set alongside a running creek, Kajem provided a scenic environment for musicians and talent to lay down their tracks. They created many hit recordings there. I have great reason to be proud of Mitch, whose ambition and drive have taken him far in the music industry. Among other things, Kajem Recording Studios helped solidify the Philadelphia area as a mecca for recording—which QVRS had also sought to do a few years earlier.

WAY AHEAD OF
THE TECHNO CURVE

Queen Village Recording Studio's 16-track Scully machine became our workhorse. Analog recording continued to rule the roost, though it seemed we never had enough separate music tracks available to us. Sixteen tracks screamed for eight more. When 24-track recording became the industry standard, studio engineers found ways to synchronize two 24-track machines together, using an electronic signal-process called SMPTE Time Code (created by engineers in the television and film industry). Hello 48-track recording!

In 1979, opting to go a route that was both daring and ahead of state-of-the art, we purchased a revolutionary multi-track recorder made by Stephens Electronics—one of only five such marvels ever produced. It could record 40 tracks on a single two-inch reel of magnetic tape. This major technological achievement startled the techies of the world because of its unconventional approach of staggering the recording head's tracks to make them all fit onto one custom-made part. Coupled with our new Neve, a beyond state-of-the-art computer-mixdown recording console, we were poised to explode right into the digital age. This was an exciting time with the record business enjoying previously unknown heights. Queen Village Recording Studios was on the leading edge. No one imagined, though, how Digital would obliterate Analog recording techniques and its apparatus, nor that miniaturization would soon rule the recording environment of our whole industry.

We had to build a new room to accommodate the computer that tracked all of our hand motions on the controls on the Neve console. The computer physically "remembered," then "commanded" those knobs and volume faders on the console to mimic all of our hand motions during playback. These components were physically moved by miniature motors interfaced to each control. Seeing all this activity on the console—without our hands touching any controls—was an eerie experience—like ghosts had taken over the control room! I liken it to watching a player piano with its keys being manipulated, reproducing an artist's prior performance. It was really spooky—all the electronic controls moving and twisting—as if invisible hands were adjusting them, just as ours had done. And, in effect, they were. The controls, receiving commands digitally from the computer, were simply replicating all of our previous moves. They'd reproduce the mechanical adjustments we'd make to our mixdown levels and equalization of the individual, original sounds being played back, all of which had been recorded onto tape on individually-assigned tracks. The electronically-mapped changes to these controls we'd make during each session mixdown were saved onto eight-inch magnetic memory floppy disks. (We'd never heard of floppy disks before getting this equipment!) Special ventilation was required to keep the computer cool. Remember, this was the dawn of music's digital realm. Music controlled by computers? Who had ever heard of such of thing?

These were the early days of computers assisting us in our everyday tape-recording applications. True digital recording apparatus was still years away. The concept of having a complete sound studio with unlimited tracks upon which to record, all compressed into a portable notebook computer, as is commonplace today, wasn't anywhere on our radar. But Queen Village Recording Studio was way ahead of the curve; we actually became the first studio in Philadelphia to be outfitted with total computer-mixdown capability. The music performance tracks were still being recorded onto analog tape at the time. But control of the final mixing and blending of these tracks was transferred to the electronic logic embedded and programmed in the computers. We were on a serious roll... quite a different one from "Roll tape!"

From my command post, I was conducting, writing, producing, arranging and managing. It was an extraordinary ride. This Go-Go environment suggested there was nowhere to go but up. There simply seemed to be no ceiling above us. The sky beckoned to just about anyone who was inclined to shoot an arrow into the music universe. A trip to the moon was no longer just a pipedream here on planet Earth, as we were all riding aboard a thundering musical rocket ship.

MAJOR LABELS AND MAJOR ARTISTS

Rydell and Gilberto: Singing Andy's Praises... and Songs

My brother and I collaborated on a total of 29 full-scale record productions at Queen Village Recording Studios for a period of nine years. We signed several new artists to major record labels. In 1974, Great Pride, a local band, was inked to MGM. Gene Leone, one of its members, became a world-class engineer who worked on dozens of hit disco records—eventually building his own state-of-the-art digital recording studio, still in operation today.

Walter produced a cover version of Paul Simon's song "Loves Me Like a Rock" with the legendary Dixie Hummingbirds, which won that group the 1973 Grammy for Best Soul Gospel Performance. Our association with the Dixie Hummingbirds brought Stevie Wonder to QVRS. He recorded a few tracks for their Gospel LP on ABC Records. Stevie Wonder! We figured we had really hit the Big Time.

We became a recording haven for groups who'd been signed to the Gospel division of the ABC label. Calhoon, a New York band on the forefront of blue-eyed soul and disco, came to us. Record mogul Phil Spector signed them to his label distributed by Warner Bros. Calhoon's single "Dance, Dance, Dance" is recognized as one of the early disco records responsible for introducing this new rhythmic dance music into white nightclubs—moving beyond its Rhythm and Blues roots. I took on new projects with established artists like Bobby Rydell and Astrud Gilberto. Both of them recorded new songs I'd written for them.

Bobby Rydell was a joy to record and to have around our studio. He was a native Philadelphia artist who brought zero attitude into the studio along with plenty of musical talent and a deep appreciation for our efforts to produce him. His natural warmth made all of our sessions together run smoothly. Bobby was always looking for new material for his nightclub act. He added a ballad I wrote with lyricist Linda Blackburn "Strangers When We Wake Up" to his live performance repertoire. That made me very proud. Bobby recorded another song I wrote called "Free to Be in Love." It was a unique pleasure to work with such a true professional.

I'd met Astrud Gilberto when I was about 15. She lived near me in a Philadelphia suburb. Riding my bicycle to her home, I was lurking around its perimeter one day, trying to catch a glimpse of this superstar, when I was collared (literally) by her second husband, Nick LaSorsa. When he inquired why I was hiding in their bushes, I said I wanted to see the great Astrud Gilberto. He suggested that I didn't know anything about her music. I proceeded to rattle off a list of the songs on her first few albums. Obviously impressed, he led me out of the landscaping to meet her. And there she was, "The Girl from Ipanema," lounging around the pool, in a bikini—just a half mile from my house!

We struck up a friendship, fanning the flames of my dream to one day write songs and play the piano for her. A decade later, our friendship provided the opportunity for my dream to become a reality. I sent a demo with a few of my songs to Astrud. She'd been planning to do a cover version of the theme song from the movie "The Last Tango in Paris." She thought this would be a good opportunity for us to work together in the studio. Of course, I was delirious with anticipation and joy. I eagerly agreed to her request that her son Marcelo play in the rhythm section we'd put together for her recording session. Plans were made to lay down tracks for the four songs we'd record with her.

Following her 1964 surprise, break-out, international smash-hit "The Girl from Ipanema," Astrud developed a reputation for being difficult to manage. This problem began during the period when she was signed to Verve Records. I personally never encountered any problems working with her in the studio. But it was while I was working with her that major friction occurred between my brother Walter and me.

One day, Walter entered the control room and made some discourteous remarks directed at Astrud. They had to do with her expectations regarding the legal rights to the tracks she and I had been recording. Astrud showed her anger at his abruptness, which spoiled the warm and comfortable mood we'd been experiencing. Much to my embarrassment and subsequent outrage, a short, heated exchange ensued between the two of them. By then, Astrud was in tears.

Her husband escorted her out of the studio, firing back a salvo that we shouldn't expect her to return anytime soon to work on our project. His words were prophetic. We never worked together on anything professionally again. However, Astrud and I maintained personal contact for a few more years.

The last time I was with her was in 1979, after a trip I took to Rio de Janeiro. I met one of Astrud's cousins there who gave me some things to bring back to Philadelphia. My partner Bruce Cahan (we had just started what would become our lifelong relationship) and I visited Astrud at her home. She was not particularly warm toward either Bruce or me. Feelings over what happened a few years earlier in the studio were still smoldering in her. She said she'd call me with her review of a recent recording of mine—an album that included sounds produced from instruments I'd picked up in Brazil during their annual Carnaval celebration I just attended. It saddened me that she never called. Obviously, the gulf between us remained.

I saw her perform with her son at a small club in downtown Philadelphia a few years later. But this also didn't renew anything professionally or personally between the two of us. Subsequent attempts I made to contact Astrud never panned out. She remains an extremely private person today and doesn't perform anymore. She prefers to live quietly, out of the limelight and fame she once enjoyed. While I honor her decision to withdraw from the business, I miss our friendship, which was real and founded on mutual respect and honesty. Stan Getz's historic recording of "The Girl from Ipanema" with Antonio Carlos Jobim and Joao Gilberto (Astrud's first husband) featured an unknown 24-year-old, shy, young woman who delivered the English lyrics with lovely innocence. That internationally-acclaimed, bossa-nova (translated as "new beat") hit altered the very tilt of our planet, standing the entire music world on its head in the summer of 1964. Astrud

Gilberto, possessing a sound no one had ever heard before, changed everything! I get goosebumps over my entire body every time I hear it played. How I'd love to see her again.

After the Astrud Gilberto incident at Queen Village Recording Studio, I knew I had a huge decision to make. Was it time to break up my business partnership with Walter? As brothers the dynamics between us had always been strained. Several times this friction spilled over into both my artistic and personal affiliations with other artists. This last incident drove a permanent wedge into the hugely important relationship I'd cultivated with Astrud. Things were certainly changing fast for me. After that sad and unpleasant incident with Astrud Gilberto and my brother, the decision I had to make became clear.

Bruce Klauber: *I played on one of the Astrud Gilberto sessions. Perhaps Andy wanted a jazz-oriented guy on the drums, or maybe he correctly believed that I just wanted to be in the same room with a gorgeous jazz legend. Astrud was wonderful and, yes, beautiful. Of course, like millions of others, I fell in love with her. It was an easy recording date, with everyone finding their own way, even with the last-minute changes in keys we had to make. Astrud made some good suggestions. We did a couple of Andy's songs including "Strangers When We Wake Up"—which I think could have become a standard— and the theme to the "Last Tango in Paris." I remember that her husband Nick was in the booth and that her teenage son played guitar on a few tracks, making the date a joyous family affair. Astrud's final public appearance was in 2001, and that was it. What a shame. No one sounded like her. And no one looked like her.*

DISCO

Disco music surfaced from the underground, enjoying a strong presence, but limited mainly to gay and black nightclubs. When it finally went mainstream, everybody suddenly wanted in. And they wanted to be there in a big way. The record companies saw unlimited opportunities as this genre literally took over the record business. Every artist from Barry Manilow to Paul McCartney, from David Bowie to Barbra Streisand, rockers from Rod Stewart and Linda Ronstadt to Harry Nilsson and Mick Jagger and even Broadway's Ethel Merman jumped onboard the Disco Train. There wasn't a popular song or theme that couldn't be "disco-ized," with the hopes that it would instantly find its way onto discotheque dance floors. The disco signature—a "four-on-the-floor" kick drum beat and hi-hat cymbals sizzling on backbeats two and four—became commonplace on almost every new release by the independent and major record labels. Classical symphony melodies by iconic, old-world composers got remade—with "The Beat." Country music's chart-topping hits suddenly included a thumping bass drum, four beats to each measure. Rock stars began incorporating disco-style versions of their hit songs into their concert performances. They even began creating new compositions that paid homage to this musical phenomenon captivating and covering every square-inch of the world's record business real estate.

Never before had the music industry experienced such a rapid run-up in sales figures and total media exposure. The buying public demonstrated an uncanny agility in scrambling over to record retailers for the latest hits they'd heard in clubs and on the radio. Fans would hear something new, and the next day all of the record stores were besieged with buyers looking for it. Rarely was it in stock because the clubs were often playing "promo" vinyl pressings of these latest releases, brought directly to the DJs by an army of in-house and independent promoters working for the record companies. They weren't yet released for sale.

Record stores wanted to get their hands on the new mixes being played in the clubs. But the newest versions either hadn't been shipped yet or weren't even planned for distribution. This made attending discotheques paramount for fans wanting to keep up with the latest and greatest special club mixes retailers likely hadn't even heard about yet. Because disco was closely associated with the gay clubs, where this sound had first totally taken hold, they became fashionable destinations for "straight" fans of the music. It was not uncommon to hear people saying that the best music could only be heard in the gay clubs. The novelty hits and generic versions were played in the straight clubs, but the gay clubs offered versions of songs that simply could not be danced to anywhere else. Stores receiving a hot new single found them selling out immediately, and the rush was on to replenish stock of a release that had suddenly caught fire.

When imported disco product landed on American shores, club-goers went absolutely berserk. This caused a whole new wave of clamoring to get one's hands on these esoteric dance club productions. Imports began filling up spaces in record store bins—under their own classification. It seemed the whole world was dominated by the disco dance phenomenon. There was no way of keeping up with the demand for newly-released product. All of this represented a lot of new territory for the record executives to reap and sow. They were dazzled *and* overwhelmed by it. The world had become stricken with dance fever, and it was getting uncontrollably hotter every day—with no apparent cure in sight.

Suddenly, DJs in dance clubs became the new go-to people for the record labels' promoters. The DJs, varied individuals, often having little professional experience, became the ones "breaking" new records—not radio programmers. Hits were being created at world-famous nightclubs like Studio 54, Xenon and Paradise Garage in New York, The Second Story and The DCA Club in Philadelphia, Chez Paree in Atlantic City, Studio One in LA, The Warehouse in Chicago, Dreamland and The Trocadero in San Francisco and The Limelight near Miami. Dozens of clubs popped up across the country and around the world. Disco was firmly in control of the nightlife.

DJs had become the new stars—a phenomenon that began in the late 1970s and one that continues in earnest today. Club DJs hold tremendous clout regarding every label's promotion of a release. They are wined, dined and sometimes drugged, receiving special attention and favors they had never received previously. The clubs became the new conduit for recordings being introduced to the public.

The frenzy of activity in a club was centered on its DJ, some of whom became internationally famous for their "spinning" abilities. Those who became recognized as having special talent for keeping crowds enthralled all night long were assigned "residencies" at a club. Regulars became acquainted with which DJs would be performing on a particular night. They'd plan their late-night activities each week around that schedule. DJs who developed a name gave clubs new opportunities to create a special event with a visiting guest performer, promoting them the way rock stars are hailed prior to their concert tour appearances.

A guest New York DJ always guaranteed a large crowd in Philadelphia. With regard to the 1970s disco scene, New York was Ground Zero for hipness. The legend surrounding Studio 54, with its glamorous A-List guests, only fueled that fire. Everyone wanted to get into 54. Most people weren't on the list of glitterati granted access to this famed club, however, so going to hear a guest DJ who came in from New York to spin at a local club was the next best thing.

DJs were inspired to come up with creative ways to drive club crowds crazy. They started "mixing" on-the-spot, actually creating new versions of popular recordings, using two or more turntables playing the same song. Through this action, the 12-inch extended single made its appearance—the result of the creativity of a few clever DJs who became very famous for creating "extended mixes." This led to shifting an already-completed production back into the recording studio for remixing. There, it was remade and then re-distributed as a specialty—a lengthier mix of a hit song already released. Because there were no computers at this point, the recording studio remained the only place with the equipment that allowed a DJ to edit and supplement "his" mix with new sounds—in order to create a unique, longer "club" version.

These multiple mixes of popular songs were being snapped up by a delirious public that couldn't buy enough new versions of a hit song they'd heard and already liked. The 12-inch extended single-DJ mix pumped tens of millions of dollars more toward sales of what started out as a single release. The record business had never experienced anything like this. And it never would again, as this was destined to be a once-in-a-lifetime opportunity for the industry to grow exponentially in a very short period of time.

In 1977, I sought out one of those special DJs. Kurt Borusiewicz was a Billboard magazine award-winning spinner in Philadelphia. A cousin of mine Joel Pesko (aka Joel Peters) told me about Kurt and took me to the club where Kurt was working full-time. I spent the next five late nights and into the early mornings at the DCA Club, a Philadelphia after-hours club. I listened, studied and observed everything. I had never before seen crowds react as they did to someone spinning records. And, it occurred on a Tuesday night just as it did on a Saturday night. The place erupted after Kurt mixed into each song, one after the other. He had the magic touch. He knew what would make people scream. He understood this music better than anyone I'd ever met or heard. And I knew, more than anything else, that I was going to work with him.

After the closing song on the fifth night of my staking out this man, I approached him in his tiny DJ booth. I simply informed him: "I own a recording studio, and you are coming with me." Not long after he finished his cigarette, his cocktail and popped a quaalude into his mouth, he followed me to my car. I drove him to Queen Village Recording Studios for what would be a historic evening during which we became musical collaborators. I played him unfinished rhythm tracks, songs that had not yet been signed, others that were signed but never released by the labels. I played some songs I'd written that had not yet been recorded—on the Steinway in the studio. Kurt's eyes widened with each new composition. Considering it got to be 6 a.m., it was amazing that we remained so focused. From the get-go, it was clear that we were both "juiced" and sensing that something very special was clicking between us. One can only imagine the looks on the faces of our engineering staff when they arrived a few hours later, encountering Kurt and me, both bleary-eyed and still sitting behind the console in the control room.

HOT SHOT

A local promoter was dying to have a hit record and had hooked up with my brother to accomplish just that. They created a few tracks together, for which I wrote the arrangements. This promoter then conjured up a novel concept for a disco record. He approached me with the idea of employing a musical instrument that would not normally be featured on a fully-orchestrated studio production. Giving it some thought, I suggested a tuba. That remark shot us right out of the starting gate toward what ultimately would become known as "Sousa's Salsa—That Tuba Thing."

I contacted Jon Dorn, a schooled tuba player with both the personality and dexterity to play against a heavy dance rhythm track. His brother was Joel Dorn, famed record producer for the Atlantic label, responsible for discovering Roberta Flack—among other stars in the entertainment world. Playing these unfinished, rough tracks of the tuba record for Kurt, I had him laughing uneasily. He didn't think this record could take the world by storm. We decided, however, that if nothing else, it would prove our ability to work together in the studio. What's more, it was on someone else's dime. So, my first project with Kurt Borusiewicz as my co-producer was to release a 12-inch extended-mix disco record featuring a tuba.

Pressed onto vinyl and released by the promoter's newly-formed independent record label in 1977, my 29th record production at Queen Village Recording Studios created some "noise" in Philadelphia and New York clubs. Although our tuba concept never really caught on, it did cement the bond between Kurt and me; we became a powerful marriage of talent and ability. Poised to make a great deal more "noise" the following year, we produced a very loud "shot heard 'round the world." My 30th record production would pry loose any doors that were previously only cracked open. These doors revealed a glittering world—one that this 26-year old musician from Philadelphia dreamed would finally open invitingly for him one day.

A year earlier, I'd written all the arrangements for the album by the NYC group Calhoon, which my brother produced for Phil Spector's Warner/Spector label. I'd also written an original song called "Stop Sign" as part of Calhoon's album, which was never released. Following the band's first and follow-up single, the label dropped them before becoming contractually required to release the rest of the tracks on an LP.

"Stop Sign" was clearly not meant to see the light of day with Calhoon. But it was "Stop Sign" that opened Kurt's sleepy eyes during the fateful wee small hours one morning in 1977. Suddenly he proclaimed, "This sounds like a hit record." Because it was entirely my composition, I was delighted over this, of course!

We made plans to meet again the following day—to rewrite the lyrics. Our plan was to create a new song that we'd lay over the existing "Stop Sign" rhythm track, which was never going to be released as it was originally recorded. That track, minus its vocal parts, had an amazing groove. Here was an unmistakably hot sound, infectious from the first two measures of music, with a lead guitar lick being duplicated on the bass guitar and piano, coupled with a driving high-hat, opening and closing on the upbeats of one and three throughout each bar. If you couldn't get into the rhythm of this song, it's likely that you were either dead or deaf. Or both.

We decided that whatever the song's storyline, it absolutely had to have the word "hot" in it, as everything in 1977 was either "hot" or "not." Playing with these two words, searching for the rhymes that were best coupled together, we came upon two and then stopped speaking—a rarity for me at any time of day. I don't know how long we were silent, but it was evident "Hot Shot" would be our title. We next focused on finding words to describe the feelings one has regarding their receiving a "hot shot"— and the race was on. We wrote the lyrics and constructed the rest of the song, straddling each other's ideas and phrases, finding the whole occasion funny— both of us giddy from the start. When the song had been written and tested against the "Stop Sign" instrumental track, our next hurdle was to locate our artist.

Kurt Borusiewicz and I had shared a number of mind-boggling coincidences. Just two years earlier, I had been living only one floor above him in Society Hill Towers. He used to hear my piano from his apartment. He'd then come up and hide in the fire-escape stairway next to my front door and listen to me playing. At that point, Kurt didn't know me at all. And I never knew that someone was nearby and listening. Apparently this went on until I moved away. Kurt was still living there when we finally met. We discovered this incredible connection on the night I introduced myself to him. Regarding "Hot Shot," we both knew that our artist simply had to be a female. What neither of us realized was that we were both considering the same performer; we didn't even know that the other one of us knew her. When Kurt asked me if I'd heard of Karen Young, I stared in disbelief. Karen's voice was all I kept hearing in my head while we were rewriting "Stop Sign" into "Hot Shot." I just knew it would take a powerful and energetic performance by a singer to pull this song off. Karen certainly fit that bill. Another one of a series of coincidences regarding Kurt and me? I maintain that there are no coincidences.

FOR THOSE WHO THINK YOUNG

I met Karen Young for the first time when I was about 10 years old—at an annual Kahn Family Chanukah party. Each year, at some point during the night, I would entertain my relatives by playing the piano. Joel Pesko, the same cousin of mine who introduced me to Kurt at the DCA Club years later, brought one of his school friends to that holiday party. She knew how to get attention playing a keyboard, and she sure knew how to belt out a song. In the middle of my playing some show tune, Karen Young came over, pushed her way onto the piano bench and barked, "Let's do a duet together!"

I'm sure I was not particularly amused at having some big girl come over to steal my spotlight. But I do remember vividly thinking afterward, "Wow, she can really sing." Her piano playing was forceful and not my style at all, but it was clear she knew how to draw in an audience with her robust talent. Karen Young and I were a hit together, even way back then!

Our paths were set to cross again 10 years later. Karen was hired to sing background vocals at my recording studio for one of our artist's productions. Kurt knew Karen from her days playing piano and singing at Equus—a gay cabaret nightclub and piano bar in Philadelphia. She developed a large local fan base who loved her ability to be raunchy and uninhibited, making her a local celebrity. Karen could wail and sizzle like Janis Joplin, scat and soar like Ella Fitzgerald and bring down an entire room like Aretha Franklin—with a voice just as huge. But she was an original. Influenced by those three superstar vocalists, Karen developed a sound and style that would remain uniquely hers throughout her performing career.

Kurt and I harbored no doubt. It simply had to be Karen Young who would sing "Hot Shot." No other singer was even considered. We were convinced she would tear it up better than anyone. Discovering she was singing in Hallandale, Florida, at a bar in a racetrack, we knew we had to take this powerful song directly to her. Off to Florida we went to inform her that she was the vocalist meant to sing it.

I love to watch the faces of people listening to "Hot Shot" because it reaches out and grabs them right away. From the moment Karen heard the demo with my singing the song on top of those rough instrumental tracks left over from the Calhoon sessions, she proclaimed this would be "her" song. We asked her to fly back to Philadelphia with us to record the vocal track. With no hesitation, the three of us left the next day. We went right into the studio to record her "demo" vocal. It was her demo performance that we hawked to record labels in search of a deal to fund finishing this track—and the other unwritten songs that would make up her LP release to follow the single. It was all beginning to unfold before our eyes.

As an award-winning Billboard Magazine DJ and Reporter, Kurt had developed strong contacts at all the major disco-oriented labels. His buddy Ray Caviano at TK Records in Miami had racked up a long string of disco hits for that independent record label. Ray turned us down when he discovered Karen was a heavy, white girl who performed at piano bars. Imagine Atlantic Records not signing Roberta Flack because of her weight and that she played and sang in piano bars around Washington, D.C.! Ray thought the tune was great, though, and suggested we find another "hot-looking" female artist to take a stab at it. Kurt and I thought, "No way!" "Hot Shot" was tailor-made for Karen Young. It was her song.

Next, Michele Hart at Casablanca, the high-flying record label responsible for launching Donna Summer's career, said she was dying to have this record on her label. But Casablanca's release roster was full, and they wouldn't put it out until sometime in the fall of 1978. It was already March. Kurt and I were keenly focused on "Hot Shot" being released just before the summer season. Having ruled out major labels, we now wondered if we'd be able to pull off a rush-release with another independent record company. A large company like Columbia or Atlantic would never be able to release it quickly. We stuck to the independents, hoping we'd find one that "got it" in the same way we did.

West End Records in New York City informed us they wanted to hear it. We warned them we'd only bring it to them if they could deliver a summer release. Mel Cheren, the label's president, offered his assurance. When we met in Mel's office, he popped the cassette with Karen's demo vocal of "Hot Shot" into his tape deck. He stopped it after Karen sang the first four lines ending in "I need a Hot Shah-h-h-h-t!" I thought, "Oh shit! He hates it." His first words were, "I must have this record." We suggested he listen to the rest of the song. His response was that the rest of the song didn't matter because he already knew what this record could be. He repeated that West End simply had to have the song and asked for our deal terms.

We were dumbstruck, of course. Not anticipating this, we didn't know how to answer. We asked Mel to listen to the rest of the four-minute demo while Kurt and I adjourned to the lobby. "What do we do now?" was all we could keep asking each other. We heard the cassette stop. A minute later, it was playing again. Back in Mel's office, we encountered his business partner Ed Kushins and Alan-Michael Mamber, the label's Artist & Repertoire guy, whom Kurt knew well. We waited until the tape ended, and the deafening sound of silence commenced. But not for long. Never known as being one to keep quiet for more than a few seconds, I asked, "So what's your deal?" Ed Kushins retorted instantly with, "So, what're ya' looking for?"

We reminded them of our commitment to having this out by Memorial Day. They said this would not be a problem. Their label was well-known for breaking out new artists and also for pioneering the 12-inch extended club-remix on vinyl. They wanted to know how much money we expected up front, as was customary when either a major or independent label bought a recording master's worldwide rights. There were many details and legal terms thrown around—including the industry-standard of the artist being signed to the label in a binding production contract for the initial release with options for more singles and an album.

The deal would have to include options for subsequent tracks, based on sales parameters and a host of other intricate details. These kept changing during an assortment of topics discussed—not limited to us hearing about the quality of a sexual liaison the label head experienced ten minutes before we arrived. We told them we'd have to talk to Karen, then consult with our music attorney to draw up a draft agreement.

Having found a label offering us a summer release for "Hot Shot," we called Michele at Casablanca, hoping she might reconsider matching our release date priority—but to no avail. West End was the only label agreeing to the single most important thing we were seeking: getting "Hot Shot" released right away. "Hot Shot" and Karen Young would be West End's in short order. And what an order for the 12-inch single they'd soon be seeing–from everywhere in the world—and all at once!

Though not the most lucrative one by any measure, our deal was struck. Kurt and I were just getting ourselves out there as a new production team, bringing along an unknown artist to an under-capitalized, independent label that was about to have both its first number one record and its first million seller. (Casablanca and TK had done that dozens of times.) Karen, who'd gone back to her gig in Florida, returned the following month to Philadelphia for another vocal session, delivering her finished recorded performance. That session secured "Hot Shot" its rightful place on the mantle in the Disco Hall of Fame.

Karen's vocal session took almost 30 hours. It included two naps by the artist, a corned-beef special, which required us putting up a "food screen" to capture coleslaw flying out of Karen's mouth during her scatting section and a pepperoni pizza with mushrooms. Karen at one point insisted on taking a bubble bath in my home—next door to the studio. She had one more stipulation regarding that bath: that she share it with a very young, sexy rhythm-track musician whom she'd fancied from the moment she'd laid eyes on him. It's a good thing he had a terrific sense of humor and agreed to hop in the tub with her. That must have been some ride! When I asked him about it later on, he refused to divulge any of the details.

Achieving Karen's "Hot Shot" performance was exhausting and grueling. But I was relentless in holding her to perfect diction, to staying in tune and keeping her energy pinning the meter. Kurt, cool as ever, lit cigarette after cigarette in the control room, nodding his head or shaking it side to side depending on what his expert ears heard from the JBL monitor speakers. Karen headed right back to Florida. We hammered out her single-release-with-an-option-for-one-LP agreement between West End and our Sunshine Productions company. A summer

1978 release it was, kicked off in three strategic locations: Philadelphia, where by our taking it to clubs, it had already developed a following in gay and straight discos; New York City; Fire Island. If "Hot Shot" caught on in the dance clubs at these locations, we knew we'd be on our way to achieving a hit record. What occurred with "Hot Shot" made pure disco history.

We ruled the charts for the first half of the summer, peaking for two weeks at number one in Billboard Magazine. West End had their first hit record, as did vocalist Karen Young, DJ Kurt Borusiewicz and I. Celebrating my 26th birthday was amplified with the news that my 30th record production had become "The Hot Shot heard 'round the world." A birthday gift like this doesn't come around very often. The owner of the DCA Club gave his approval for me to throw myself a birthday party there, because his club was where the record "Hot Shot" was literally born. This was some party. The usual club-goers mingled with my huge list of invited guests. Flamboyant drag queens, cross-dressers and high-fashioned gay men shared the dance floor with my straight friends, studio business associates and clients, cousins, aunts and uncles, members of my immediate family and even Astrud Gilberto with her husband Nick. Everyone was there. It was just awesome, a word I reserve for when it is truly deserved. I was on top of the world.

Who knew how short-lived this "party" would be? How could we have known that the record business was reaching its limits? It would soon come crashing down, leaving tons of debris to be picked through by those few remaining players who had the stamina to breathe the fumes of a rotting trash heap. Absolutely no one suspected that the end of an extraordinary era of the music industry was just one year away.

WHAT A BUSINESS

The recording business, like many within the performing arts, is filled with parasites and would-be promoters who smell quick money. They move in on an artist, promising fame and riches beyond comprehension. With a surprise hit record sitting at number one, Karen Young became an easy target. Local promoters contacted her and engaged her parents in discussions. Parents often serve as a performing artist's most vulnerable conduit for promoters. Some promoters tossed around some pretty unreasonable dollar figures that Karen could get by working with them. They said she'd never receive as much money while being managed by us. Getting "Hot Shot" to this point was something Kurt and I had done against all odds. Our team, which included my brother Walter and the club owner who was Kurt's silent partner, had paid for everything up until then—all on speculation. The leeches knew all this and preyed on Karen.

Karen's level-headed, career-long attorney Lloyd Remick offered some sensible ideas to us, designed to satisfy Karen's parents. But even Lloyd, whom they trusted, was unable to persuade them to settle crucial matters now hanging in mid-air, jeopardizing our tour schedule which was set to start in just a few days.

With no investment on their part, promoters find it easy to appear out of nowhere and make wild and unrealistic promises. Karen was told she was being ripped-off by her current management. In fact, the opposite was true. A serious monkey wrench had now been thrown into our plans at the eleventh hour. We were faced with the nearly impossible task of undoing the damage these promoters had instigated. We desperately tried to convince Karen and her parents that we had always been looking out for her, working with her best interests at heart—and that it was our team that got her here, not these promoters. Her parents demanded one thing through all of this, and they wouldn't waver. We would have to come up with a sizable amount of money before they would let her go out on tour. Frustrated and worn out physically and emotionally, we came to realize that we simply had no other choice.

The alternative would have produced an uncooperative artist receiving advice from less than honorable sources—and from her parents who were led to become suspicious of our intentions—all of whom were applying pressure on Karen now. We paid up. Never mind that these shenanigans were comparable to extortion. The tour was back on. One hurdle had been removed, albeit, an extremely important one.

Next, our record label tried to pry our artist away from us. We'd produced West End's first hit record, and they rewarded us by making private innuendos to Karen. This served to confuse her parents and her once again. They advised, like the others before them, that they'd do a much better job handling her career than Kurt and I. Mel and Ed tossed out names of well-known record producers they'd hire to create Karen's next studio recordings—if she'd just give us up. This is an age-old entertainment industry ploy, a routine that continues to plague new talent when they begin to get recognition—especially those plucked from obscurity, who find themselves suddenly thrust onto the international stage of stardom. West End continued making their presence felt throughout the tour, applying pressure on Karen every step of the way—making it extremely difficult for us to keep her focused on our schedule and the plans we'd made on her behalf. She was impossible to manage the entire time we were on the road promoting "Hot Shot" for the label, touring with a new band we'd put together for her "live" show. It was a tough tour, but it was an amazing and educational experience I wouldn't have traded for the world. This was on-the-job learning that simply could not be acquired in any institutional setting.

Bruce Klauber: *Corruption, dishonesty and greed have always been part of the music business. Andy and I experienced our share of double-dealings at a young age. Clubs in which we worked ended up having padlocks on them when we showed up to perform the next night. Payments promised from some pretty big names never came through. On one occasion, we had to go to the Pennsauken, New Jersey, branch of the Musicians' Union to collect money owed to us. We found ourselves standing in line right behind jazz trumpeter Dizzy Gillespie, who was trying to get paid from the same club! Andy and Kurt were* *not naïve, but they were scrupulously honest and trusting in an industry that was anything but. They could have taken the easy way out by becoming shysters themselves. To their everlasting credit, they did not.*

We booked a club date appearance at a discotheque in Connecticut. Karen was scheduled to perform "Hot Shot," singing "live" against an instrumental track—much more effective than lip-synching a performance. The fans become more engaged when they see—and hear—the artist for "real." It also prompts the artist to put on a great performance. When we arrived, the owner of the club took one look at Karen and said, "Who dat?" This was a club that catered mainly to black patrons. The sight of a white girl, whom most people just assumed was black after listening to her, took this man totally by surprise.

Our road manager told the owner of the club who she was. The man insisted she could not possibly be Karen Young. When he was told again that this, in fact, was the artist to whom he'd agreed to pay $2,000 for a live performance in his club, he took us all aside. We were sternly told that Karen would not be performing in his club that night. When asked the reason, he replied without hesitation that his club's attendees expected to see a black female vocalist. If Karen got on stage, he was certain that she would be booed off the stage and harassed. We told him that he was overreacting and that he'd be pleasantly surprised once he heard her perform. We said that Karen's voice had a powerful effect on every audience, and she should be given the opportunity so he could see and hear that in person.

He wasn't buying it. We brought up the issue of our signed contract for Karen's appearance there. He again, now more forcefully, told us that there was no way she'd be appearing in his club and that he had every intention of avoiding both a riot by his patrons and a lawsuit by our management company. He reached into his pocket, pulled out a large billfold, peeled off 20 one-hundred dollar bills, pressed them into our road manager's hand and said, "Now, go on! Get that white bitch outta here before things get really ugly." Pointing toward Karen, he added, "And they're ugly enough already!"

We were dumbfounded. Not one of us was prepared for a scene like this to unfold based on a racial issue. We hustled Karen out the back door. Unable to grasp why this was happening, she kept protesting that she went there to sing. Karen loved performing for black audiences. Everywhere she went, they responded well to her. When she opened her mouth to sing, she was overwhelmingly accepted as one of their own. When she went on stage, many would look at her quizzically. But when she began to sing, boiling hot lava erupted from her vocal volcano and she won them over every time. I know. I was there each time it happened. I often remarked that Karen was simply a black woman who'd gotten trapped in the body of a heavyset, white, Jewish girl from Northeast Philadelphia. That club owner in Connecticut made the wrong decision in paying her off and demanding that she leave. He should have given Karen the chance to prove that music truly overcomes racial prejudice. He'll never know what he missed by sending her out the back door of his club. She would have killed everyone there that night.

I cannot claim to be without any form of prejudice. I don't know anyone who's able to claim they don't have prejudices on any level. I do know, however, that when the walls of color are eliminated and art is allowed to take control, amazing things unfold. I watched this happen again and again while touring with Karen Young. Legions of "Hot Shot" fans, who simply had no idea that she wasn't black, were won over the instant she began singing onstage. Her talent was a beacon that overshadowed every other beam of light in a room. Getting her onto the stage was always a challenge, though. She was terribly afraid of heights. She didn't do well climbing any number of steps. She seemed to experience stage-fright right before going on; a wild look came over her face and fear gripped her eyes. But when the intro to "Hot Shot" came on, her world suddenly turned beautiful again. Her panic dissolved, as did mine. I was one of the two men who did everything we could to get Karen into the moment when her voice would take command of a room. Even as I breathed that welcome sigh of relief, I knew I would to have to face the identical scenario the following night—in a different venue, before a different crowd of disbelieving fans—all astonished that this white girl could actually sing like that. And sing like that, Karen Young certain did!

While on tour, Kurt and I had to cater to Karen to such a degree that we found ourselves wondering how we'd ever gotten involved with such a mess of an artist. Of course, we didn't need to be reminded that we were the ones who handpicked her! Now we wondered how long it would take us to have had enough of her. Karen needed pampering and attention 24 hours a day. Locating her became an exhausting exercise each day on the road. We always kept a spare key to her hotel room because knocking on her door typically produced zero results. If the hotel had a lounge with a live group entertaining its patrons, Karen would go there and perform onstage with them. Long after closing hour, she'd usually hang out with the band members. If she found any of them attractive—usually a black or Latino musician would catch her eye—she'd just disappear with him. Karen found ways to elude us any chance she could.

I can't count the number of times she managed to actually leave the hotel without telling us. We would panic when we realized our star had vanished. She would return eventually, hours later. Several times, it was only a few minutes before we had to leave for her next tour destination. A vehicle would suddenly drive up with several people inside waving at Kurt and me, while we were grimacing at them as we stood in front of the hotel. The door would fly open, and out would pop Miss Karen Young with a huge grin on her face—rivaling any that Alice in Wonderland's Cheshire Cat might offer. We were furious and she knew it. And in a matter of moments, we were off to do it all over again at our next stop. Being on the road with Karen Young meant providing her with plenty of food, a room of her own and keeping track of her stage wardrobe, personal clothing and the medicines she needed. This required meticulous management.

To regulate her mood, Karen took drugs that doctors had prescribed for her since she was a child. Ritalin was one of them; when she took it regularly, she was clearly more focused and easier to manage. I wouldn't say that Karen never mixed any other substances with Ritalin. She certainly loved her Southern Comfort, and she was known to party along with a crowd as much as any of us did during those wild days of disco. However, I feel obliged to say on the record that Karen Young was not the drug addict and uber-alcoholic for which she'd achieved a widespread reputation.

I was right there with her. While on tour, Kurt and I literally lived with Karen. She was a true artist. Artists often have wild looks in their eyes. They have talent that extends beyond anything mere mortals can be expected to comprehend. Their gifts captivate them, often making it seem as though they're possessed. Well, they *are* possessed—with an artistic ability needing to be expressed. That is what makes them unique, so very different from the rest of the world. Too often, human beings ridicule and poke fun at those who do not conform to convention. Karen Young was not born to conform to any type of convention. Her special gift was to dazzle through her enormous artistic talent. She succeeded in doing that at every turn. The electricity visible in her eyes, that awkward way she walked, her physical clumsiness from being a large-framed woman gave the impression that she was always "on something." Having spent a huge amount of time with her, I cannot disagree more with that assessment. I do agree, however, that she was "on"—onto something that the rest of the world finds difficult to comprehend. She was on an artistic trip, not so much a laboratory-induced one.

Karen Young was on a journey that few people would understand. I shared that journey with her. Being a performing artist myself, I'm on a similar journey. Every artist is different. Some can handle their special talents at all times. Others can't handle them at all, resulting in their self-obliteration. And then, there are artists who sit somewhere in the middle. Artists are rarely understood. This doesn't make them less than true artists. I believe that the only people who can really understand artists are other artists.

DINAH SHORE'S BARE FEET

One individual who understood Karen was superstar Dinah Shore. Karen Young was invited to be a guest on the singer/talk-show host's daytime television show. Dinah had already extended invitations to a number of musical artists making names for themselves through disco music. In Los Angeles for the show's taping, Karen was fixed up by the best stylists in the business. They did her makeup and rearranged her hair. Their magic made our artist look just short of glamorous. We were all thrilled that Karen was about to make her national television debut. Just before going on stage with Dinah, Karen started to take off her shoes. Karen Young hated wearing shoes while performing—and also during just about every other hour of the day. (Retrieving her shoes onstage after a performance was a regular task for her road manager!) Kurt and I warned her sternly to keep her shoes on—or else! She reminded us that she always sang better when she was barefoot, smirked, gave us the finger and then promised she would keep her shoes on.

Having witnessed Karen record her vocal track for "Hot Shot" in bare feet at the studio, I knew all about this idiosyncrasy. Performing on stages and in clubs during this tour, she often told her audiences that she could sing much better without shoes. Of course, the crowds loved this display of informality and urged her to take them off, which she obligingly did. But we told her this time had to be different. This was national television. This was going to be seen across America. This was Dinah Shore! So, with both shoes still on her feet, Karen walked on the studio set. She was to perform "Hot Shot" and then chat with her host. Dinah asked Karen what inspires her to let go with that exciting, electrifying singing voice. Until this point, Karen had been conversing in her normally quiet and shyly reserved manner. She answered that she simply removes her shoes, adding that doing so "grounds" her, allowing her monster voice to come through. I think Kurt and I experienced combined heart failure at that moment. Dinah Shore looked at Karen briefly, said she could understand this concept and thought she'd like to try it out herself. So off came

Dinah Shore's shoes. Not needing any more encouragement than that, Karen quickly followed suit. They then ad-libbed an acapella duet of "Stormy Weather," and the audience lost its collective mind. Still in shock, I don't recall ever actually hearing them sing together. This antic is just one of the many unpredictable events we encountered on a daily basis from our lovely artist. Karen had certainly created a true "moment" in television history. Score for Andy and Kurt: Zero. Score for Karen Young: One.

Appreciating the many difficulties of being on tour with an artist who in the end always knew how to win her audiences over is what kept us at it. One day though, we just couldn't rationalize doing so any longer. Kurt and I had set our sights on creating great music together with Karen. But if her tour was any indication of how much angst the future held for us, we knew we'd become burnt out cinders in no time. It didn't take us long to begin making plans to leave her tour. We'd created a dream project for ourselves, hoping to turn it into a reality during the coming year. Our success in the record business, following our production of Karen Young's "Hot Shot," seemed guaranteed. We firmly believed that 1979 would be the year we'd break through into the musical stratosphere. In fact, this was really just ahead of the Great Implosion.

Bruce Klauber: *Dinah Shore came off as a warm, friendly and tuneful country girl from Winchester, Tennessee, though she was a lot hipper than most imagined. She had romances through the years with some pretty progressive partners including Gene Krupa, Frank Sinatra and a controversial one with a years-younger Burt Reynolds. She sold millions of records in the 1940s and 1950s with an astounding 80 charted hits. Although she appeared in some motion pictures, she never really conquered that medium. She was made for television and she knew it. Early on, she proved herself to be one of the rare female stars not afraid to headline a regular television series; she was one of the few women to achieve major network tube success as the star of a comedy/variety series. She was among the first pop artists to record with jazz musicians like Ben Webster and Red Norvo, and she invited them to be guests on her program. Dinah Shore was on television, both network and syndicated—*

though rarely in bare feet—almost continuously from 1956 until two years before her death in February of 1994.

Despite the insanity of Karen's tour, "Hot Shot" was the number one disco record in the country, and no one deserved that success more than Andy and Kurt. They achieved it the hard way: They worked for it. The excitement surrounding the activities of Karen, Andy and Kurt was irresistible, and I couldn't help but become a bit of a hanger-on—often visiting the local discos with Andy to hear Karen's show and to join the party. And what a party it was! Andy did something during one of those disco nights that, in my estimation, guarantees him legendary status. Karen, Andy, Kurt and the gang took their road show to a disco on New York Avenue in Atlantic City. I cannot tell you the level of partying that went on that night, much of it pharmaceutical in nature. Several of us—not Andy Kahn, by the way—spent more than a few hours in the toilet paying for our excesses. By the time daybreak came, a couple of us were looking somewhat green. We must have hit the street around 6 a.m. and watched the sky lighten over the Atlantic Ocean. Before getting in the car for the drive back to Philadelphia, Andy decided he had to have a cheesesteak. All I wanted to do was throw up. Again.

THE GIPSYS IN OUR SOUL: KINGS UNCROWNED

At the end of 1978, even though Kurt and I had just begun writing and recording the first tracks for our next project, we both really needed a break from the action. No longer on tour with Karen Young, we decided to go to Rio de Janeiro for their annual world-famous Carnaval celebration. It was an opportunity to relax—and be amazed simultaneously. Rio is a city of unparalleled beauty. Set upon the sea, it hums with the energy of its citizens' non-stop dancing and singing. Carnaval served as an electrifying inspiration for both of us. We went out each night to amazing nightclubs where the music was as infectious as the people were sexy and uninhibited. There is no way to avoid getting caught up in the scene that is Carnaval in Rio every year. We were out drinking and dancing all night long. Then, like everybody else, we collapsed on a sparkling beach in the 100-degree heat sometime during the morning hours. Our beach was directly in front of the hotel along the Copacabana section of this outrageously decadent and sensual city.

During our three weeks in Brazil, we hung out a few times with Jacques Morali, the successful songwriter and producer who, among his other credits, was the creator of The Village People. Jacques had gotten to know Kurt fairly well through his numerous visits to the DCA Club. He was providing Kurt with advance promos of his records long before they hit the streets. Jacques had scored many number one disco records, all of which were recorded at Sigma Sound in Philadelphia. He went there specifically for that "Philadelphia Sound," and boy did he get it!

In Rio, Jacques Morali introduced us to Régine Zylberberg, undisputed queen of the international disco jet-set—and to her husband Roger Choukron. This couple owned opulent, celebrity-drenched discotheques around the world. They wanted Jacques to produce a group from France they'd fallen in love with—and had signed to a management and production contract. The group, several authentic Gypsy-born guitarists and vocalists, brothers and cousins who'd been performing their own compositions throughout the south of France for years, had not yet recorded in a professional studio. The brothers' father José Reyes was a Gypsy guitarist who never achieved worldwide commercial fame, but he was widely regarded as a superstar in France and Spain. One night, in front of Jacques' business partner Henri Belolo, while we were all sitting by the Copacabana Hotel's pool having cocktails, Jacques announced to Régine, "Baby, I am too beezy! Kurt and Andy created 'Hot Shot!' They weel produce your gypsies!"

Listening to a cassette tape of songs performed by the group, we were amazed at the infectiousness of their rhythms, punctuated by synchronized hand-claps delivered in 16th note repetitions, creating a syncopation we'd never heard. Conventional drums were not part of this group's sound. Their rhythms, played on multiple acoustic guitars, were captivating by themselves—allowing one to feel their groove. With disco still ruling the charts, we were expected to supplement their sound with a traditional rhythm section, something the group lacked. Strings and horns—augmenting their gypsy guitar music with "The Philadelphia Sound" that everyone, everywhere was copying—were a must-have, we were told. The couple wanted their group to be "disco-ized," and we were elected to pull this off for them.

It was decided that these gypsies from Arles, France, would come to Philadelphia to record at Queen Village Recording Studios. We made a deal whereby we, with our arrangements and production, were contracted to complete an album by this group of outstanding musicians. It would be Régine and Roger's task to then sign the group and the tracks we produced to a major record company. Our trip to Rio marked the beginning of a musical journey that, for me, remains unrivaled. Words like "unique," "extraordinary," "overwhelming" and "spectacular" do not give justice to the sound created by these musicians and singers.

In October 1979, the gypsy group arrived in New York from France and were driven to Philadelphia. They checked into a hotel near the studio with their road manager—the only member traveling with them who spoke some English. A limousine was at their disposal 24 hours a day. They arrived at the studio wide-eyed and eager to meet us. These guys spoke only French and Gypsy-Spanish. Thankfully Kurt and I were both conversant in traditional Spanish, so we were able to communicate with all of them on some level.

Escorted into the main studio, they unpacked guitars, stood in a staggered line and immediately began playing the original songs to which we'd be adding new arrangements and producing them as disco tracks. Our jaws dropped during the first four bars of their pulsating rhythm. After they'd performed three songs, our chins were on the floor. We were in a state of astonishment. Never before had either of us heard such music. This group was producing pure magic. The studio was alive with the sound of music—their music.

Our in-house rhythm section musicians were contracted to record a strict-tempo dance track beneath the gypsy group's guitar strumming. Recording the rhythm track was an experience defying description. Much of the gypsy group's music is constructed on its "feel." The players often added an extra two beats or even a full measure of music, based solely on how they *all* "feel" while playing together as one rhythmic unit. No matter what one of the players does to change it up, they all fall right into that groove. This is a music arranger's nightmare! Their performance was unstructured, but it felt so right. I had to figure out ways to make their live-playing work within some established written boundaries. Because it was their "sound," I was forced to invent ways to make it fit both mathematically and musically—without disturbing their essence. I had to establish a common musical ground by putting their songs into a structure that would be both acceptable to the group's members—and to Kurt and me.

These young musicians inspired my string and horn arrangements. I was both overwhelmed and excited—beyond anything I'd ever experienced. The challenge of keeping all of their raw energy in place while conforming to a structured arrangement was daunting. Writing long hours into the night to accomplish this, I let out a big sigh of relief when I received unanimous approval from the group on all the enhancements that my orchestrations brought to their unique sound.

The group, who had never been to the United States, stayed in Philadelphia for almost a month. At their hotel, they became instant celebrities—to management and guests alike. They hung out in the hotel's lounge (shades of Karen Young) and thought nothing of jumping in to play with the musical groups performing there. They took their guitars everywhere. All of them. At a restaurant, the guitars would sit under their chairs, like children clinging to a parent, ready at a moment's notice to be summoned for playing. Unannounced, they performed at almost every restaurant we dined in together. We became close friends with these musicians, introducing them around the city, taking them to both gay and straight nightclubs and discotheques where they terrorized all the patrons with their good looks, charm and total lack of inhibition. It was a very sad day when they left for New York to catch their flight back to France. We'd all become very close and knew that what we had created together was something special. We delivered our final mixes to Roger Choukron in New York City, leaving Régine and Roger to the job of signing this group to a label and getting these gypsies' amazing music released. A piece of cake, so we thought.

Alas, The Gipsy Kings were not ready for Prime Time. Perhaps it was the other way around. The sheer talent and exciting sound we discovered while producing these extraordinarily talented artists in 1979 would not hit pay dirt for another eight years. By then, Régine and Roger were no longer contractually involved.

All efforts by Régine and Roger to sign Los Reyes, as The Gipsy Kings were known in 1979, did not bear fruit. In retrospect, we were given an incredible opportunity to share our talents while we were still young—most of us still in our 20s. We applied the universal language of music in creating magic on the group's recorded tracks. That alone provided me some comfort. The saying "Timing is everything" certainly applied to this band's ultimate nod of approval from a world they eventually took by storm.

It's sad that throughout the history of the arts, original participants in a creative project find themselves left out in the cold when their work finally receives acceptance—often many years after the creative work had its genesis. The amazing music we produced with the gypsy group was ahead of its time. It seemed that only we knew what it truly was in 1979. "World Music" had not yet been recognized internationally. The Gipsy Kings' sound defined that musical genre, but it took almost a decade for the planet to catch up with their artistry. I'm honored to have played an integral part at the beginning of their professional recording careers. Arrangements I wrote for The Gipsy Kings are still being used in their onstage performances and on their live recordings. I consider that a great tribute to the work I created with them.

Fifteen years later, I again came in contact with The Gipsy Kings. They were appearing at the Tropicana Casino Hotel and Resort on Atlantic City's famed boardwalk. I went backstage after the show, where we renewed our former "love fest." They told their new manager that Kurt and I were the only people they'd ever worked with professionally who treated them with respect for their artistry—and also as human beings. Regarding their authentic gypsy background, corporate entities controlling their management and creative output often mistreated them and did not reward these men with true appreciation of their unique artistry and talent. I felt extremely proud learning how they felt towards Kurt and me. We worked with these incredibly gifted artists before they became in great demand as superstars. I can only imagine what might have happened had our studio tracks served to catapult them onto the music world's stage.

Réginé, Roger, Kurt and I were nearly a decade ahead of a huge trend that occurred in popular music. What we'd all heard in The Gipsy Kings' sound would eventually evolve into a worldwide musical phenomenon in 1987 with the release of their song "Bamboléo." This kind of thing happens way too often in the arts. And it's always a great disappointment for those to whom it happens. The slight glimmer of hope in that disappointment, though, is knowing that you were aware of something before the rest of the world signed on. After that moment of positivity, though, these good feelings tend to dissolve into thin air!

"Bamboléo" soared to the top of all the charts around the globe, heralding The Gipsy Kings as the acknowledged ambassadors of what was now being labeled and merchandised as "World Music." Their previously unknown sound had finally achieved universal acceptance; The Gipsy Kings had hit the Big Time. By then, these talented musicians and singers had gained a tremendous amount of experience in recording techniques and in many other aspects of the music industry—both good and bad.

BIG BAND DISCO

Kurt and I returned from our trip to Rio infused with rhythmic ideas inspired by Brazilian music and rhythmic dance. AKB was our next brainchild. Derived from our initials AK and KB, the project was part Busby Berkeley musical—a "Ferrante and Teicher style two-pianos-go-disco" parody—and part orchestrated dance-music-extravaganza. After writing six new songs and arrangements for a large group of musicians and vocalists, we began producing it in the studio. Our ultimate plan was to take our "show" on the road. This would be a monster fantasy traveling orchestra—with Kurt and me conducting it from two concert grand pianos out in front. Big dreamers were we.

Following our dramatic international success with "Hot Shot," ears attached to the heads of major record labels began to lean in our direction. Kurt and I formed AKB Productions, which marked my independence from my business relationship with Walter and Queen Village Recording Studios. While my brother kept expanding QVRS, my recording creativity was blossoming through my association with Kurt. And that creativity was precisely what would dictate my future in the music industry.

The first thing we did was produce "Stand Up Sit Down" and "We Got Rhythmic Feet" on spec. They would be the centerpieces of a project that would include four additional, even larger, orchestrated numbers to complete an album. Al Coury, president of RSO (Robert Stigwood Organization) Records, whose label had The Bee Gees heading up its roster of fine artists, flipped out for "Stand Up Sit Down." He handed us a generous deal with lots of front money—enough to reimburse us for the two songs we'd already finished and also to cover the additional full-scale production numbers we'd planned for the album.

Kurt and I employed the same formula for testing "Stand Up Sit Down" that we'd used when producing "Hot Shot" a year earlier. We tested every new mix put together in the studio at the DCA Club, where Kurt continued to work as resident DJ.

Now paying for our studio time, we'd spend hours each day at QVRS, adding new sounds to the song we planned as our next dance-single release. Then we'd crash at home before going to the club to try it out on the dance floor—which would be packed by 1 am.

While Kurt was clearly the star of the DCA Club, I'd also become a bit of a celebrity there. As one of the elite members allowed to stay at the club long after its official 4 am closing, I often didn't leave until the sun was up. A typical evening found me listening and dancing to Kurt's music, drinking at least a half dozen vodka and cranberry drinks, smoking marijuana at the bar and, on occasion, even dancing on the bar! This didn't shock anyone at this outrageous nightclub. Like Studio 54 in New York, anything and everything was going on at any given moment. I thought I was quite the "Hot Shot" and soon developed a reputation there for being a bit smug, very much taken with myself and a little out of control.

One person who shared this opinion of me was a regular club-goer named Bruce Cahan. Bruce was extremely popular; he could be seen at the DCA every evening. He was always flanked by admirers and friends gathered in the same area of a bar where I liked to hang out. Despite opinions of me that he'd developed over the last year following my success with "Hot Shot," closely associated with the DCA Club, on March 25, 1979, Bruce Cahan decided I was approachable. Making his move, he tapped me on the shoulder and asked, "So, when are we going to get together?" My response was, "Call me." And so, he did.

Bruce and I made plans for a dinner date three nights later at The Borgia Café, the spot where I'd been a featured pianist until Karen Young's "Hot Shot" tour took over my schedule. Bruce started coming to our long recording sessions, often bringing me food. Having observed that dozens of hours would tick by before I'd eat anything, one time he showed up carrying a small Gucci duffel bag. Inside was a delicious chicken that he'd roasted and a bag of strawberry licorice sticks. Thanks to Bruce, I made it through extended, arduous studio sessions with some real food in me. Otherwise, it would have been the usual pizza, burgers and gallons of coffee that was fueling me.

Seventy-four musicians complemented by four terrific vocalists were assembled. The huge string and horn sections, normally recorded in independent sessions from one another at QVRS, were assembled simultaneously at Alpha Studios in Philadelphia—a facility large enough to handle recording more than 50 musicians at a time. We recorded "live" human tap dancers on the song "We Got Rhythmic Feet," a sparkling, unique sound-bite providing an outrageous "visual"—a sound that would carry through, we believed, onto our AKB tour.

Gene Leone, the drummer and leader of Great Pride, from one of the early record productions (signed to MGM) that I'd worked on with Walter, was now the head engineer behind the recording console at Alpha Studios. Philadelphia, though a large metropolitan city, has a way of reconnecting its people through the years. Gene engineered the huge studio sessions on our AKB recording project. His expertise as a musician and, more recently, as a producer, made these recording dates special for me. This time, I didn't need to include engineering as one of my many duties on the project. With Gene, I could limit myself to being only the writer, arranger, producer, conductor and keyboard player! It was great having him onboard again, though this time, he was positioned on the opposite side of the control room window.

We made sure there was plenty of Latin percussion. For some of these exciting sounds, Kurt and I played some of the unusual percussion instruments we'd purchased in Rio. The final four songs for AKB were mixed to blend together into one long continuous medley on the "B" side of the album. The entire project was completed for $12,000 under budget. When Al Coury (a well-respected music industry veteran with lots of hits delivered on his watch) heard the finished album and discovered we'd done it with money to spare, he asked why we didn't bill the remaining amount in our budget to the label under "other production costs." We answered that doing so meant we'd have that much more to repay the label from our first sales. Astonished and praising us for our honesty and integrity, he commented that in his three decades as an executive in the music business, this was the first time he'd ever encountered billing to the label coming in under its original budget—by any artist or producer. Did we feel good? You bet!

With plans to hand deliver our master tapes to RSO, we flew to Los Angeles, with arrangements to master the AKB LP tracks at the internationally-respected Kendun Recorders in Burbank. Mastering is the final step before a record's release. It is a critical, technical operation that balances high and low frequencies of sound on the recordings. It incorporates electronic apparatus designed to enhance the overall aural imaging—creating the most presence possible. It's the last step before distributing the final product of a record, tape, CD or DVD. Mastering is an engineering art in itself. Because it is very technical and generally not very exciting to witness, it's a step in which producers usually do not participate.

I wear many hats related to making a record; one of them is as a recording engineer. I never miss the opportunity to be involved with the mastering phase of my recording projects. There are only a few over-the-top mastering facilities in the world. One of these is Kendun Recorders. When Al Coury gave his approval for us to use Kendun on the AKB project, it was like handing me a slice of vinyl heaven on a solid-gold platter.... all puns intended. Kurt and I got to visit this true inner-sanctum of the record industry—a high-end, off-limits sound laboratory that most music people have never heard of, let alone been given the opportunity to spend five hours in, tinkering with sounds in order to achieve audio perfection.

Another reason we went to California was to shoot the AKB album cover. Al Coury came through again, pledging sizable RSO funds to hire Elliot Gilbert, the L.A. photographer who shot the award-winning debut LP cover for the group The Cars in 1978. Inspired by their second LP, 1979's "Candy-O" cover, with an image first created by the 1950s icon, painter Alberto Vargas, it featured a female model draped across the hood of a Ferrari. The front cover of our LP featured a female model's shapely legs draped over the front of a gleaming black grand piano, dangling onto the keyboard, wearing bright red Capezio tap shoes! (As mentioned previously, the album's title song "We Got Rhythmic Feet" featured real tap dancers whom we'd recorded on one of the song's instrumental breaks.)

Kurt and I envisioned performing on matching pianos for the AKB Orchestra tour (which never happened). For the back album cover, two shiny black grand pianos were rented and brought into the photo studio. The two of us, dressed in white tie and tails, posed at the keyboards in front of Elliot Gilbert's clicking camera. One of these shots made the final cut, but it's the front cover with the model wearing those bright red tap shoes that got us noticed. In 1979, "We Got Rhythmic Feet" by AKB was nominated by Billboard Magazine for Best Disco Album Cover of the year.

During the summer of 1979, "Stand Up Sit Down," the single released from our AKB album rose through Billboard Magazine's Disco chart, taking up a commanding position at Number Two, remaining in the Top Ten for a few weeks. While "Stand Up Sit Down" fell just short of reaching Number One, it was recognized as one of the disco anthems characterizing that summer's music. This record's haunting theme captivated cities like Miami. It ruled the roost in all their discotheques for months as the dance record that was played in that city's nightclubs most often. Once again, Kurt and I believed we were right on the money.

We'd created another signature release and felt we were on our way to fame and fortune. We'd achieved our objectives after being given the incentives and capital to pull off this extraordinary recording project. We took this achievement as a green light to begin converting into a reality our AKB tour, which had until then been simply a dream for both of us.

Disco music enjoyed a fantastic summer in 1979. It occurred despite the news media's widespread coverage of a planned rally that was negatively aimed squarely at the music industry. "Disco Demolition Night" was staged at a White Sox game in Chicago's Comiskey Park Stadium on Thursday, July 12. Thousands of 12-inch vinyl single records (the benchmark of a disco release that was a hit in the clubs) were destroyed in a huge bonfire event occurring during an inning break. A serious, fiery campaign to kill disco music had been unleashed, planting the seeds for a revolution that was about to affect a lot of high-flying players in the music world. Television's network news programs covered this event, affording this stunt plenty of exposure. The announcers joked about it, calling it a prank, but it struck a nerve in many people across the globe. When we learned what happened, we all laughed about it heartily. Those were just a bunch of punks, we thought. How could they expect to wield enough power to change the very face of music?

THE RIGHT TO
REMAIN SILENT

While in California, I went to San Francisco to visit my younger brother Billy who'd been living in Haight Ashbury. Kurt remained in Hollywood at The Continental Hyatt House on Sunset Boulevard. Music industry people have long favored that hotel. Flying up from Los Angeles and back the same day was a breeze, and I returned around midnight. Shortly after exiting LAX in my rented Camero Z-28, I was pulled over by the Los Angeles Police Department. By the time two officers reached my door, two more squad cars with flashing lights had surrounded my car. I was asked to step out of the vehicle. When I inquired what I'd done wrong, two officers got out of their cars and pulled out their weapons. They arranged themselves on the hood of the car, facing the windshield, pointing their guns directly at me from crouched positions. The officers again asked me to get out of the car. I obliged, my heart pounding rapidly. They threw me against the side of the car and abruptly handcuffed me—advising me of my rights. I again demanded to know what I'd done wrong. Their only reply was I'd find out at the station. I asked them what I was supposed to do with my car. They suggested I lock it up and then get in the squad car with them—NOW! Having a pair of handguns pointed in your direction makes a real impression, and I decided in very short order that I would do well to follow their instructions.

At the station, I was fingerprinted and photographed. After being told to strip down naked, they looked up my anus for drugs. I was instructed to grab a mattress from a pile in the hallway and drag it to the cell where I'd be detained until detectives arrived at 8 a.m. the next morning. What? I had to wait eight hours to find out why they'd locked me up? Yep, that's the deal, I was told. I'd be given a chance to discuss my case when the detectives arrived. My case? What case? I was locked in a cell with two other men who kept looking longingly at my footwear. I was wearing a new pair of Martegani perforated gold lace-up shoes. When one of them blurted out, "Nice chooz, man!" I knew I was in deep trouble.

I asked an officer if I could make some phone calls. He casually wheeled over an old-fashioned pay phone attached with huge steel bolts to a cart. The receiver wire was barely long enough to reach into my cell. I called Kurt at the hotel. Thankfully, he answered. When I told him to come bail me out of jail, he said he'd call me right back. He hung up quickly. Something told me he wasn't going to come through. I found out later that he took a quaalude (a surefire method for rendering himself completely useless) and promptly passed out for the rest of the night at our hotel.

I called my parents and was informed by my father that it was past 3 a.m. in Philadelphia. I shouted I knew exactly what time it was and that I needed his help—explaining what happened to me. His response was plain and simple, so typical of him. "Andrew, there's nothing your mother and I can do for you right now. You'll have to wait until 8 a.m. and find out why they arrested you. I'm assuming you weren't drunk. You weren't smoking that grass were you?" I answered no to both allegations, adding that the police wouldn't say what the charges were. His final statement was, "So you'll wait and find out. Consider this a new life experience, another page to put in your book someday. Let your mother and me know what happens." He hung up. I found myself staring at the phone's receiver in disbelief. "Another page to put in my book someday?" Boy, was he ever right on the money!

The next phone call was to my new life-partner Bruce Cahan. Bruce had come home a few hours earlier from seeing the movie "Midnight Express" with two friends. Of all the movies they could have picked that Sunday night, this was certainly apropos. He told me how disturbing the movie was and how strange that I'd be calling him from jail. This was not to be believed. He said he was trembling, thinking about the movie and the coincidence of its main character having been thrown into jail in Turkey—and now this just happening with me in L.A. Bruce and I had been a couple for only two months, and now I was calling him from a jail cell 3,000 miles away. After saying he realized that he wasn't dreaming, he had an idea and said he would call me right back after I gave him the number.

The phone rang about five minutes later but it wasn't Bruce on the other end. It was the brother of one of Bruce's friends who'd been with him earlier at the movies. This man was a detective with the Long Beach, California, police department. Long Beach and Los Angeles apparently had reciprocity and cooperation between their law enforcement agencies. He said, "I don't know you. But my brother vouched for you and said I could trust you. If I get you sprung, you must come back to the precinct at 8 a.m. and talk to the detectives—without fail. I'll get you released on your own recognizance, but swear to me that you won't make me sorry I'm doing this." One glance at this mean-looking Latino standing next to me looking down at my expensive Italian shoes was all I needed to shout out, "Yes, of course, I swear to you! I'll be back at 8 a.m. Make that 7:30. Just get me outta here!" He told me to sit tight.

I called Bruce back and told him I'd heard from his friend's brother. Less than five minutes later, a uniformed guard came into the area and shouted out "Prisoner Kahn!" I answered, "Yes," and he came over to unlock the cell door and told me I was free to leave. He didn't even tell me to report back at 8 a.m. The fact that I could go was all I needed to hear. I never looked back to see the expressions on the faces of the two guys who were sharing my cell. I gathered up my belongings and called a taxi to take me back to the hotel. Kurt was still unconscious, under the influence of the quaalude(s) he ingested. Such a help, he was.

In the morning, after having a taxi take me back to the LAPD precinct, the detectives revealed that my rental car had been listed as stolen a year earlier in Connecticut. When I told them I had a legitimate contract from Budget Rent-a-Car, they drove me to the car, saw my rental documents and called Budget to confirm my rental. They discovered that when the car had been recovered, it hadn't been removed from the national list of stolen cars. They apologized curtly and said they would close the case—all charges dropped. No kidding! I inquired about my fingerprints and the mug shots they had taken. They said they had no power to remove these from their system. "Sorry, Mr. Kahn. And you have a nice day!"

My other two run-ins with the law were as a minor, so no arrest data had been kept on record. This time, though, as an adult, I was screwed. I contacted my attorney in Philadelphia who asked if I wanted to file an action against the LAPD for false arrest. If we prevailed, I could demand that my record be expunged—having all the identification they'd taken from me removed and my file destroyed as if it never happened. I instructed him to file suit and requested damages relating to the harassment and discomfort they caused me. Appearing in person would have meant returning to California a few months later, likely yielding a larger cash settlement. I opted to stay in Philadelphia. The case was settled out of court. Clearly all the evidence was in my favor.

THE PARTY'S OVER

The entire music industry was about to suffer a series of blows centered on bringing down the white-hot musical genre known as Disco, a style that originated as "The Philadelphia Sound." The publicity stunt at Comiskey Park in the summer—designed to kill disco—had begun to gather steam nationwide. Word on the street that disco was dead began invoking fear among many of us in the business; we suspected that a lynching was underway. How could any of us anticipate what was bubbling just beneath the surface?

The industry had become a $4,000,000,000 Godzilla by now, and we'd thought there would be no end to the heights it was capable of achieving. Meanwhile, a mixture of fear and loathing used on a grand scale against the entire disco phenomenon became a new and powerful weapon in the hands of those wanting to see it all come to a screeching halt. Rhythm and Blues had been closely related to Black/American culture. Having surfaced from underground gay nightclubs and threaded its way into the mainstream, Disco was widely regarded as "gay music." This stigma created problems for disco with conservative groups across America. They believed it was designed to promote and impose a sexually uninhibited, gay lifestyle on this country's youth. That presumption started a tidal wave of campaigns designed to "Kill Disco." The movement was strengthened with slogans like "Disco Sucks," and it took no time to catch media attention.

Compounding the problem was a disease that suddenly manifested during this time, and it seemed to predominantly affect gay men. Campaigns against disco grew in numbers, bolstered by news that this horrific "gay disease" was likely the result of blatant homosexual promiscuity—cultivated in the alleged hedonistic atmosphere of the disco club scene. Free love was certainly not a new concept, having already helped loosen attitudes about sex during and after the Hippie Movement of the late 1960s and early 1970s. Because promiscuity among homosexuals was fingered in the media as the primary method for contracting this unknown disease, the movement's flames were fanned vigorously. AIDS, as the disease was later named, was killing off gay men, drug users and hemophiliacs. With this perfect storm, the battle lines were drawn. The war to combat AIDS, a disease associated with a community whose music had captivated the world and supposedly promoted promiscuous sex, ramped itself up to a fevered pitch. The movement grew in strength, its advocates gaining tremendous ground internationally over the fear prompted by this disease.

Overnight, Disco was chased back underground. Legions of individuals had embraced the conservative thinking. It seemed that mass psychology was being used against the gay population; they were the scapegoats—just as other groups had been blamed for other scourges in human history. This time, it was "gay music" that was killing people, threatening to poison the Earth and wipe out humanity altogether. Panic caught on in a flash, like wildfires burning down forests. And just like that, Disco was dead. The record labels ran for the hills. Recording budgets were cut to zero. Projects were canceled instantly. Acts were left holding onto worthless contracts, wondering how this could possibly have happened. Not even a whimper of the word "Disco" was heard within the music industry for years to come.

Music that had gotten the world up onto its collective feet, playing to an audience that sang and danced joyously like never before, was slaughtered with one razor-fast slash. It was over. Disco wouldn't be heard from again up on the surface until it was resuscitated and renamed "Dance Music" a few years later. Dance Music had the same boom-boom-boom-boom of the kick drum and the sizzling hi-hat played on the upbeats. But the name "Disco" was forced underground. It would never again be referred to as "Disco" by most industry professionals. It will always be called "Disco" for me.

Bruce Klauber: *Though perceptive and eye-opening, Andy's theory about the death of Disco is not unique. A good part of it certainly had to do with the Carter/Reagan politics of the day. Instilling prejudice and fear among the multitudes has been a part of the entertainment industry for decades. This ranged from the treatment of black entertainers through much of the last century, accusations that swing and be-bop music in the 1930s and 1940s—and rock in the 1950s—were corrupting* *the morals of our youth and McCarthyism in the 1950s. Some industry Monday-morning quarterbacks, however, maintained there was another component to Disco's disappearance. They claimed that too many acts were signed too quickly in order to capitalize on a money-making fad, a la Elvis and Beatles' clones, the cha-cha, bossa-nova, comedy records, the intro-duction of stereophonic sound and the Twist. Something, they said, eventually had to give. But Disco was no mere fad or nov-elty that lasted a few weeks. It was artistically valid, and no music had touched so many facets of international culture for so long since the Swing Era. History books will show that no form of music was so effectively and literally wiped off the map in such a short period of time. In line with Disco's contribu-tion to music history, for the first time, recordings had become a producer's medium. And those producers, like Andy Kahn, were often the composers and engineers also. Think about it. How many Disco artists have remained in the limelight today? Even its biggest star of all, the late Donna Summer, turned into something of an "oldies act," as did Gloria Gaynor and The Village People. But it was the producers who made Disco, and they finally were receiving the credit they deserved for chang-ing how recordings were created and marketed—and for the many technological advances they helped pioneer. The pro-ducers are the ones in Disco that are remembered today.*

THE ORIGIN OF BRUCE

Bruce is a very popular first name for men (#67 out of 1220) and also a very popular surname name (#541 out of 88,799). (1990 U.S. Census)

A Scottish surname since medieval times, it is now a common given name. (Wikipedia)

People named Bruce have had a distinct impact on me. The name has a lot of character simply in the way it sounds aurally. For me, though, it is more complex because of the character the name embodies. When I was nine, Bruce Klauber appeared on the "scene." The miracle of our musical collaboration is the longevity it continues to enjoy. Somewhere, maybe as late as the early 1980s, bassist and all-around nice guy Bruce Kaminsky was added into the mix that defines my life. He's still with me, still performing with Bruce Klauber and me. Always, we have been swingin'. Definitely swingin'. And we're still swingin' together after all these years. Yes, sir. I am so grateful for having these two Bruces with whom I swing!

Yet, these two lovely and talented men named Bruce were still not The Bruce of my life—My Bruce.

I got him by default. Because, as I am fond of saying: there were no men left on the social landscape for him to capture. So, he elected to get me. And when his immediate family—his mother Jayne and his father Earl—each left the building, there was really only me left standing by him. And that remains today.

My Bruce is the most charming man. He is stunning to view—and to study. He's easy to love, so everyone loves him. But not like I love him. No, my Bruce is for keeps, and my Bruce is very real. At this writing, more than 39 years have elapsed since the night I met Bruce Harry Cahan. Our eyes locked on each other on one of the first nights I went to the DCA Club. That was 1978. The Year of "Hot Shot" by Karen Young. I acted so silly to both Bruce and the entourage of admirers forever flanking him—those fortunate enough to hang out within "his" space at the bar. Frankie Vacca's Bar, I'm often reminded by my Bruce. It was at Frankie Vacca's Bar, located on the north wall in the front section of the first floor of the DCA Club, where everyone wanted to hang. Right next to Bruce Cahan.

At the bar's front seating, just a few feet from the lighted white dance floor, anyone could be a star. A real star! And there were plenty who planted themselves there, in front of Frankie Vacca's Bar, which was his on the weekends. The rest of the week, this bar was tended by Bill Wood, aka Woody, who offered patrons nothing less when it came to delivering bar service with an impact. "Hollywood," "Cowboy" and Robbie also ran this bar on other days of the week. If you wanted to be somebody at the DCA Club, this is the one bar of several that populated the club where you were guaranteed to be seen. I discovered early on that the back section of this bar, along the wall, was really the In Place. It was narrow, cozy, sexy, slightly invisible and offered a clear view out to the mobbed dance floor in front of it. Of course, my Bruce was right there that Sunday night when I climbed up onto Frankie Vacca's Bar sporting a fuzzy, unruly, full beard. Frankie Vacca, always Mr. Nonchalant, was attending to his regulars that Sunday. It became known that I would pass around pre-rolled joints from my gold cigarette case. On this particular night, after a half-dozen Stolichnaya and grapefruit juice drinks, I jumped up onto the bar-top and began dancing, hanging onto mirrored slats embedded in the ceiling above the bar to maintain balance. Yep, that was me. Andy Kahn, Mr. Hot Shot himself, always putting on some kind of show.

Bruce admitted to me not long into our relationship that he initially thought I was just plain obnoxious. Looking back, I couldn't agree more. Basking in the brilliant limelight of "Hot Shot," a song that owed much of its wildfire success and recognition to the DCA Club itself, I was having the time of my life. Years of wanting something I'd create to be appreciated on a world-wide level had turned into exactly that.

It's really easy to get caught up in the rush that comes with the excitement of a big hit record. I stand "guilty as charged." For a 26-year-old, it was overwhelmingly intoxicating. Without the pot, booze, pills and powder, I was already cocksure of myself. But under the influence of one or more of these "additives," I became pretty comfortable acting obnoxious. It all worked for a while. But there was an obstacle barreling toward Earth, something horrible that would soon have a devastating effect on the health of millions of this planet's human inhabitants. And because the script was already written, it was no accident that Bruce and Andy would become, well, Bruce and Andy. Something had to be done to ensure that we "persevered." A drastic change in social lifestyle practices for both of us offered the solution to keeping us alive through an about-to-happen debacle—and being able to fulfill our supreme purpose in living.

I'd already tasted his chopped liver. Passed around on a foil tray one Sunday night in 1978 by the ever-smooth DCA Club staff member John Wallace was this delicious appetizer—my favorite. It was accompanied by John's repeated narration, "Bruce Cahan made it."

It certainly *could* have been made by Bruce. I've consumed many pounds of fresh chopped liver made by this man since then. John had also tasted Bruce's "own" homemade chopped liver during some festive holiday dinner parties at Bruce's well-known apartment, nestled deep inside 1914 Spruce Street on the 3rd floor. Therefore, it stood to reason that the chopped liver John Wallace was passing around the DCA Club that night at 4 am was made by Bruce Cahan himself. I announced that I must tell this Bruce Cahan how delicious "his" chopped liver was. So I did.

This particular chopped liver, the reason I actually talked to him, following 11 months of our smiling, nodding and waving to each other, was actually made by his mother. It would have been impossible for me to know right then that I would have many opportunities to eat his mother's chopped liver in her home, in other homes and in mine, during years yet to unfold. But, of course, none of this was an accident. What was happening that night was simply written in the script Bruce and I are still reading.

Chopped liver prepared from scratch. Yum. I was so accustomed to the institutional chopped liver we'd buy at Hymie's Merion Delicatessen or Famous 4th Street Delicatessen (just up the street from Southwark Paint Company). This occasion, believing I was enjoying a real, home-made version fashioned by this handsome Jewish guy named Bruce Cahan, someone that everyone adored, a man who maintained his station on the north side of Frankie Vacca's Bar, began with me sitting on a bar stool, facing the dance floor on the south side of the bar. The police had already come and collected their "taste" for the night. And they had already removed hundreds of club patrons who were not welcome to stay for the evening's un-der-the radar segment about to begin at the DCA. Before the lights went down, signaling Kurt Borusiewicz to begin spinning music again, John came up to me with that broad grin of his and offered me that delectable leftover from the Passover din-ner Bruce's mother had served earlier that evening. For me, this scene remains indelible. My taste buds were delighted. I was smiling broadly. It was obviously time for Bruce Cahan and me to elevate to "our" next level.

I was charmed by him immediately. Everybody, I've learned, is charmed by this delicious man. To this day, his in-famous allure and charismatic style are unmistakable. I appre-ciated his radiance the very first time I saw him; this skinny, adorable, gorgeous man, was always dressed and groomed far better than any other individual among the hundreds of DCA Club characters in residence that night—or on any other night. Words passed between the two of us. And there have been many millions of words—actually billions—since that night now known as The Chopped Liver Affair of 23 April, 1978.

A little more than 11 months passed before the die was cast or, more factually, consummated. At the very end of De-cember, I was contracted to perform with my trio at a house party in Queen Village, near the recording studio. Coinciden-tally, Bruce Klauber was not playing drums with me that night. Only one Bruce was allowed in that night, I presume! It was a holiday party, attended mostly by straight people who were friends or colleagues of the homeowners. Sure enough, in walked Bruce Cahan.

Bruce worked in the same real estate office as the wife of the couple giving the party. He was accompanied by a strik-ingly handsome Jewish guy named Randy Harburg. Randy complemented Bruce very well. The two of them were adorable together. Bruce, upon seeing me, started a conversation. He asked where I'd be playing on New Year's Eve, only a few days away. I told him my society band was booked at Woodcrest Country Club in Springdale/Cherry Hill, New Jersey. He smiled broadly and remarked that his mother (The Chopped Liver Queen) would be there that night. I asked how I might recognize her. Bruce said she'd be the "pretty blonde" being twirled around the dance floor.

Bruce anticipated that my band's music would be peppy. With that in mind, he knew his mother would be dancing to it and she'd be easily recognizable from his description. Knowing the demographic of this country club, I suggested it was likely that several other blonde women would be there who'd fit that profile. Bruce added she'd be there on a date with a man named Irv Nahan. How ironic. Jayne Seifert (last name from her second marriage), who had once been Jayne Cahan when married to Bruce's father, was now being squired by a man whose last name was Nahan! Astonishingly, Irv Nahan was the man who personally booked my five-piece band to play at Woodcrest on New Year's Eve. He'd been dating Bruce's mother now and again. So Bruce and I were talking about his mother—again! With Nahan so close in spelling and sound to Cahan, the infamous chopped liver connection was fortified now, much more than just an Appetizer.

Sure enough, New Year's Eve 1978, Jayne was there. Blonde, sexy, gorgeous and twirling on the dance floor with Irv Nahan, just as Bruce had said. During one of our breaks, I went over to Jayne and introduced myself. I addressed her as "Mrs. Cahan!" I didn't know she no longer carried the last name of Bruce's father and that Bruce's father would soon be a man with whom I'd enjoy a very close relationship. I said to Jayne, "You have a very nice son!" Her instant reply, as she held up a glass of white wine in a toast clearly directed toward her son (a gesture I'd see many more times in the future), was, "I know what I've got!" She smiled coyly, Marilyn Monroe-style, and wiggled away. Oh, that wiggle!

Bruce has the same wiggle, though in its masculine form. But it's Jayne's wiggle, just the same! It didn't take long to learn what it meant when saying she knew what she had. Because I was going to share in the "having" of Bruce Cahan, I can say with certainty and assuredness, that "I" similarly "know what I've got." I have a profoundly deep understanding of Jayne's quick turn of phrase that night. There was no way, however, I could have known the depth of meaning in her statement on the 31st of December in 1978.

Three months later, on another Sunday, this time the 25th of March, 1979, Bruce and I would exchange words again. Not an inauspicious day, it was Bruce's mother's 57th birthday. Mother and son celebrated it together—always. Jayne was not married then, though she would become a bride for the third time two months later. Our conversation took place sometime during what Mr. Sinatra would refer to as "the wee small hours of the morning." Bruce and I were hanging out independently at the DCA. I was deep in the throes of the AKB recording project with Kurt. We'd signed our album deal with RSO, and the upcoming AKB "Stand Up Sit Down" single was due for release in May. Kurt and I were living pretty high then.

The crowd was thinning out, and Bruce Cahan came up behind me. I was sitting on the north side of Frankie Vacca's Bar, looking out toward the dance floor. He tapped my shoulder. I turned toward him, surprised that he'd approached me. I'm sure I started tingling right then. (Bruce still makes me tingle.) "Don't you think it's time you and I got together?" he asked. Did I hear him right? I do know that I replied quickly, believing I was still in control. I must point out that one is not typically in control being around Bruce Cahan. He serves as automatic pilot, making sure you're steering down the right track, the one that will always present you in the best possible light. He acts as the voice of reason when reason seems to have slipped away unnoticed. It's just the way he presents himself. If you're destined to navigate through some space and time with Bruce and you're even slightly aware of anything, you learn this early on! I snapped back, "Okay, call me!" What a lame comeback. I gave him my card.

The real estate office Bruce worked in was on South Street in Queen Village. Of course, it was in Queen Village— the same geographical sphere with my recording studio and my home—Ground Zero in my life. That center of gravity was about to change forever. Bruce performed a real estate search on me—easily done in his office. He discovered that I was—amazingly—a real person! I owned property. I was listed and rated. I wasn't some late-night phantom living on the fringe of the system. I was actually IN the system. Further intrigued, Bruce called me. We made a date for the following Wednesday night, the 28th of March.

The plans were that I'd pick him up on Walnut Street following his evening real estate class. He emerged from 1616 Walnut Street—the striking Art Deco edifice that once housed the Pew Family's corporate headquarters of their behemoth Sun Oil Company, complete with a huge penthouse apartment rumored to be unrivaled anywhere outside of New York City. I was waiting out front; my car was parked a half a block away. I was wearing a belted camel-hair wrap trench coat. (With Bruce, one learns to be very aware of what to wear.) He was dressed in a solid-color dress shirt and a pin-striped suit-style vest that was casually unbuttoned. I drove to 2nd and Pine Streets in Society Hill to The Borgia Café, that charming, atmospheric, below-ground, grotto-style bar and restaurant where I played before going on tour with Karen Young months earlier. The Borgia was the most romantic spot I could conjure up for our date.

We drank Stolichnaya and grapefruit juice, poured by heavy-handed Howard Hess, the Borgia's gay bartender in this not-so-gay, subterranean lounge. Howard knew Bruce from the bars. He knew me from when I had performed there. We ate delicious Linguine and White Clams, one of our absolutely favorite dishes. I'm sure we were stumbling a bit upon leaving restaurateur Edward Bottone's bistro. It must be noted that this was the night the Three Mile Island nuclear power plant in Pennsylvania experienced a partial, yet nearly total melt-down of its main core. (It remains the worst nuclear power accident to occur in the United States, though not as catastrophic as it came close to being.) It was a noteworthy night for any kind of meltdown! Bruce and I went back to my house. I parked my black 1977 Oldsmobile Toronado on the sidewalk of Leithgow Street, opposite the house I owned at 402 Catharine Street. Bruce Cahan and I spent our first night together in this house—next door to my recording studio, just across the alley from Weccacoe Playground, where my father, uncle and uncles-to-be played ball together every moment possible.

The next day, after putzing around my office on the third floor of this small three-story home, I drove Bruce back to his apartment. He told me he rarely spent the night with someone unless it was in his own apartment. He added that he usually couldn't wait to escort them out after a liaison, fiercely hoping he wouldn't have to wait until morning. Yet, here he was, having slept "out" with me. When he exited my huge car (one of the last extra-long General Motors vehicles, outfitted with only the "finest" crushed, red velvet seats–just one step away from being a Pimpmobile), I said to him softly, "Don't be a stranger!" I'd never said that to anyone before. I haven't said it to anyone since. Nor will I.

The following Sunday night in the waning hours of April Fools Day (Uncle Lloyd's birthday), I called Bruce. He had just come home from being out in the bars and already had eaten an entire pizza that was delivered to him. He was now enjoying a bowl with his favorite ice cream flavors: chocolate, vanilla, strawberry and coffee. I told him I wanted to come over. There was a brief pause. Then he said, "Come on!" In my Massetti purple shirt, which I'd purchased from the now-defunct Gatto, a wonderful Italian men's clothing store on Walnut Street, I shot up to his apartment. He buzzed me in and called down to me that he was all the way up on the third floor—in the rear of the building.

I was dazzled by the interior of this three-story townhouse one block south of Rittenhouse Square. Its wooden staircase was a thing of exquisite beauty and extraordinary craftsmanship. I was totally mesmerized by the leaded, stain-glassed windows encountered as I ascended the steps leading up to Bruce's residence. I was moving up the steps very slowly, and Bruce was wondering why it was taking me so long to get up to his apartment. All the guys to whom he'd previously granted access had apparently scrambled up those steps, simply because Bruce was waiting for them! That's all they needed to know. Finally, I arrived at his stunning, long, narrow, beautifully furnished, huge one-bedroom apartment outfitted with antique, tiled, twin fireplaces in the living room.

When I opened the door, which he'd left slightly ajar, there was Bruce—far, far away—at the very rear of this classic building constructed out of masonry, wood, glass and pure charm. He was sitting on his bed—way beyond a long foyer, the bathroom, galley kitchen and past the large living room. On the other side of a portal framed by two white, louvered French doors was the bedroom. And there, looking simply adorable, sitting on his bed, was the one and only Bruce Cahan. He was watching something on a television nestled onto a low-wheeled, metal cart—a signature period accessory typical of the 1960s. We spent a beautiful night together.

That night marked the beginning of our relationship, one that formidably has endured to this day. With the exception of a few sporadic nights we've been forced to spend apart, because of illnesses and brief hospital stays, and more recent occasions requiring our geographical separation, we have continuously been together since that Sunday night when I first visited Bruce in his apartment. In fact, it was and remains odd whenever we're not together. It took both Bruce and me a great deal of time getting used to those rare occasions. Our understanding of any separation has deepened considerably. But it still seems strange when we're apart for more than a few days, especially during the longest period of time that occurs annually in mid-July. That's when I travel to Maine and Bruce remains in Atlantic City. The first time, in 1997, was very difficult. It's still an odd feeling each time I go. Engaged with many people at an annual conference each summer at Orgonon in Rangeley, Maine, I'm well-entertained there—and distracted from Bruce's absence. On the other hand, he spends a week, sometimes longer, without the person whom he's shared nearly every day for more than 39 years—a man rarely not by his side, day and night.

Were Bruce and Andy meant to be? Of course we were. Little has changed when it comes to thinking about our incredible relationship. There's no volume big and fat enough to contain all the details describing who we are together. The quality that stands out most for me surely has to be endurance. We've participated in a great number of family lives, deaths, tragedies and struggles together. As a devoted couple, we've confronted adversaries, some who have threatened our stability. We've been fortunate, though, to have established solid relationships with people we cherish, which endure to this day. It is our mutual love, respect, admiration and true friendship with each other that hold together the very core of "Bruce and Andy." It is ours—alone. We belong to one another. Until death do us part, we agreed. No law, government, constitutional amendment or proclamation by any state, province or other authority could ever alienate Bruce from me—or me from Bruce.

It took a decision by the United States Supreme Court regarding same-sex marriage for Bruce and me to tie the knot. We both agreed, even after a good number of states in our country legalized same-sex marriage, that we wouldn't follow suit until all 50 were in concert. Even when New Jersey and Pennsylvania, states where we maintain residences, made same-sex marriage legal, the rest of the states where it remained illegal held us back. We find it ridiculous that it took a ruling from the highest court in our land to open the door for our marriage. But marry, we did, on November 15, 2015. With 20 of the dearest people in our lives assembled at historic Dante & Luigi's Restaurant on the northwest corner of 10th & Catharine Streets in South Philadelphia, Former Philadelphia District Attorney and Judge Lynne Abraham officiated. Following the ceremony with all of our guests as witnesses, a stunningly beautiful and delicious affair ensued. Produced and Directed by Bruce and Andy, of course.

A terrific guy, Fred Thimm, former president of the parent company of the Palm Restaurants, once remarked that "Bruce and Andy" is like a brand! www.bruceandandy.com

THE FOREST OR
THE TREES?

The music industry hasn't recovered from the loss of actual sales experienced when its huge bubble burst in 1979. It was a bubble that had clearly become bloated. Many people were thinking the industry's future had become uncertain. Disco wasn't the only "enemy" to pummel the music business. A new technology appeared on the horizon. Digital computing would offer fantastic opportunities for the recording industry to reinvent itself. But music executives buried their heads very deeply below the sand. Others just couldn't recognize the marvel of digital recording as a true gift-horse when it trotted in their direction. Rather than embrace this new technology, the major labels—holding on to archaic corporate sales philosophies—believed they'd always hold all the cards. They refused to see that this technology would totally change the business. They balked at the concept of instantaneous file-sharing and allowed music to get passed around all over the globe—for free. It was as if they weren't looking. And the major labels thought that the computer geeks, as they were often referred to, would never be able to understand their business. "We're the record industry. They're a bunch of computer nerds. We legally control the music, not them. They can't hurt us!" Through a series of legal maneuvers by the record labels, Napster, the original free, online file-sharing platform was forced to close. The executives thought they'd won the online digital war. They were so wrong.

It was the corporate "suits," not seasoned music professionals, who were running large record labels for even larger corporate entities. Huge entertainment conglomerates had purchased the labels during the run-up of acquisitions in the 1970s. The heads of these companies held the line, maintaining conservative attitudes toward effecting serious changes in the distribution of music. It was going to be "business as usual." Meanwhile, a forward-thinking computer company named Apple viewed the industry titans' one-track approach to file-sharing as an incredible new opportunity. Apple created a unique business model for legally selling music cheaply over the internet. Not long afterward, it became obvious the record labels had ALL missed the boat. Computers were capable of delivering music to anyone, anywhere, anytime—and reliably. When Apple's iTunes became a worldwide success, it was too late for the labels to sign on. They'd left the barn doors ajar—and all the horses had run. By the time the industry heads realized what had happened—inviting the online innovators to a deal-making table—it was clear that those horses had no intention of returning home to that old, dilapidated barn.

With the advent of digital recording and digital downloads, the traditional record business lost its longtime compass. The executives were no longer able to maintain firm control in disseminating an artist's recorded performances or control an artist's career through the tight management of purse-strings. The foresight shown by Steve Jobs at Apple shook the entire recording industry to its foundation. It's been reeling ever since—with no stability in sight. Why would anyone think there'd be a way to return to the old methods the public used to get its music? That's long gone. What a 180 the music business did! They say change is good. This was more than change. This was a total reinvention of its wheel, effected by one savvy, intuitive electronics company. That company is the largest corporation in the world today. Bigger than Big Oil. Bigger than the Automotive Giants. Bigger than anyone. And the start-ups that followed on Apple's coattails created a whole new world of online shopping and information-gathering, becoming the next largest companies in the world. Technology rules. Long live Technology.

Any financial success realized from the re-release of "Hot Shot," as it is with most music out today, has been measured strictly by radio play—broadcast and internet—and club play. This is where the potential to generate real sales exists. But sales are a pittance of what they used to be before digital took over the music industry. Today, you can get almost any music that's been released—for free. And you don't have to look very hard to find it. Spotify and Pandora, popular digital subscription streaming services offering unlimited access to music, contribute very little to writers' and artists' incomes—unless a recording becomes a monster hit. The streamers are overloaded with music, sporting an inventory from artists that's overwhelmingly diverse. People hear something they like, and then they dip right back into the wellspring of music created by both legends and unknown artists, looking for something new. Everything can now be found on the web. CD sales have become nearly nonexistent. Download sales are tanking. Streaming services are the only outlets with paid subscriptions. But at $10 per month for unlimited access to vast libraries being offered to their members, a tune needs to be streamed thousands of times to produce a single penny for its creators.

The digital-version "Hot Shot" Remixes of 2007 had tremendous amounts of exposure—with very little income yet to be derived. The original analog version of "Hot Shot" on vinyl in 1978, however, offered a vastly different scenario yielding substantial earnings. In addition, "Hot Shot" was played several times on network television during NFL halftime breaks. The broadcast royalty for a single inclusion on network television is huge.

The following are examples of how popular a recording can be without producing any significant income for its creators:

"Hot Shot" became one of the most widely used workout recordings during aerobic classes worldwide. It is still used to help people grunt their way to a better body.

"Hot Shot" sheet music was printed and distributed by Polydor.

"Hot Shot" was included in the 1979 Casablanca Records release "A Night at Studio 54." This was the first sanctioned compilation of original master recordings of major hit disco recordings. Because it contained major hits of the Disco era, the two-disk album went gold quickly.

"Hot Shot" was re-created in a 1989 episode of "The Benny Hill Show." It was performed as a new musical and vocal production during a sketch featuring the zany star and one of his "girls" playing at a pool table.

"Hot Shot" was inducted into Billboard Magazine's Disco Hall of Fame.

"Hot Shot" was used by permission for a pivotal scene in the 1990 motion picture "Reversal of Fortune" starring Glenn Close and Jeremy Irons. It was the song being played during a flashback to July 1978—when Karen Young's "Hot Shot" reached number one in Billboard Magazine. It was unquestionably one of the disco songs that significantly defined that summer's music.

"Hot Shot" was re-released in the 1994 Hot Productions-sanctioned compilation CD "The Best of Karen Young."

"Hot Shot" was sampled by permission in 1996 by the musical group Daft Punk on their "Homework" album within the song "Indio Silver Club" released by Virgin Music.

"Hot Shot" was covered in 1996 by vocalist Barbara Tucker, released initially by Tycoon Records, a Canadian company, and then reissued on other compilations worldwide.

"Hot Shot" was remixed in 1997 by DJ/Producer Gary Quinton, released initially on Mo'Bizz recordings, which included the "Rollercoaster Mix" and "Da Techno Bohemian Radio Mix."

"Hot Shot" was included in the 1999 Rhino Records release "Boogie Fever." A four-CD boxed-set, it was a sanctioned-compilation containing the major hit recordings of the disco era.

Another version of "Hot Shot" was covered in 1999 by the group Blondie featuring vocalist Deborah Harry. It was released on Epic/Beyond Records as part of Blondie's "No Exit" album. This album marked the first reunion for Blondie as a group. It had been 17 years since they previously recorded together.

"Hot Shot" was included in the 2001 West End Records release "Masters at Work: 25th Anniversary Edition Mastermix." This was a sanctioned compilation of original master disco recordings released by West End Records. This label signed Karen Young as one of its artists and released the original version of "Hot Shot" as a single in 1978, also releasing her album "Hot Shot" the same year.

Mel Cheren's 2001 autobiography "My Life and the Paradise Garage: Keep on Dancin' " details the story of West End Records signing Karen Young and "Hot Shot" becoming the label's first hit record. Mel Cheren was a founding partner and the head of West End Records in New York City.

"Hot Shot" was featured in an award-winning 2007 documentary film "The Godfather of Disco," based on the life of Mel Cheren and his company West End Records. Mel narrates the story of the rise and fall of disco in the 1970s and the effect AIDS had on the music business.

REALITY CHECK AND RECAP

Widespread exposure and financial gain do not always follow the same curve. As mentioned earlier, the advent of the public being able to obtain music for free—or nearly free—by going online—caused the demise of music being purchased the way it traditionally had been. Napster enabled free file-sharing for its subscribers. Eventually the government instituted regulations that forced Napster to shut down. This paved the way for Apple Computer's iTunes providing music to consumers at a nominal cost. Today, perhaps 10% of recorded music sales are derived from retail, while those who get music for free constitute the other 90%. Through iTunes and other such services spawned by Apple's innovative thinking, writers and artists actually continue receiving something for creative output, though it's solely from the 10% of documented sales. In contrast, prior to digital downloading and streaming, income to music creators was generated by 100% of the recorded music distributed to the public. The record companies held all the cards then. Realistically, they did not always give a fair and accurate accounting of the sales to the creators. But music was distributed through a fiercely-controlled network. Its creators had no choice but to participate. In addition, the public had no choice when obtaining recorded music for personal enjoyment. They BOUGHT the music they wanted. Before file-sharing and streaming, the system was simple, straightforward and reasonably fair to the artists, writers and the consumers who bought their product.

Income that songwriters, publishers and recording artists receive now is derived from a tiny sliver of the amount of recorded music that entertains this planet's inhabitants. Music's creators now rely on a hodgepodge of digital retail outlets strung across the internet. And those retailers account for a small fraction of the music people enjoy. As for the hard copies of music still being made today in the form of CDs—and even vinyl records in some markets—sales are minuscule compared to the vast stockpiles of music available via download or streaming outlets like Spotify and Pandora. The streamers "count" the number of times a title is requested from their overstuffed libraries. A tune is released through subscribers' pre-selected playlists or an actual request for a specific art-ist/title/performance. The few dollars generated from one of today's medium-sized hit recordings can't begin to compare to the actual living a creator might have been able to make from a single tune just four decades ago—long before online distribution.

Artists who rely on recorded music to make a living today must hope they attain the level of a few dozen or so superstars who rule the music industry today. Those fortunate souls ac-tually do sell a lot of product. At their concert performances, hard merchandise that attendees snap up bolster an artist's income. Everyone else—the writers of songs and the artists who record them—simply starve. Even so, never before have there been more individuals trying to make it in the music in-dustry. Writing a song that becomes a hit has always been nothing less than supremely alluring. The rewards, however, are now reserved for a precious few. And this follows a similar pattern of the totally lopsided wealth hierarchy in the U.S. to-day—in which the top 1% of the population controls 75% of the wealth. Unfair? You betcha.

Bruce Klauber: *Andy got a real double-whammy, what with the professional and personal problems at Queen Village Re-cording Studios and the fact that a bunch of artists and pro-ducers like him lost their recording contracts when disco went bust. I felt very bad for my friend, who wasn't even 30 when all this happened. Few people will experience having international fame one day and seeing most of it disappear the next morning. That is how quickly it happened. Though he certainly had the right to be, Andy was not bitter—more startled, surprised and a bit depressed—unlike many in the industry who could not be-lieve this incredible turn of events. For a short time, Andy was indecisive about his future. He was realistic enough to admit that disco was not coming back anytime soon. In the history of popular music, something like this had only happened once before: Swing music ruled the land as the popular music of the day from 1935 to 1945. Then, one day, it was over. Regarding disco, I don't think we'll see an industry phenomenon as pow-erful as this again. Contemporary music is too fragmented for the demise of any one form of music to find itself rejuvenat-ed in the recording industry's marketplace. After considering* *his future and his options, Andy ultimately decided to join his family's business, which he eventually took over and ran for 25 years. Given his passion and dedication to everything he has ever done, it's no surprise that he ended up having another hit. This one was called Southwark Paint and Decorating Company. The good news was that after his quarter-century of running Southwark, he would have the time to start playing jazz once again.*

BACK IN THE FUTURE

In the mid-1980s, analog recording techniques universally yielded to the digital format. With analog quickly swept out of the picture, recording studios and engineers either made the conversion to full-digital technology, or they found themselves out of business. With the exception of a few worldwide locations that specialized in the preservation and restoration of magnetic analog tape recordings, this represented a wholesale revamping of every recording studio on the globe. Digital was anointed king. I did not involve myself in any facet of the record business while this was happening. The digital age of recording was clearly poised to pass me by. And so it did for more than 20 years.

With the much-ballyhooed demise of the disco era in the record business beginning in 1980, I took a hiatus from recording and composing. I occasionally played the piano for profit—and also to benefit certain charitable organizations with whom I'd developed personal relationships. What I had intended would be a brief hiatus became a 25-year break from doing any work in a recording studio or songwriting.

In order to keep up my skills at playing piano and performing, I began a series of solo piano gigs during weekday cocktail hours. Returning to The Saloon—my first piano gig when I was 15, you may remember—was true déjà vu. This was followed by a stint at the Not Quite Cricket Lounge in Philadelphia's Latham Hotel on Walnut Street. That dimly-lit spot set the stage for a new wave of newspaper exposure for me.

To keep my name alive as a performing artist, I hired our old friend Sam Bushman. I'd begun investing in the stock market in 1980, hanging out during the day at a center city brokerage house, watching the ticker and making a few shrewd investments. Sam thought this activity would play well in the newspapers.

Blurbs in columns referred to me as "the best-dressed saloon singer in town," a jazz and standard song stylist who "performs in a $500 suit" (considered to be a very expensive suit in 1983), someone who'd become a successful investor after having had a hit record. The columnists ate up this juicy stuff like it was Thanksgiving dinner. My personal "stock" and street "cred" shot up exponentially. A lot of what was being written about me was exaggerated and twisted—to elicit as much glamour as possible. I played the Not Quite Cricket Lounge gig for almost a full year. Next, I played one block away at the Warwick Hotel's Brasserie, the newest favorite watering hole for downtown's after-work crowd. I think my professional notoriety expanded because my music and personality lent itself to this downtown clientele. I rode this delicious media-fueled ride for another year, at which point I turned another 180 degrees to tackle a life-changing business opportunity. It was totally unrelated to music, but it deeply reconnected me to the affairs of my family.

In 1983, I entered the private sector and took over the helm of my family's paint business. It was still directly across the street from Queen Village Recording Studios, which Walter now owned and operated alone. My life-partner Bruce H. Cahan, whom I'd met in 1979 near the end of my first career in the record business, joined me in running my family's business. Together, we expanded it to include window treatments and interior decorating. Started in 1918 by my grandfather, we continued to operate Southwark at its original South 4th Street location. We didn't close the retail paint store until 2010. Even then, Bruce and I continued running the decorating arm of the business. Southwark Decorating and the legacy started by my grandfather at 4th & Catharine Streets survives today. To have this business still operating in 2018—marking its 100th year, remains one of our most beloved achievements. Southwark will always be deeply embedded in my consciousness.

After dropping out of the record business, my public piano-playing was reserved for charitable organizations. I performed in events set in public venues and privately in my home. In September of 1990, I arranged to perform at an event at the Mandell Theater on Drexel University's campus in Philadelphia. This concert was held in memory of Bruce Cahan's mother Jayne who had died unexpectedly from an aortic aneurism a few months earlier. This event, like some others I had done, benefitted ActionAIDS—Philadelphia's premier support organization for people living with Acquired Immune Deficiency Syndrome (AIDS). Wanting it to be very special—Jayne was someone I loved and cared for very deeply—I invited several musical artists to perform with me. I hadn't played with some of them for years.

I invited Kurt Borusiewicz to attend this event. He and I hadn't done a musical project together for 11 years. He'd gone back to spinning records in clubs for a while during the 1980s and began working as a hairdresser in the suburbs of Philadelphia. After more than a decade of spurning personal requests from Karen Young to get back together and work on music again, it seemed time to bury that hatchet. I called her and asked whether she'd perform with me at this event. She immediately answered with a booming "Yes!" We didn't need to be connected by telephone; I would have heard her anyway.

The event was a sell-out. With several soloists making guest appearances, it was thrilling for all of us onstage—and for those in the audience. Guitarist Frank DiBussolo amplified our jazz trio to a quartet. Tenor Saxophonist Jerry Brody, from my Outside playing days, was a guest soloist. I saved Karen's appearance for last. She waddled onto the stage to thunderous applause, all of us musicians vamping the intro to "Hot Shot." And she tore right into it. To say she brought the house down would be understating the effect she had—on everybody. It seemed obvious to me the time had finally come for the three of us to rejoin forces. Karen "Hot Shot" Young, Kurt Borusiewicz and Andy Kahn had once been internationally-known in the music business as a creative team. Together, we planned to make every effort to get ourselves known on a scale of that magnitude again. Kurt and I decided to go into the studio with Karen after we wrote some new material for her. It was something we didn't jump into right away, however, because we were both busy in our other professions. We decided to wait until sometime "after the holidays." I've always considered that expression as one used too freely, whenever someone wants to stall something for some reason. I had no idea our concert at the Mandell Theater would be the last time I saw Karen Young.

AND SO IT SHALL BE: LEAVING THE BUILDING TOO SOON

Four months later, on January 27, Bruce Cahan and I were shopping in a chain drug store in South Philadelphia. While I was checking the expiration date on a bottle of Tylenol, we heard two young girls working behind the pharmacy window talking together. One of them asked, "Did you hear that Karen 'Hot Shot' Young died?" I'm sure I didn't hear the other's response because Bruce and I were now staring at each other—speechless—in disbelief. I put the bottle back on the shelf and went over to the window. I asked the girls what they had just said. One reiterated what she'd heard in a dance club the night before—and that everyone was talking about it. I blinked in silence. I asked whether she knew the song "Hot Shot" and that Karen Young was the artist who performed it. She scowled at me and said, "Of course I know who she is. Everyone does —and everybody loves that song. It's still played in the clubs! I heard she died of a drug overdose!" My knees went weak. I don't remember driving home. I don't remember what Bruce and I said to each other from that moment on until we were back home.

I called Karen's brother Paul and awkwardly asked him about what I'd heard. It was true. Karen Young died suddenly the day before. News travels fast, especially when it surrounds a colorful, local celebrity. Many people who met Karen or saw her perform believed she was a drug addict. Rumors that she was always "screwed up" on drugs persisted, and that reputation did not die with her on January 26, 1991.

When I hear people speak of Karen today, her supposed penchant for drugs remains the most constantly-hyped aspect of her tragic musical career. The truth is that Karen died when a bleeding ulcer ruptured after she had been rushed—in excruciating pain—to the hospital. This may have been accelerated by substances Karen took—prescribed or not. But after so many years of talk about her supposed addiction, people believed she overdosed on recreational drugs. The truth was that her early death resulted from a condition that Karen ignored for years—one that in the end spiraled out of control.

Karen's funeral was a media event attended by musicians and singers, promoters and club owners, lawyers and record industry executives, her family and a throng of friends. Kurt was a total mess, crying and sobbing uncontrollably—trembling from both sadness and the freezing weather. Standing next to me in his long fur coat during her graveside service, he kept saying, "She just *had* to die on my birthday!" Kurt had turned 39 on the day that Karen Young went to sing with the angels.

The September benefit concert at which Karen Young performed on stage for the last time caught the attention of the radio and television department at Drexel University. The university operated the Mandell Theater where we had staged that sensational show. I was offered an opportunity to play a jazz concert that the school offered to professionally record—using their student crew. In exchange, I agreed to allow them to include it in the programming on the university's television cable station. It sounded like a great opportunity to play and also gain some television exposure, so I signed on. The taping in front of a capacity theater audience on April 10, 1991 still runs on Drexel's cable TV station. I watched it recently. I can tell you that we played our hearts out. We drew a lot of inspiration from the memory of Karen Young who had performed with us on that same stage just three months earlier.

For Kurt, 1991 wasn't destined to be a good year in any sense. As mentioned earlier, he'd been working as a hairdresser. At one point, he began feeling ill; then he became so ill that he was unable to work much. His worst fears were confirmed when he tested positive for HIV. I hadn't seen him since Karen's funeral. He called to tell me the bad news. We talked as much as friends can talk about such a horror regarding a disease that seeks only to kill. Kurt was put on a strong regimen of drugs to treat the dastardly virus that was making him feel so miserable. His symptoms got worse. Unable to work any longer, he took refuge in his parents' vacation home in Delaware.

The next time I saw Kurt was on July 22, 1992, the day before my 40th birthday. Bruce Cahan and I drove down to visit him. We were shocked at the image of the reduced man we encountered: pale, ultrathin and caved-in. These would be the most accurate words to describe this once very much alive and talented man. It was painful to see how AIDS had ravaged him. Kurt bought a birthday cake for me, and we sat around reminiscing for a few hours. When I hugged him goodbye, it was terrifying to feel his frame. He was skeletal. Bruce and I were terribly shaken.

How could this have happened? Well, it was happening everywhere we looked. People who had been pictures of health were now terribly sick—dying left and right. Bruce kept a running journal with the names of people we knew who had died of AIDS. The list filled several pages—both sides—of a legal tablet. Kurt's name hadn't yet been added to it. We knew upon leaving him that night, it wouldn't be long before we'd have to add the name Kurt Borusiewicz to this growing list of unfortunate souls.

My mood was brightened considerably when we arrived at our condo on the beach in Atlantic City the next day, my 40th birthday. Bruce had purchased and arranged for a new Roland piano (my first digital instrument!) to be waiting there for me. This thoughtful and loving gift was exactly what any sensible doctor should have ordered to get me out of the funk I fell into after visiting my supremely talented and seriously ill music collaborator.

In 1992, with no cure in sight, most HIV positive individuals who began showing signs of the dreaded AIDS disease became ill very quickly; they often died after a short period of time. The only bright light in this whole situation was the disease typically spared the infected individual and his family from a drawn out nightmare of horrific medical events. Kurt, unfortunately, was not spared. His disease lingered, and his withered body continued to deteriorate. I can't imagine how much more emaciated Kurt must have been by the time he died nearly two years after we'd seen him in Delaware. There wasn't much left of him in 1992, so he must have wasted away, millimeter-by-millimeter for two more years until AIDS finally claimed his life on July 6, 1994. I had lost Karen. Now, Kurt was gone. That left me as the torch-bearer of a musical legacy the three of us created together at the end of the 1970s—before disco music died. I will never forget Kurt Borusiewicz. As long as "Hot Shot" is played and heard, no one else will either.

I helped organize a reunion at the DCA Club, where Kurt's artistry as a DJ was already immortalized. This event was held in his memory. The DJs, Reenie Kane and Michael DeCero, both protégés of Kurt's, paid beautiful homage to the man. They performed superbly in the DJ booth, faithfully mixing "his" music—the music Kurt helped introduce and popularize there. And those who used to hear him play the very best dance music anyone had ever heard "back in the day" were there that night.

For the next decade, I was immersed in running the family business with Bruce. My playing had diminished to live performances once or twice a year, mostly benefit concerts, and an annual event in Atlantic City at the condominium building where Bruce and I have a home. But I continued to practice—and I became a better pianist as I matured. I delved more deeply into my technical artistry. Being an "entertainer" was relegated to the background. But that didn't stop Bruce Cahan from taking a page out of my father's book.

In 1996, Bruce and I took a road trip along the California coast with a couple we'd befriended in Atlantic City. Our last stop was Los Angeles. At The Beverly Hills Hotel, we met up with another mutual friend living in Los Angeles who also owned a home in Atlantic City. This hotel remains reminiscent of the glamour days when songwriters, performers, producers and movie moguls all hung out there together. The chic atmosphere that pervades every corner of this fabled property is unmistakable.

During lunch—where, of course, a fine pianist serenaded the guests who were dining—our friend, who owns a magnificent house in the Hollywood hills, suggested I play a few numbers. Usually I decline such requests as it disrupts the employed player's performance schedule; I also prefer to listen rather than infringe on someone else's gig. The protests by our group were overwhelming. I told Bruce that if he made the arrangements, I'd go up and play a few tunes. That's all he needed to hear. In a flash, I'm sitting at the white grand piano adjacent to our table. Suddenly, the maitre d' comes running over, insisting that I wear a bowtie. All the pianists "must be properly dressed," he stated firmly, whether they are working or sitting in. He handed me a bowtie.

In all my years of traveling around and sitting in, this was the first time this had happened to me. I felt awkward initially. But seeing my friends hysterical over this, I decided it was better to go with the flow and have some fun rather than get annoyed. Bowtie in place, during the middle of the Gershwins' song "Our Love is Here to Stay," a female waiter rushed up to me. Startled by her face appearing just a few inches from my own, I heard the words, "I need you to play 'Happy Birthday' for that table in the corner!" "When?" "Now!" she snapped. Oh well, I WAS the piano player of the moment. And I knew very well the importance of having live musicians play "Happy Birthday" when needed. If you think my friends were laughing over the bowtie ordeal, this really took the cake. I played a jazz version of "Happy Birthday" that I'm sure no one in The Beverly Hills Hotel has ever heard anything like—before or since.

Bruce Klauber: *With the record business behind him at that point, Andy got back into playing jazz. I was honored that he called me to join him from time to time—for concerts at Drexel University, several benefits for AIDS and at his annual programs at the Ocean Club in Atlantic City. He encouraged me to trot out my saxophone and vibes, which even my music teachers wouldn't allow me to do. His Ocean Club Labor Day shows were really something, as we were joined by a plethora of guest stars including bassists Bruce Kaminsky and Benny Nelson, trombonist Richard Geven and vocalist Joy Adams. The programming of these shows was consistent from year to year. Andy would sing and play solo for a while, then do a couple of duo numbers with the bassist. Finally, the whole band performed. At some point there was my prerequisite drum solo. The crowds loved it. They especially loved Andy.*

YOU CAN GO HOME AGAIN

In 1995, Mitch Goldfarb, my lifelong friend—a partner at Kajem Recording Studios in Gladwyne, PA—informed me that their facility had been sold to world-famous recording artists Boys II Men. After years of building a formidable recording studio enclave deep in the woods, the partners were going separate ways. He invited me to record what would become the last recording session there. I jumped at the chance to play on their 7-½ foot Yamaha grand piano, lights dimmed low, microphones trained on me.

The huge studio room was barren except for Andy Kahn and his favorite instrument. The digital tape machine rolled continuously for hours. With no planned repertoire, I recorded what would become "Solo Duet," an album of whatever came to my mind. Inspired and influenced by Lennie Tristano, Bill Evans and other landmark jazz pianists, I laid down some of the most creative work I'd ever committed to recording media.

Those recordings led me to Jimmy Amadie...again. While having lunch with my partner Bruce at a small café a few blocks from our Center City home, I spied Jimmy. I hadn't seen him in more than 20 years. Just the day before, I read in the *Philadelphia Inquirer* about his return to performing and recording. Jimmy—who'd been afflicted with career-crushing tendonitis in both his hands at an early age—had been forced to stop playing piano, squelching what surely would have been a bright future as an artist. As a result, he became a music educator. When I was 18, I learned a lot about jazz from the "Prez." That's how he referred to himself; it was also what he called each of his students.

Jimmy discovered that by resting his fingers for very long periods of time, he could record one tune before the pain would overtake his ability to continue playing. Before attempting to record another song, he wouldn't touch the piano keys for several months. Over a period of a few years, he managed to accumulate enough recordings to complete his first CD "Always With Me." I went over to Jimmy's table where he and his wife Lucille were entertaining a group of associates.

After lots of hugs, smiles and introductions, Jimmy asked me to attend his CD-release party a few days later. Bruce and I were there. That's where I handed Jimmy a copy of my "Solo Duet" compilation of spontaneous jazz improvisations—and I purchased his first-ever CD. I'd never heard the Prez actually perform on piano until I played his CD. What a thrill it was for many of his students who'd also never heard him play anything more than an occasional chord or a short phrase on the vertical piano in his studio!

An even bigger thrill came when Jimmy called me a few days later to thank me for coming to his event. He added that I should come out and see him. He wanted to talk to me about my playing. I was dumbstruck. He said, "Prez, you come and see me. I've listened to your playing. It's real good. But I'd like us to get together so we can talk more. I always thought you were a great talent, Prez. You've got a lot to say, but you use too many words." "Words" was Jimmy's metaphor for musical notes.

Intrigued, I took him up on it. That personal chat with Jimmy Amadie lasted 11 years—with a few breaks along the way. I engaged myself fully in becoming a better player. I developed an entirely new approach to creating improvised lines on the piano—leaving time for each musical phrase to "catch its breath." One statement every student heard over and over from the Prez was, "When in doubt, lay out!" I had always tried to impress listeners with my ability to fill up a jazz riff with as many notes as I could articulate into a single, long, musical run-on sentence. Jimmy taught me that it's what you don't play that's often as important as what you do play.

Our deep and emotional friendship developed into a bond we often expressed to one another. My studies with him evolved into Jimmy playing piano vicariously through me, trying out his newest musical ideas and expressions that he'd been developing for his own upcoming recordings—which he created over the next 15 years. He couldn't risk blowing his "chops" before his next recording date. So I played for him. And, in so doing, I learned a great deal about harmony and how to approach executing my musical ideas.

Over the ensuing years, Jimmy eventually recorded seven CDs, releasing them under his own name. At one of our several hour-long sessions at his home in Bala-Cynwyd, he treated me to his first new group-oriented recording project. This was Jimmy performing in a piano trio setting. His playing was full and highly artistic. More important, his determination and personal motivation had paid off marvelously. At the same time, he kept fighting off illnesses that threatened to snuff him out time and again. The Prez. He sounded better on each new CD—until 2013. That's when Jimmy Amadie died from lung cancer.

Jimmy inspired me on so many levels. He used to say, "Prez, I'm not teaching you how to play piano. I'm teaching you how to think!" I say these words over and over to my own students. I feel as though Jimmy is sitting up on my shoulder—coaching me coaching them. I hear his verbal phrases as vividly as his musical ones. I sometimes tell a student," You can't play better than that! You can play something different, but you cannot play BETTER!" That's a true Jimmy Amadie phrase. I find myself saying it when a student plays something soaked in beauty—or something that demonstrates incredible artistry, true nuance, intense musical introspection.

Jimmy Amadie and I had an ongoing Push-Pull relationship. The last few years of his life, he was very angry with me. He discovered I had had a successful music career in my 20s, during that 20-year hiatus in our relationship, before we got together again in the 1990s. He was incredibly upset that I didn't keep him informed about what I'd been doing during my years at Queen Village Recording Studios. It pissed him off miserably. One day during my ride from Philadelphia to Atlantic City, I endured a 45-minute torrent of words over my mobile phone, as he delivered an angry monologue. This caused me to turn away from this masterful musical artist once again. I regret that this mentor of mine died during the period when we were not communicating. I attended his love-fest of a memorial celebration. And I've maintained a dialogue with his charming wife Lucille. She reminds me in each conversation just how much Jimmy loved me. And I, in turn, remind her how much I loved him. The way I play piano today has been shaped from absorbing much knowledge imparted by the incredibly brilliant teacher, pianist Jimmy Amadie. R.I.P., my friend.

Bruce Klauber: *Jimmy Amadie had quite a life and career. He definitely deserves respect for his contributions to jazz education and for his determination. To my ears, he echoed the sounds of the great post-bop pianists like Barry Harris and Tommy Flanagan. Amadie was a superior jazz educator through his books, recordings and teaching. When Andy said that Jimmy believed he played too many notes, it made me think about listening closely to Count Basie or John Lewis, who were masters of the use of space. I assume that's what Amadie meant when he said that Andy should simply "lay out." Given Andy's patience, understanding and respect for his fellow artists, I'm certain he learned a lot studying with Amadie, and that's what's important. And I'd bet that The Prez also learned much during his long-time association with Andy. Lennie Tristano made it a point to listen to and internalize the playing of the jazz giants, and that was the basis of his teaching philosophy. Andy has learned a great deal from listening to Tristano and other pianists. The bottom line, however, is that Andy Kahn has never sounded like anyone but himself, which is a rarity among rarities.*

THE SOUNDTRACK

In 2002, I was asked by my friend, Kevin Hinchey, a filmmaker and screenwriter, to provide the musical soundtrack for a 30-minute video documentary he was creating. It would serve as an introduction for visitors to the Wilhelm Reich Museum in Rangeley, Maine. I jumped at the chance to perform original music over the documentary's visuals—something I'd never before attempted. Kevin sent me the "rough cut" of the video, and I spent a few weeks analyzing its content. I composed a melodic theme that would recur throughout the documentary; this would be interspersed with other music I'd planned to perform for it. My music was mostly improvised— in a "live" piano setting. I recorded whatever came to mind while viewing the video footage from start to finish. Kevin approved my "theme" melody. We made plans for him to come to my Philadelphia home where we'd record the soundtrack on my Schimmel acoustic grand piano.

We used a digital audio tape (DAT) deck I owned and microphones lent to us by Mitch Goldfarb. He signed on as audio engineer for the music soundtrack of the video "Man's Right to Know." I played the entire piano part while watching video monitors suspended directly in front of me. I did several complete 30-minute performances without taking any pauses for editing. I created an emotional mood and improvised the music as the changing images and narration dictated.

Doing this filled me with euphoria and total satisfaction. We did virtually no post-editing of my piano performance. One of my full takes was incorporated into the final version of Kevin's video. It continues to be shown to visitors at the Wilhelm Reich Museum. And it's available for sale in the museum's bookstore. This remains one of my proudest musical accomplishments, a creative achievement and artistic performance unlike any I'd done to date—or since.

In 2018, Kevin completed writing, producing and directing a full-length documentary film on the life of Wilhelm Reich, M.D.—a project that took more than 15 years to complete. He told me that I'd be doing the music for this film. Kevin then informed me—a year before the film was completed—that the job was going to a professional music house that specialized in creating soundtracks for documentary films and television programs. It would have been difficult for me to produce music for a 110-minute film, which is a hugely different task from creating music for the 30-minute video in 2002. While I'm disappointed that my musically creative themes are not part of this documentary, I understand that tackling the task would have been impractical considering my current schedule of teaching and performing. As Kevin told me right before the film had its world premiere in New York City on 13 January, 2018, "It's a good film!" I was at the premiere. I met the composer and producer of the music, Bruce Zimmerman, that night. And I couldn't agree more with Kevin. It's a good film.

BACK IN THE SADDLE

In 2005, Bruce Cahan and I took our first Mediterranean cruise—on a huge ship. During one of the upper pool deck parties where 2,000 passengers were whirling around in a dancing frenzy, I realized I was hearing music of the disco era. It had begun creeping back onto DJ's playlists. They weren't only playing remixes of old songs. Instead, the original recordings were being spun individually or mixed in as samples for effect. I was amazed at what I was hearing—and also dismayed that I had perhaps let a different type of "ship" sail without my being onboard. I turned to Bruce and said, "Y'know, I could make a remix of 'Hot Shot' that would be every bit as good as the stuff I'm hearing these DJs playing." He turned his head in my direction. His response was short and sweet, "So, why don't you?" Good answer, Brucie! The stage was set for my return to the Biz.

In 2006, I contacted Mitch Goldfarb again. Mitch had set up a world-class digital studio in his home and had lots of industry experience to back it up. I told him I wanted to do a remix of "Hot Shot." He'd been trying to lure me back into the recording studio for more than two decades. He'd asked me several times to come and record piano parts on demos he'd been working on; he said that my musical contribution would enhance a production track's value. Mitch immediately signed onto my idea. This would be my first experience recording anything in digital format. I was fascinated by the ways technology had leapfrogged since analog recording techniques were euthanized. Seeing some of the original analog electronic equipment and applications we had had at Queen Village Recording Studios replicated and displayed so meticulously on a single computer screen—referred to as plug-ins—was almost more than I could handle.

What looked like vintage audio gear was now "digitally" recreated—not as actual, tangible hardware, but in exact likenesses on a screen. The same knobs and switches with their original functionality—manipulated by using a computer mouse!—were displayed. When I recovered from my amazement at this virtual equipment on the screen and the arsenal of electronic toys available for the project, it all seemed logical. This is exactly what had to happen technologically. Having unlimited tracks had become paramount. Digital recording provided for that beautifully—limited only by the speed and memory capacity of whatever computer was running the show. It was astonishing, but it represented the next logical link in a natural chain of events that the recording industry's needs dictated. Thankfully, my technological aptitude allowed me to adapt to this new technology rather easily. This was my first music project working totally in the digital realm. Mitch was already an old hand with digital. It didn't take me long to get up to speed.

When I shared my idea of resurrecting "Hot Shot" in a sanctioned remix using Karen Young's original vocals, Mitch screamed "Hallelujah!" Her performance had been preserved on a 16-track, two-inch analog master tape, which my brother Walter had kept. The original tempo of "Hot Shot" was 120 beats per minute (BPM.) We digitally converted it to 130 BPM for this remix because dance music tempos were now trending faster than in 1978. We faced the arduous task of "cleaning up" Karen's solo vocal track, removing extraneous sounds made by the artist, along with those produced in the original "live" room at Queen Village Recording Studios. For this remix, we used only one other "live" player—musician and vocal artist Jon Rottier performing on a real electric guitar. We tapped into hundreds of digital sound libraries available in endless varieties. I played all of the parts, gathering instruments accessible from these libraries, making up the new rhythmic foundation.

Karen's voice was processed perfectly, leaving its raw character intact. For those who wouldn't know better, this 28-year-old vocal track of Karen's sounded as if it had just been recorded by the artist—not 30 years earlier. Digital allows you to take tracks recorded at one speed and increase or decrease tempo *without* changing the pitch, which *would* happen by changing the speed on any analog recording. Karen's vocal was sped up to the new 130 BPM tempo, yet the pitch was preserved in the original key of her slower tempo as recorded in 1978.

Mitch, Jon, an associate named Susan Lazarus and I formed MaxRoxx Music, LLC. We were a company searching for a label to distribute "Hot Shot—The Karen Young Reheat."

Hooked on cruising around Europe, a break in the studio action found me on another ship in the summer of 2006. Because of a miscommunication between Bruce and me, upon disembarking in Messina, Sicily, I found myself alone on the dock. I began trying to find someone to share a taxi with me to Taormina—about an hour away. One person offered to join me on this journey. I introduced myself as Andy. He shot back that his name was Ralphi. I didn't make the connection that he was one of the world's foremost remix DJs scheduled to perform during our voyage. As the taxi wound through the narrow passages up in the hills, I inquired what he did for a living. He said he was a DJ, named Ralphi Rosario, and that he had just joined the ship in Messina. He would be playing the late-night party events several times during the rest of the voyage. Struck by the coincidence of riding in a taxi with the renowned DJ Ralphi Rosario, I suggested he might know one of my records from the heyday of disco: a song called "Hot Shot."

He stared at me for a few seconds—his jaw dropping wide open. He then asked," Andy? You're Andy Kahn? *You* are one of my mentors!" I didn't know what to say. What does one say riding in the mountains in Sicily during a chance meeting with a true superstar of dance music who has just announced that *I* was his mentor? He began hugging me—telling me that as a teenager in 1978, "Hot Shot" was his favorite song. It was played over and over at home when he was kid. Ralphi was too young to be out in the clubs then, but he was a disco fanatic from the beginning. He started singing the horn riffs from "Hot Shot" to me. I was pretty flabbergasted, as you might imagine. Ralphi Rosario then amazed me even further with his instant recall of the horn and piano arrangements I'd written for AKB's "Stand Up Sit Down" track in 1979. He was singing them to me in a taxi...in Sicily!

We were laughing uncontrollably at this point. If ever I needed proof that there really are no coincidences, this had to be it. The rest of the day, as we toured exquisite Taormina together, he kept saying out loud, "I'm in Sicily with Andy Kahn!

I'm hanging out with Andy Kahn!" It was pretty embarrassing. Something like this was clearly supposed to happen; and so it did. Thus began a friendship between a "mentor" and his "student." This naturally led to securing Ralphi's creation of his own fantastic remix using Karen Young's vocal track. That version became the lead track for the re-release project of "Hot Shot," which I had planned to finish immediately upon returning to the U.S.

When I got back into the studio to wrap up our "Hot Shot" remixes, I sent out Karen's vocal track to a few other well-respected DJs in the USA and the UK who had expressed interest in providing their own remix versions for this project. When all the remixes—which took nearly a year to assemble—were completed, Mitch and I went to New York to see Mel Cheren, the now ailing, former head of West End Records, whose label had originally released "Hot Shot." This was late in the summer of 2007.

I hoped Mel would show an interest in releasing "Hot Shot" once again, this time on his newly-rejuvenated West End Records label. He listened intently to all the tracks we brought him. After a pregnant silence, he gave us his assessment. First, he said, Ralphi Rosario's mix was the only track that would carry this project into hit status—a prophesy that Mel never lived to see come true. (Mel Cheren passed away from AIDS-related illness on December 7, 2007.) He insisted that we'd only achieve success by distributing the tracks ourselves. Digital download was the only way to go. He added that finding an existing record label to distribute this would be a waste of our time. As we no longer had a "live" artist—and remixes of this nature usually proved to be a financial dead-end, he implied that we'd come out better doing the work ourselves. The labels wouldn't do anything significant to promote our release. He made it clear that we should not give this project away, that we would be more successful distributing these tracks on our own. Following Mel's advice, we released all the remixes on our newly-formed MaxRoxx Music label. Positive club reaction to the new "Hot Shot" was immediate.

With the help of an independent promoter we hired, "Hot Shot" was back on the charts! In just a few weeks, we landed in the top ten section of Billboard Magazine's Dance chart. We spent five weeks there, peaking for two weeks at number seven. I was informed that remixes of deceased, famous, disco-era artists had yet to accomplish this feat. In early 2008, the sheer spirit and magic of Karen's extraordinary performance, coupled with great remixes from club DJs Ralphi Rosario, Wayne G., Paul Goodyear and those by our own Max-Roxx studio team brought "Hot Shot" full circle. Thanks to the settlement Walter had arranged with West End years earlier, the worldwide rights to the original master of "Hot Shot" were ours again. As a result, we decided to include the original 1978 extended club version, a track that hadn't been available for sale in almost two decades! The new remix release continues to sell on iTunes and through other worldwide digital retailers. Karen Young and "Hot Shot" live on—thanks to the advent of digital recording, digital downloads and that incredible digital online wonder—YouTube.

That summer I was visiting a small club in Atlantic City. Local DJ Joey the Hatt, a longtime friend and permanent fixture on the club scene in this New Jersey resort town was playing one of our new remixes of "Hot Shot." A very young, exuberant guy was dancing with a few of his friends, mouthing the words perfectly in sync with Karen Young. Because he appeared to be no more than 20 years old, I was astonished when Karen began her scat portion; he knew every lick. When another song was mixed in, I went up to the DJ booth where this young man was now talking animatedly to Joey. I leaned into the booth and said, "Do you believe this kid? He knows every single vocal bit of "Hot Shot." This "kid" looked at me quizzically for a moment, then pointed and proclaimed, "Wait!! YOU! You're Andy Kahn!" (Having recently gone through a similar experience with Ralphi Rosario in Sicily, I was stunned—again.) "What? What did you say?" I asked him. By now Jimmy DePre had flown out of Joey's booth and was standing right in front of me shouting over the club's sound system. "I saw an article about you in the paper recently. It was about your remix project of "Hot Shot," which is my favorite disco song ever! I LOVE Karen Young! I loved the original! And I love what you did with all of those remixes!"

There'd been a recent resurgence of interest in the 1970s and the music that had gotten the whole world dancing. But this fellow was so young; how could he know so much about "Hot Shot"? He proceeded to tell me of his passion for Doo Wop and Disco music. He'd researched them both to the point that he became a walking encyclopedia of them—demonstrating total recall about these two musical genres.

Jimmy was working toward becoming a professional DJ. He'd already played at Philadelphia and southern New Jersey clubs and events. Still in shock over the energy I was feeling from him, I set to thinking about my own young career and how I'd also absorbed those earlier musical styles with a voracious appetite that seemingly could never be satisfied. I realized that art serves as the bridge for generations, tying them together—a common thread that communicates through a universal medium that knows no boundaries. Consider how young people currently have become so interested in Frank Sinatra's music and career, along with the Golden Age of Music a.k.a. the era of The Great American Songbook.

Why shouldn't "Hot Shot" have the same effect on a 20-year-old in 2008 as it did 30 years earlier? The groove was still there. Karen was still singing her heart out. People still have a pulse. (Well, most of them do, anyway.) Even though it dawned on me that I'd written and produced a song that now qualified as a Golden Oldie, this is what's supposed to happen when a composition and its performance are that good. The music legend that was Karen "Hot Shot" Young was still very much alive. And one of her youngest fans had just proven that to me in Atlantic City on a warm, summer night in 2008.

Jimmy DePre has since become one of the most sought-after club DJs in Philadelphia, California and New York. His love for 70s disco music is local folklore. He certainly is one of the reasons that people in the future will know the magic of disco. Thank you, Jimmy!

A RENDEZVOUS WITH DESTINY: A "LIVE" ARTIST

In 2009, following the success of the "Hot Shot" remixes, I decided to put out a song that the world had never heard before. Karen had recorded "Rendezvous with Me" in 1979, a song that I'd written for her right before her national "Hot Shot" tour. The production was never finished, however. And because of the tensions and complications that arose between Karen, Kurt and me while we were on tour together, no form of it was ever released. Remaining safely tucked away in my tape vault for 30 years, it was now time for "Rendezvous with Me" to finally surface. Following many of the same technical procedures we employed on the "Hot Shot" remixes, we set about creating a brand new production from two independent 2-inch master tapes. The release this time would not be a remix. Instead, it would be a previously unheard, virtually NEW song. One thing for sure, it was not going to be easy putting it together.

What made this project so technically challenging was that Karen's vocal track was recorded as a demo at Queen Village Recording Studios in 1979 against a basic rhythm section of piano, bass, guitar and drums. It was one of the last sessions recorded on our 16-track, hit-making machine—before the studio upgraded to the 24/40-track Stephens tape recorder. Back in 1980, when it became clear that Karen was not going to be involved in our professional lives anymore, Kurt and I began looking for another singer—someone with whom we could develop new productions. We found a girl with great potential and took her to Mitch Goldfarb's Kajem studios. While recording a few demo tracks of new songs with her, we decided to also try her out on "Rendezvous with Me." Kajem was not equipped to run older 16-track masters. We had no choice but to re-record the song from scratch on their 24-track equipment. We assembled musicians to lay down a brand new set of rhythm tracks. And for the first time, a "live" horn section was brought in to play my new arrangements. As it was, the vocalist did not pan out for us and "Rendezvous with Me" got shelved—again. Shortly afterward, I abandoned my involvement altogether in future record productions.

Fast-forward to 2009. We now faced the challenge of synchronizing Karen's demo vocal performance extracted from the 16-track QVRS master tape with the new horn section arrangements extracted from the 24-track Kajem master tape. These sessions had been recorded almost a year apart. Thankfully, humans don't play in perfect time. Musicians play together with a groove, a rhythmic "feel" that wavers faster and slower than the original counted-off tempo—without being digitally aligned in perfect spacing. On the other hand, computer-generated rhythms from sound libraries do not waver. They remain perfectly aligned to an electronic grid, making even the slightest tempo variations a thing of the past.

While some people complain that rhythms created this way have no "soul," this is how all dance music is produced today. You either get with the program or the program gets you! Mitch Goldfarb's expertise, garnered from years of digitally producing and engineering at Kajem and his personal studio, was the key to marrying these tracks together. He began digitally stretching, editing and refining the linear lengths of hundreds of tiny, individual, analog-recorded vocal and horn segments. This microsurgery needed to be done bit-by-bit in order to allow all the pieces to sync up with the new digitally-produced, perfectly-aligned rhythm tracks we created for this project. Those rhythm tracks were built around a foundation linked to Karen's QVRS 1979 vocals. Kajem's 1980 horns needed digital surgery to incorporate them into this new production of "Rendezvous with Me." The procedure was something to marvel at—a true and miraculous engineering achievement, painstakingly pulled off with precision and expertise.

Hundreds of hours can easily be eaten up using the digital recording platforms today. Because everything is bare-naked, there is no room for error. Allowing a vocalist's pitch to be out of tune is a thing of the past. Everything is "fixable" now. There's an electronic plug-in operation called Auto-Tune that can repair human pitch deviations. When we all played together in years past, flaws in performances like that got "hidden in the mix," a term freely used in the analog recording days.

Because mistakes can actually now be corrected with digital tools, that's a procedure that must be followed. That's why it takes so long to produce a complete track.

We invested more than 400 studio hours making just one remix track of "Rendezvous with Me." All those hours for just that one track. A year earlier, the MaxRoxx "Hot Shot" remix required nearly as many hours to create. Tedious work it is— and not for those easily bored by repetition. It is not uncommon for one 4-measure piece of music to be worked on—over and over, often hundreds of times, until it's right. This meticulous process takes nerves of steel and tons of patience.

This new MaxRoxx mix of "Rendezvous with Me" includes the Kajem studio-produced "live" horn stabs and flares from 1980 synched up to Karen's extraordinary, energetic vocals recorded at QVRS in 1979. It utilized many of the tools producers now employ in digital environments. This was not your father's Oldsmobile. We used a modern-day rocket ship to blast Karen Young back into the musical universe. This time, she was singing a "new" song—albeit in a performance she delivered at the mike 30 years earlier!

Again, we hired an independent promoter. We released "Rendezvous with Me" in the beginning of 2009 using remixes by DJs Paul Goodyear and Zathan Radix and by our own MaxRoxx production team. While this song did not enjoy the equivalent worldwide success that the "Hot Shot" remixes did, the late Karen Young was once again on Billboard Magazine's Dance chart. "Rendezvous with Me" spent ten full weeks on the chart. It reached number 28, and we considered it a respectable recording accomplishment.

I'd been invited to perform on a South American cruise in early 2007. Dance Music vocalist Pamala Stanley was performing on that journey, and we became good friends along the way. Pamala had several modest dance hits in the early 1980s, but it was her 1983 song "Coming out of Hiding" that took the clubs by storm. It became a monster hit and remains a dance classic today. She's a bundle of raw energy and superb talent. She makes sure she's always working. Pamala plays piano, sings, dances and puts forth incredible effort on stage, always entertaining and delighting her audiences.

In 2009, I co-wrote a song "The Bank of Love" involving three young talented guys with whom I'd begun working. Two of them, Mark Kuryloski and Rick Reinhart (the son of my life-long friend Fred Reinhart), had been making music tracks in Mark's home studio. DJ Zathan Radix, whom I'd collaborated with for the first time on the "Rendezvous with Me" remix project, joined me initially in writing this song, which we then took to Mark and Rick to help us complete. This foursome became a creative record-making team. I knew "The Bank of Love" would be a perfect vehicle for Pamala's voice and personality.

Pamala came to Philadelphia to record her demo vocal in Mark's studio (shades of Karen Young coming in from Florida to do her demo vocal on "Hot Shot" in 1977). How nice it was to be working with a live artist again. DJ Manny Lehman, a mutual friend of Pamala's and mine offered to contribute re-mixes to this project. "The Bank of Love" came out in May 2010, marking MaxRoxx Music's third release. It took a few months to catch on. It was aided by a new "Soulful House Mix" I created with music-industry veteran Gene Leone whom I first met in 1974 at QVRS, when we signed his group Great Pride to MGM Records. I'm astonished how musical artists and personalities from my past keep popping up. Club and radio play of "The Bank of Love" increased with the addition of that new mix, and it began receiving immediate DJ record pool chart action. Pamala's voice was back in the clubs. One of my songs—this time a brand new title—was being played on the radio and heard on dance floors again. It felt terrific to be back in the saddle again.

"The Bank of Love" was successful creatively. But it offered no guarantees of substantial income for any of the principals involved. An artist used to have a hit record when their released single sold a million copies or their album sold a half-million copies. Today, if an artist sells 10,000 CDs or 20,000 digital downloads, it's considered a hit! The royalties associated with 99-cent-per-copy sales don't yield much profit for an artist. They're forced to make livings from live concert appearances and merchandise sold at those events. They also profit if they're the writer of the song, as those royalties continue to be monitored and distributed in America through performance rights societies like ASCAP and BMI. The recording industry needs to create a future in which the public will again buy recordings—and feel comfortable paying for them. Artists and writers cannot make a decent living through their craft today. This serious problem is plaguing the industry, and no one seems to be offering solutions based on positive change.

Only a handful of recording artists ever get to become superstars. So much creativity exists in the world—and those that have it rarely make a dime, these days, from their extraordinary gift. And an unfathomable amount of talent remains undiscovered. Talented individuals, more often than not, slink away into obscurity.

That's not the way it used to be. Talent was uncovered by record labels—literally every day. There's a plethora of talent out there now—more than ever! Digital devices allow people, young and old, to express themselves in new musical formats that were previously unimaginable. What a shame that these creative individuals seldom get heard. And should they actually manage to find a listening ear—maybe even land a recording contract!—they can only hope to eke out barely enough to make a decent living. This is an industry that offers them next to nothing for all of their efforts and creative output.

LEARNING A LESSON

On December 31, 2009, we closed Southwark Paint and Decorating's retail operation. This had been my family's primary source of income since 1918—and Bruce's and mine since 1983. I decided that the Window Treatment and Decorating segments of the company could continue, as these required no inventory or a store where customers could make a purchase. Shop-at-home was how we sold most of our window treatments anyway—bringing samples to customers and taking orders onsite. Very little in-store Window Treatment retail business occurred during the 25 years we offered those products at Southwark. But the retail paint operation—the focus of the company my grandfather Abraham started with his brother Aaron—went kaput. The advent of large retailers like Home Depot and Lowes killed off the growth needed to sustain such small operations. Our business had stalled and nearly caused personal financial ruin for me.

Our longtime bank would no longer extend credit to the business because it hadn't been showing a profit. To pay our employees, whom we did everything possible to keep onboard for more than 15 years, Bruce and I poured in all of our personal savings and accessed our personal credit lines to their limits. While all business indicators showed us we'd continue to chalk up losses each year, we stayed with it.

For a few years, our accounting firm had advised that we would not survive unless we cut our expenses by more than half. They advised closing the paint store. We ignored this advice and did everything possible to keep Southwark Paint's retail store open. In 2009, despite being recognized as a Philadelphia institution with a stellar reputation, it was time to let go of my family's presence at 4th & Catharine. We'd already pared down our staff; we had let our longtime manager go a few years earlier. By then, it was just Bruce, our driver Tracy Rivers who'd been with us for 25 years and me manning the operation. Retail business was evaporating. Wholesale business, without my father around (he had been our star salesman in the field), had all but dried up. We became another local enterprise casualty. We were entering the history books of old-time Philadelphia businesses that had simply run their course.

With great sadness, we began the arduous and exhausting task of shutting down our retail location. Southwark had been in continuous operation at 801 South 4th Street in Philadelphia for 92 years. Upon closing the store, Bruce decided he would retire. Without having an office to go to or retail receipts and weekly payroll to handle, he simply said "I'm done!" I had no intention of retiring. It wasn't because I hadn't reached the qualifying age to receive Social Security. I was still involved in plenty of music-oriented projects. These ensured keeping me busy after closing the paint store.

Since then, I've created projects in recording studios, collaborated on writing new songs and performed many more gigs in public than I had during the quarter century of running Southwark. In 2010, I didn't know what moves I'd make to begin the next phase of my musical life. But I was certain that I'd plunge deeper than ever into the music industry. I didn't have a clue then about two things that would propel me to a new level in that world. But I was certain that I had to find my way back into the musical arena. I believed—as I did when I was 18—that this would be both my primary source of income and artistic satisfaction. What concerned me was that during the 25 years I ran the family business, I did very little in the field of music other than keep my "chops" in good shape. Still, I had never stopped playing the piano at home regularly, ensuring I could continue to play well.

I spent the year evaluating how to reinvent my life. On December 16, 2010, I got an unsolicited call from Al Rinaldi, Jr. He was little more than an acquaintance of mine at the time. Somehow he'd heard we had closed the store at 4th & Catharine. He asked me flat out "What are you doing?" My answer: "Driving my car." (My typical frankness, as usual.) "What are you doing this afternoon?" was his second question.

Al was the owner of Jacobs Music Company, the Steinway & Sons and Yamaha representative for the Tri-State area of Pennsylvania, Southern NJ and Delaware. I couldn't imagine what he had in mind. But I had always been intrigued by this self-made man. Although physically small and unassuming in appearance, he commanded tremendous respect in his field. Starting with the flagship showroom on Chestnut Street, he expanded his business, becoming one of the largest and most respected piano retailers in America. Al did this singlehandedly. He gobbled up most of his competition by acquiring piano retailers in the area. Jacobs Music commanded six retail operations selling the world's finest acoustic and digital pianos.

Following the usual pleasantries that start any business meeting, Al asked me "How would you like to be our Artist-in-Residence at Jacobs Music?" When I replied that I didn't know exactly what that meant or what such a position entailed, he said, "We shall see." He went on to enumerate areas in the company in which he thought I could be an asset. He wanted me to join the staff as a part-time employee with vastly different responsibilities from his full-time staff—some of whom had worked for him faithfully for more than 30 years. Surprisingly, I didn't have to think this over or consult Bruce. I accepted right then and there and asked when I would start. That was a Friday. Al said, "You start Monday."

I reported to work that Monday, December 19, 2010, having little or no idea where this commitment in the musical workplace would lead. I knew, however, that my decision to join Jacobs Music was in keeping with my goal of staying in the music industry. Jacobs Music offered me high visibility and a professional position with their well-established company. It provided me with new industry credibility along with reliable and ongoing income each week—which I truly needed. By gaining the prestige and status associated with Al's company, I became directly connected to both Yamaha pianos and, more importantly, those manufactured by Steinway & Sons.

The stage was set for a new phase in my musical life. I had no idea what being associated with a store that sold the finest pianos in the world might lead to, but it turned into something entirely beyond my expectations or understanding at the time. I went on to become a Steinway Spirio Artist, joining a unique roster of renowned Classical and Popular pianists who hold that title. It gave me the opportunity to produce live piano recordings for Steinway & Sons at Steinway Hall in New

York City. My performances will always be included on every Steinway Spirio Acoustic piano manufactured by this truly great and enduring American institution. Steinway & Sons has been making pianos in the United States since 1853. I am truly honored to have entered the ranks of Steinway artists who contribute to moving that iconic company boldly into the future—ensuring that acoustic piano manufacturing will continue (in the midst of a sea of digital pianos that threaten to take over the piano industry).

One day, not very long after I started at Jacobs Music, a young man entered the showroom and asked if he could play one of the pianos. I asked him if he was interested in purchasing one, the standard opening line from any salesperson in this area of retail. He said, "Eventually, but I have to save some more money." He said he had an old Knabe grand piano that had outlived its life expectancy and that he would love to have a new grand piano someday. When I asked what he did professionally, he said he had graduated from Philadelphia's Temple University School of Finance and Business and was working in the Derivatives Department at J.P. Morgan. During the day, he was an active trader on the floor of the Philadelphia Stock Exchange. Today, on his break, he had finally succumbed to the nagging lure by our gorgeous array of pianos—visible through the display windows at Jacobs Music's 1718 Chestnut Street showroom.

He began to play. What I heard knocked me off my feet. Lush chords and exquisite harmony were not what I'd expected from him. What I heard at one point made me exclaim, "Hold that chord right there! Don't move! What is that? Let me see it!" The look on his face was one of great surprise. What I'd heard was a heavenly sound, something one would expect to hear while ascending to the angels! There was this extraordinary suspension of sound that seemingly didn't belong down on Planet Earth.

This majestic sound seemed to float above the piano's soundboard—suspended in mid-air. It was a unique voicing of a Dominant 7th Suspended 4th chord. I had to ask him, "Where did you get the chord's voicing? Who taught you that?" He replied that he came up with it himself, as he had with all of the

251

harmony and melodic lines he played. Dominant 7th Suspended 4th chords were not foreign to me, as I played them myself. But the sheer magnificence of this particular construction of harmony completely blew me away.

He went on to say he had been the accompanist for his church's gospel choir on Sundays since he was 6 years old! That explained everything. If you have never experienced the joy and spirit of an African-American choir rocking out, it would be difficult to understand how this man's ear got such deep musical training. But my brother and I had created gospel albums for ABC Records in the 1970s. We worked with The Dixie Hummingbirds and other gospel groups. I experienced that angelic phenomenon of this music then—and the infectiousness and overwhelming effect it had on one's soul. I immediately understood how this man's early musical experiences had imbued his universe with a purely natural quality, born of sheer spirit. I was clearly moved by his playing and gushed about it to him.

I told him I was the Artist-in-Residence for Jacobs Music and a performing jazz musician. I wasn't surprised to learn of his interest in jazz—with its solid roots in African-American culture. He asked if I would play something for him. When a serious customer is in the process of selecting a piano, I rarely play. My music can be daunting to a sales prospect who might end up thinking, "Shit, I could never play piano like THAT!" This has been known to cause prospects to turn away from making a purchase. I was so bowled over by this guy's natural musical talent, however, I couldn't wait to show him both my style and approach to the keyboard. I happily slid onto the piano bench and launched into a standard tune I thought he might know. His eyes lit up immediately, and I could see he was digging what I was playing. When I asked him if he'd heard the song "I Only Have Eyes for You," he shook his head while saying "No."

What astounds me is young people's lack of knowledge regarding The Great American Songbook—their total unfamiliarity with it. When I ask a 20-something if they've ever heard of George Gershwin or Cole Porter and they blink their eyes in an obvious "No," it shocks me right to my core. After recovering, I move the musical period forward a few decades, asking if they're familiar with Burt Bacharach. When they again answer in the negative, I'm reminded that I must seem very old to them, despite my convictions that I function like a 30-year-old man— one who's continually learning and experiencing everything into which I choose to immerse myself. Nathan Burns, the fellow with whom I'd been interacting, was completely unaware of the Great Innovators in American music and their compositions. This was mind-blowing to me, but still very true. After listening to me play, he asked me flat out, "Do you teach?"

I'd been asked this question many times. For more than thirty years, when someone asked me to teach them, I simply said no. I would state that my preference was performing over teaching. With the exception of one "student" whom I saw with some regularity in the early 1980s, I never attempted teaching anyone how to construct chordal harmony or how to improvise new melodies over a structured set of harmonic chords. Yet I'd been asked to do this by aspiring and professional musicians countless times. The one "student" I *had* taught happened to be a loyal fan of mine who came to The Saloon religiously on the evenings I played.

The irony of returning to that venue at the age of 29, fifteen years after I'd played there as a teen, has never been lost on me. That fan, who years earlier had told me he "noodled" around the piano and wanted to learn more about chords, intrigued me. I figured, "I'm back here playing piano at the Saloon after all these years. Perhaps there is a reason for that, and maybe it's simply that I should teach this guy some of what I know."

He and I met for a year or so, sporadically, allowing him time to practice. Those lessons were usually at his home (a few blocks from Southwark Paint and only one block from The Saloon). My level of understanding of how—and what—to teach him was way below what would be considered an acceptable academic standard. Still, he was thrilled with what he learned—so much so that he presented me with my first copy of "The Real Book" for my 32nd birthday. The Real Book remains the gold-standard "fake" book, the absolute Go-To bible of songs for aspiring and professional jazz musicians alike.

Fast-forward to 2011. The idea of teaching Nathan, this young pianist who came into Jacobs Music one auspicious day, who'd been given an incredible gift of music and was imbued with outstanding harmony in both his head and fingers, intoxicated me. Without much additional thought, I suggested we meet at my home on 18th St. There I could evaluate his playing and determine exactly what I might be able to offer him that would improve his understanding of what he was articulating on the piano. We could then, perhaps, begin to work on expanding his knowledge of harmony and improvisation. I explained that this would make him a more credible artist, pianistically. What happened in that first session became the springboard that changed my professional life yet again. A serendipitous meeting of two artistic forces occurred. Of course, to me, this was just more proof that there are no coincidences.

The challenge I faced with Nathan was figuring out how to teach modern jazz harmony to someone who had very little experience in reading music. Whatever he retained from grade school represented his entire knowledge regarding musical notes written on paper. The prospect of taking someone back to Square One—starting at the very beginning—was not attractive to me. Just the same, I knew I could figure out how to do it. The question beleaguering my thinking was "Did I really want to do it?" If I were to teach someone wanting to play in the modern vernacular, I was more inclined to plunge right into the core. Such a student would already have a basic understanding of the relationships notes have to each other—intervals. This also required having the ability to read notes printed on a music staff.

Teaching the basic fundamentals was very unappealing to me. It was the significant reason I never wanted to teach what I knew—despite legions of friends, fans and family suggesting that I should. Even with these reservations, I looked forward to my first and what would perhaps be my only session with Nathan. Although he had little idea what the elements were that made up the chords he played so beautifully, I knew his ear was finely tuned and that his concept of harmony was superb. When he arrived for his "evaluation" lesson—which I offered at no charge, it was exciting to hear him playing those rapture-filled chords and counterpoint melodies once again. These were trademarks of the style he'd developed on his own over two decades—just from listening to music and playing piano for his church choir.

That's exactly how I had started. Listening. Hearing music in my head. I'd then trot over to our grand piano and pick out the melodies I'd heard. Next, I began to form left-hand harmony in chord formations to support that melody. This came naturally for me. And this method carried my playing until I was 18. That's when I was forced to learn how to synchronize myself to the other musicians with whom I was playing. They all had the ability to read music. They understood a language that everyone involved also understood—and used when playing together. I was the "faker" who relied on his ear to skate through—which I did well. But there came a time when it was obvious I'd have to get with the program. Nathan was another individual who'd learned to play piano the way I did. His fundamental knowledge of music was right where mine was at age 18. He knew—as did I—that it was time for him to learn the common language that musicians use to connect the dots (pun intended.) How truly exciting that first session with this man was—for him *and* for me!

After his lesson, when I went upstairs, Bruce said, "Wow! Look at you! You're beaming." I did feel as if electric sparks were flying off of me! I was energized, all right. That session opened up my thinking to a level I had never experienced. I began constructing harmony in keyboard positions I didn't usually select. I was well aware of the elements that went into these "voicings." But I expanded them as I ran through concepts for chord progressions that were already in my mental music inventory. I realized I hadn't used them very often—if at all. It seemed as if I was *relearning* things I knew but hadn't been incorporating in my playing.

This brought to mind my 7th grade Science teacher, a fascinating man with stark-white hair—then in his 60s. A highly-regarded educator in the Lower Merion School District, Leon Perkins and I became friends instantly. Every Monday morning, he wrote a new slogan in chalk on the upper left-hand corner of the blackboard. He never mentioned them. They were just there. A few weeks into the school term, one slogan fascinated me the moment I read it: *"You know more than you know you know."* I loved that expression. That Wednesday, I noticed the slogan had been erased. When class began, Mr. Perkins announced there would be a pop quiz. It was mostly about the science experiments we'd begun studying. But one question on the test was *"What is this week's slogan?"* Only two people in the class knew the answer—and were lauded by Mr. Perkins for that. I was one of them.

What I found with Nathan—in my first real teaching session—was that I really did know more than I knew I knew. I started implementing musical constructions, ideas, chord patterns, harmony—all of which had been in my mind's "storage"—though rarely used in my playing. (One of Leon Perkins' other prize slogans was *"An open mouth is a poor listening device."* He was a great man who wielded tremendous influence on me. Both of those slogans have remained with me since 7th grade.)

I told The All-Star Jazz Trio's longtime bassist Bruce Kaminsky what happened to my own thinking about harmony during my first teaching session with Nathan. Bruce teaches a Music History class at Drexel University in Philadelphia. He replied, "An old saying regarding teaching is: 'The best way to learn something is to teach it.' " That could easily have been one of Leon Perkins' slogans on the blackboard 50 years earlier! What a revelation! This said it ALL to me. It explained how I was able to pull dormant information filed in my memory that I didn't access regularly when performing or practicing. I really knew much more technique than I was employing in my regular playing. It made me realize that teaching could become a critical and important aspect in improving my own musical artistry.

From what I discovered about myself during that first session with Nathan, I realized I was destined to teach. I became super-excited at the prospect of expanding my own musical education through teaching. The timing could not have been more perfect. Performing gigs and concerts has always been a tough road in the music industry. While I knew I'd continue to perform, teaching now seemed to be more tangible and sensible. Teaching facilitates fresh thinking, allowing my musical ideas to remain relevant in the industry. I announced to my Trio mates that I was actively looking for potential students—offering a free evaluation session to determine if a student and I might be a musical match. I hoped to begin building a client roster that would allow me to be an active participant in this aspect of the music business. I was really psyched over this new beginning!

It didn't take long to acquire a group of students. Each had a different musical background. They ranged in age from age 8 to 82; they demonstrated various levels of performance and knowledge regarding Jazz Harmony and Improvisation. My association with Jacobs Music brought people into my sphere of influence. Most people coming to Jacobs for piano lessons are beginners. The majority of them are looking for Classical training. Jacobs offers only Classical music lessons in their stores with teachers on staff. Occasionally people do walk in who want to play American Standards and Jazz. They are referred to me. I offer to evaluate them in an initial private session—as I did with Nathan. I teach them privately at my studio—with the utmost gratitude to Jacobs Music for channeling them in my direction. I advertise my professional services online. This has garnered some terrific students who've been studying with me for several years. Word of Mouth and Referrals are a great source for Jazz and Modern Harmony students.

The joy and satisfaction I get from every one of my students—regardless of how they played and what they knew before studying with me—are nothing less than overwhelming. I look forward to each student and session—of course, some more than others! But they all seem to *get* it. And I see to it that they do get it. I am unusually patient with them even though I'm not generally a patient man. I do have a quick temper. My father always referred to me as having a "short fuse." But there is no room for a hot temper in the world of teaching. I found that age is irrelevant in the realm of teaching, although not so much in the performance arena.

For the last 20 years or so, I've become keenly aware of the fact that clubs and other venues presenting jazz on a regular basis tend to book youthful performers. Natural Selection is a fact of life in mankind. It's in all professions and artistic disciplines. It exists throughout the Animal Kingdom. But it could not be more evident than in the world of performing artists, where youth is actively and continuously sought. Image is paramount in the world of entertainment. How an artist presents himself, how attractive he or she is and the personality they exude all are critical in the performing arts. In teaching, though, I sense that I could be 95 and using a walker. I could still be considered relevant as long as I'm able to impart the knowledge students seek. And so, I plan on teaching until it's over. (Not anytime soon, please!) But if you're thinking that by teaching, I'm planning on giving up performing—well, "Fuhgedaboudit!"

I do not teach by the Text Book method. Each student is handled individually. I base my approach on their ability to absorb and learn critical concepts, sequences and constructions that make up Harmony and Improvisation of standard tunes. I'm able to jump from one platform of teaching to another on days when I have six students scheduled back-to-back—all with different needs and desires. And I never tire of showing them something new—even something I'm developing in my own playing. It might be a concept that I've reprocessed—something in my personal "inventory" that's been lying dormant until recently being rediscovered—that reemerges through my teaching someone something!

There is an endless stream of thought and awareness that I bring to the table with each student I teach. And they keep coming back to me. So I figure I'm doing something good for them. And their progress—some at an accelerated rate and others more slowly—delights me to no end. The satisfaction of passing on what I've learned—and what I continue to learn—simply enthralls me.

While I hope I'll be able to continue performing for years to come, I expect to be teaching until such time as it would be physically or mentally impossible for me. I truly believe that I'm spawning many new "stars" on the horizon of popular music and jazz. It has always been my fashion to "teach" audiences during my concert and club performances. I always include some history about the brilliant composers—those incredible innovators who created The Great American Songbook. Little did I know that I was setting the stage to become an educator—someone who distributes a wealth of knowledge and experience accumulated over decades of listening and playing. I truly hope that I'm helping to spawn tomorrow's noteworthy musicians, composers and arrangers. That has now become my singular goal in teaching.

NOTE: I considered making this next section a separate book. Its subject is worthy of having a work entirely devoted to her incredible life story. Because she has figured so deeply in my professional life since we met in 2013, there simply was no way I could leave her out of this work.

BUT DO YOU KNOW THE VERSE?

Peggy King has been referred to as a national treasure. That she is one cannot be denied. Frankly, no performing vocalist—male or female—on the planet today has achieved all that she has. She's covered just about every area as an entertainer: Big Band Singer, National Television Show Appearances, Weekly Television Show Featured Performer, Night Club Singer, Movie Actress and Singer, Stage Actress and Singer, Advertising Jingle Singer, Recording Artist and Mentor. That she continues at age 88 to sing effortlessly makes everything about her surreal.

Her memory is simply jam-packed with all of the music and lyrics constituting that vast body of material known as The Great American Songbook. There's only one song I played for Ms. King that she did not know (which initially baffled me)—Jimmy Van Heusen and Johnny Burke's "Oh, You Crazy Moon." I was astonished that such a charming composition had eluded this exceptionally knowledgeable vocalist. Then it hit me. Mr. Sinatra had recorded that song first for his "Moonlight Sinatra" LP on his Reprise record label in 1966. By then, Peggy King had long vanished from the music world, following a heady decade that witnessed her singing, acting and appearing on stages everywhere. She had given it all up five years earlier when she married into Philadelphia's celebrated Rudofker family and raised her own family. She was certainly a staunch Frank Sinatra fan; she knew him personally during her meteoric rise to fame.

Peggy was a multifaceted player in the remarkable decade that introduced television to America. But by the early 1960s, she was no longer paying much attention to Frank Sinatra's recordings—or those of any other vocalists. She was creating what she never experienced growing up in Greensburg, a small mining town near Pittsburgh, PA—or during her teenage years in Ravenna, Ohio. As an only child, Peggy King always wanted a real family. She'd suffered the travails of having an abusive, alcoholic father and a mother who took the role of obedient and passive wife. Peggy yearned for a loving husband and to raise privileged children in a sprawling residence—the idyllic comfortable suburban life.

Her parents were shocked when their determined, starstruck 18-year old daughter landed a job singing in a Cleveland hotel. Next, Peggy joined a touring swing band. It didn't take long before she became a super-hot, nationally-recognized household name. With fame and money, she gifted her parents with a fine home on the West Coast—an accomplishment for which she remains regally proud today. Her celebrity was hooked onto an ascending star; she launched a brilliant, but intentionally-shortened career in show business. She cut it short herself, because of a man named Sam. As she tells it, hers is a true story of rags to riches. "I grew up dirt-poor," she vividly recounts. "Having food on the table for the three of us was always a nagging issue. Plenty of nights, we were pretty hungry! My father drank heavily and abused my mother. This didn't make life very pretty for me. I vowed I would find a way to save myself and then save them. And that's exactly what I did."

Despite warnings from her parents about being on the road—traveling in a crowded bus with a bunch of guys and being the only female member of a band, she signed on with bandleader Charlie Spivak. "Charlie was a real schmuck," she says with total abandon. "But boy, did I learn all about the business from my experiences with him—and from all those great musicians of his!" Learn, she did.

When opportunities appeared, Peggy snatched them up at every turn. She got noticed and moved up the rungs of a ladder being grabbed at by hundreds of aspiring female singers. They came from every corner of America—and even beyond its shores. Someone suggested she audition for a new primetime NBC network television show starring Mel Tormé—the first full-length, weekly program to be broadcast in "living color."

Taking advantage of a break between two afternoon shows the band was performing in New York City, Peggy traveled across Manhattan–eager to get to the audition. There, she found herself surrounded by dozens of female singers. She barely got a chance to sing "The Boy Next Door" before having to run back for her next show with the band. (She was late and was scolded by Spivak.) But according to Ms. King, before she left the audition, a man came running out of the booth, picked her up, twirled her around and said, "They're crazy if they don't hire you as Mel's sidekick!" Shocked, she asked him who he was. "I'm Hugh Martin, and I wrote that song!" Peggy King was hired on the spot. Bye bye, Charlie.

One of the most significant and powerful producers at MGM, Arthur Freed, caught on to Peggy's sizzle. After hearing her in a small NYC club called The Blue Angel, he signed her to a film contract with multiple-year options. Although Freed was known for making inappropriate advances toward women, Peggy never played that game. Nevertheless, he flipped for her. Freed's master plan was to groom her to become the next Judy Garland whose life was publicly falling apart. While Peggy King never starred in a major movie produced at MGM, she claims she was introduced to everything else in the movies an aspiring actress/singer could dream about.

She had the opportunity to study The Great American Songbook with legendary pianist/accompanist Bobby Tucker from whom she took daily vocal lessons on the lot at MGM. After hearing Peggy sing one song, Bobby said to her, "Well, you're just about the best girl singer I ever heard!" Bobby elevated Peggy "from a band singer into a star singer." MGM also provided her with a daily regimen of dancing, acting, speech, diction, makeup and poise lessons. She became what an aspiring starlet needed to be—a true product of what was known as The Studio System. From the time she first auditioned for that hotel-lounge job in Cleveland, Peggy King (which happens to be her real name) found herself many times in the right place at the right time. She never looked back—only forward, and always up. Way up. Big Time up. This was Peggy's intention from Day One.

While listening to the radio in his car one day, Columbia Records' Artist & Repertoire icon Mitch Miller heard a female vocalist singing a catchy jingle advertising Hunt's Tomato Sauce. "The Beard," as he was affectionately or unaffectionately known, desperately wondered who she was. He wanted her and would stop at nothing to get her. Using his immense power in the industry, in short order he was able to discover it was Peggy King.

He got her telephone number and called her personally. When she answered her phone, he politely introduced himself saying, "Peggy, this is Mitch Miller." Knowing full well how much power that name wielded in the record industry, she didn't believe him. She retorted, "Really? Well, this is Snow White!" and hung up. She figured someone was just playing a joke on her. Mitch had an associate call her right back to confirm that she'd really been speaking to The Beard himself. On the phone, Miller said, "Peggy, we'd like to have you on the Columbia Records label." Peggy shot right back, "When?"

In no time, Peggy King became the newest female vocalist on Columbia to gaze out at buyers from the bulging shelves of record stores—from coast to coast and abroad. Her adorable looks didn't hurt sales one bit. Her albums marched right into America's homes and were being played on phonographs everywhere. Peggy had a string of hit recordings at Columbia while under the tutelage of Mitch Miller. He was difficult, demanding and stubborn—especially when stationed at his position behind the control booth's glass divider in a recording studio. Many hits were created through the genius of this extraordinary record producer and Artist & Repertoire mogul.

Miller made a serious blunder with Peggy, however. He refused to allow her to record the song "Cry Me a River," which had been written specifically for her by composer Arthur Hamilton. The reason given seems unbelievable. He told Peggy: "No song with the word 'plebeian' will ever be on the Columbia label." And it wasn't. Instead, Julie London was offered the song, which countless numbers of vocalists and instrumentalists covered after it became an immense hit. Peggy will emphatically tell anyone today, "That's MY song! It was written for me!" Despite this obvious miscue by the man in charge, Peggy King still benefitted enormously from her musical association with Mitch Miller and Columbia Records. They gave her a boost in her journey to stardom and helped propel her rapid ascension into the stratosphere of the entertainment world.

Singer Gary Crosby, son of famous crooner Bing Crosby, became a dear friend of Peggy's. She claims that Bing, who was also fond of her, suggested she be hired by his Hollywood neighbor George Gobel. Gobel was putting together a new weekly television variety show. Positioned in Saturday night's Prime Time slot of network programming, the George Gobel Show became hugely popular in the mid-1950s—commanding a huge audience. Pretty, smart, talented, spicy and a marvelous singer with impeccable timing and uncanny intonation, Peggy King proved the perfect on-air foil for George. He gave her the moniker "Pretty, Perky Peggy King" and, in no time at all, Television Land knew her by that name.

The George Gobel Show enjoyed a multi-year run, garnering the nation's largest viewing audience every weekend. Peggy was featured posing with Gobel on the cover of TV Guide, literally forehead-to-forehead with this huge television star. That image became one of their trademark interactions during the show. Peggy sang. She kibitzed. She flirted with George. And audiences flipped out for her. She was given her own solo song during each telecast and also sang with the show's other guest performers.

Peggy King became a bonafide American star. Her face was plastered on all the entertainment and gossip magazines. Everyone in Hollywood was calling for her to be a guest on their shows. And Peggy accepted all their invitations. She also made appearances on a number of television series filmed in Hollywood. In one, she was paired with handsome James Garner, acting and singing in an extraordinary episode of Maverick: "The Strange Case of Jenny Hill." She was also written into a unique episode of "Dragnet" starring Jack Webb. In it, she performed the song "Any Questions?"—another tune written for Peggy by "Cry Me a River" composer Arthur Hamilton.

"No way THIS song was going to be cut!" she retorted. In fact, this was the only time during the entire run of the Dragnet TV series that a song was ever featured. The rest of the music heard on Dragnet was strictly for background or to achieve a special effect for action occurring in the storyline.

Peggy landed small roles in substantial films alongside huge movie stars. She was featured in "The Bad and The Beautiful" with Kirk Douglas, Lana Turner, Dick Powell and Walter Pidgeon. With Dana Andrews, Linda Darnell and Sterling Hayden, she played her most significant and important acting role—in the film "Zero Hour." This was a corny, well-liked film that became the inspiration for the movie "Airplane" years later. Peggy even showed up as a sultry singer during a marvelous club scene in the venerable film "Abbott and Costello Meet the Mummy!" Her roles in these films, while not remarkable, showed her versatility as an actress and how extremely photogenic she was. Her personality definitely did justice to celluloid.

Well-liked and widely acknowledged for her unquestionable singing, acting and comedic talent, Peggy King was invited to tour with Bob Hope. Her longtime Hollywood pal Debbie Reynolds joined her on some of Hope's world-famous USO shows overseas. They visited wounded soldiers in military hospitals in embattled areas and entertained the troops during the Korean War. She dazzled the soldiers as a featured celebrity in star-studded shows performed in front of thousands of men in uniform.

Peggy was invited to perform Irving Berlin's "Count Your Blessings" from the movie "White Christmas" during the 27th Academy Awards telecast in 1955 hosted by Bob Hope. It's hard to comprehend how famous she had become in such a short time. Her name was instantly recognizable to tens of millions of people in America and around the world. Yet today she remains in relative obscurity to generations of viewers who came along following that incredible era in entertainment—a time affectionately known as The Golden Age of Television. That era ended in the early 1960s.

Peggy King was a frequent headliner at the infamous Mocambo nightclub in Hollywood. During the last half of the

1950s, she performed solo in a number of other high-end night-clubs across the country. During that time period, while being cast in movies and stage productions of musicals and dramatic theater, she continued receiving invitations to perform as a fea-tured guest on TV's biggest stars' variety programs. One week, she appeared alongside Jack Benny. Milton Berle and she were then seen camping it up live in front of the television cameras the following week. A host of other luminaries who "owned" the airwaves during that glorious era of live television insisted on having Peggy as a frequent guest. She even appeared as the famed Mystery Guest on the CBS television network pro-gram "What's My Line?"—watched by millions of viewers every week. Even using a squeaky voice to conceal her identity, Peg-gy King was unable to stump the panel of stars from figuring out exactly who was their celebrity guest.

At the end of 1960, Peggy was booked to appear at the famed Chicago jazz club Mister Kelly's. On a business trip to Chicago at the same time was a man named Samuel Rudofker, Chairman and President of Philadelphia's After Six Formal Wear. An avid lover of classical music and opera, Sam was asked by his good friend, Chicago journalist Irv Kupcinet, to join his party at Mister Kelly's one night. Rudofker initially balked, saying he was not particularly fond of jazz. Relenting for the sake of maintaining good relations with his friend—and considering After Six's stellar reputation needing to be upheld in the press, Sam joined Irv and his colleagues at Mr. Kelly's. To say that Sam was smitten instantly by Peggy King's on-stage performance would be—according to the vocalist her-self—"quite an understatement." He insisted on meeting her. "The chemistry between us was unmistakable. I felt it immedi-ately!" Peggy said.

As their feelings for each other grew exponentially over a very short time, they began to travel between Los Angeles and Philadelphia to see each other. And soon they began talking about marriage. Peggy insisted she'd exit show business en-tirely so they could start a family. Sam protested strongly, say-ing he didn't expect—nor would he even suggest—that she give up her stellar career. She responded that if he anticipated her continuing to perform, she wouldn't marry him—though she adored him. That matter settled, Peggy and Sam made plans to get hitched.

Peggy was warned by influential honchos—the true big shots who occupied the highest echelons of the entertainment industry—that were she to quit, there was literally no chance she could ever return to her career. Ms. King didn't acquire her show biz moniker—Perky Peggy King—by acting timidly or being easily swayed from her convictions. Her mind was made up. And the decision, she insists, was hers alone. With a career that could not have been more flourishing, Peggy knew she was leaving the road to superstardom.

Despite the intensity of her love for Sam, it must have been excruciating for Peggy King—barely past her 30th year—to simply disappear from Hollywood and New York. Everyone, including Peggy, knew she was headed for a gigantic career in The Biz. But love changed all that. And it happened quickly. Peggy bid adieu to Hollywood, where a new star on the Hollywood Walk of Fame with her name under it had already been permanently installed. Peggy's star was one of the first 100 such permanent markers installed there! And thus ended the storybook career of one of the most promising female stars ever.

Peggy and Sam made plans to set up house in Philadelphia. She moved to the East Coast and began an entirely new life as Peggy King Rudofker. Sam was a member of an iconic Philadelphia family—one with vast wealth. And he was known far and wide for his artistic and cultural philanthropy. Soon after they were married, two children were born, one right after the other. Pretty, Perky Peggy King was now a mother of two—just as she had planned.

There is a plethora of information on Peggy King's extraordinary and brilliant career in show business. The internet is full of photos, stories, videos and anecdotes about her. I've simply outlined the sequence of events that led up to her performing career—describing the highlights. She orchestrated and carried this off all on her own.

Peggy was first married in the 1950s to musician Knobby Lee, a trumpet player in Liberace's orchestra. They produced no children and divorced in less than two years. "People always confused Peggy Lee and me back then," she told me. "When I married Knobby," Peggy added with a twinkle in her always-sparkling eyes, "I actually—and legally—became *Peggy Lee!* Imagine how Hollywood's Gossip Columns kept getting us twisted up! Peggy Lee and I joked about that for years!"

With her star firmly embedded on the Hollywood Walk of Fame, history cannot overlook Peggy King's incredible accomplishments. She became an American entertainment legend. But the public—always fickle when it comes to entertainers—often demonstrates its uncanny ability to turn on a dime toward new artistic expressions, styles and performers. It's easy to see how Peggy's name faded just as rapidly as it shimmered while she was making a name for herself. Gossip columnists in Hollywood and New York found nothing glamorous about a starlet who decided to trade her incredible career to become a wife and a mother in Philadelphia. No one can be certain where her career might have led had she not bid farewell with one astonishingly quick wave goodbye. Insiders were shocked. Colleagues were in disbelief that she chose to vanish at the moment her career was exploding. But vanish she did. Peggy King was gone from the limelight. Coincidentally, American Standard tunes were beginning to decline in popularity.

The music certainly changed in the 1960s. Rock 'n' Roll had come on the scene in the late 1950s. It morphed substantially with the onslaught of Rhythm & Blues and the new music imported from across the Atlantic Ocean. Before the Liverpool Invasion, it was Elvis Presley who knocked everybody a few rungs lower on the ladder of stardom. When the Beatles and other groups from the U.K. arrived on America's shore, they garnered the interest of millions of young fans. This changed the face of the music industry in a very big way.

Composer Alec Wilder wrote "American Popular Song: The Great Innovators," which serves as the consummate textbook regarding the importance of The Great American Songbook. He nailed it. In Wilfrid Sheed's "The House That George Built," he states that during the era of the Great American Songbook, the brilliant composers "tripled the world's total supply of singable tunes." As the 1960s unfolded, the output of the Great American Songbook composers slowed considerably. However, Frank Sinatra, Ella Fitzgerald, Tony Bennett and Sarah Vaughan were among a handful of singers responsible for keeping the songs of Cole Porter, Irving Berlin, George and Ira Gershwin, Harry Warren, Jerome Kern, Johnny Mercer, Richard Rodgers and Lorenz Hart, etc. alive through that decade. These performers continued to record those fabulous compositions imbued with the American vernacular and spirit. There should be no dispute on this matter.

But suddenly there was a new engine driving the music industry. In a frantic scramble, record labels were forced to endorse fresh, new sounds and forgo those that had kept an industry rolling in dough for nearly three decades. The upstart newcomers became the sought-after artists who'd control the styles of music heard over radio receivers, selected by radio's program directors. In no time, these artists also took over the airwaves delivering popular shows to millions of viewers glued to their television screens.

The record companies were forced to get onboard with the new sounds dominating record charts. Did Peggy King see this paradigm shift coming right before it actually occurred? Was this the reason she insisted on leaving show business? Was it a coincidence that all the incredible Songbook tunes crafted by those supremely gifted American composers— compositions that captivated the world for more than a quarter of a century—were now relegated to be heard solely in nightclubs and large public venues? They became the only reliable performance centers for artists the public associated with the Great American Songbook; in fact, those entertainers could still draw huge and nostalgic audiences in Las Vegas, New York and Los Angeles. And they could go on national and world tours and command standing-room only audiences. But everywhere else this music was dead. Radio no longer paid attention to it. The Golden Age of the Great American Songbook was finished after having defined a long and prominent era in musical history.

The music scene was under assault, precipitated by seismic shifts from early rock 'n' roll artists. Hits were pouring out of Bernie Lowe's Philadelphia Cameo-Parkway label. His independent record company pointed the way for other independent and major record labels. An onslaught of new recording artists was now captivating both young black and white audiences for the first time. This paved the way for Detroit's Motown Sound—created by visionary record mogul Berry Gordy. Adding to this mixture of new music was the viral invasion and virtual conquest swept across the Atlantic from Liverpool. The Beatles kick-started an entirely new era of hit-makers. What perfect timing Peggy King showed by leaving the industry!

She was now free to pursue her dream without professional encumbrances. She married an adoring husband and gained fabulous wealth. Samuel Rudofker had been married before and had two grown sons. The couple produced son Jonathan in 1962. Daughter Suzanne followed—just a year and ten days later! According to Peggy, Sam's two sons from his first marriage spent a fair amount of time with the new family. The Rudofker agenda was filled with children and never-ending social and business engagements. While Sam ran After Six, his family's huge apparel-manufacturing conglomerate, Peggy created a new role for herself at his company. She wrote musical shows for its trade conventions—and participated in them, traveling across the country and beyond its borders.

Peggy and Sam frequently traveled abroad for pleasure. They often spent their summers in Italy. They toured the world as a glamorous American couple and drew attention wherever they went. This was the life Peggy optioned by walking away from the one she'd carved out for herself as a television, theater, recording and movie star—as well as a high-profile nightclub vocalist. It was as if her own crack-team of Hollywood fantasy writers had created the scenes of the family life she had longed for.

After Peggy and Sam's two children reached adulthood, she no longer produced musical shows for After Six. Instead, she began performing at benefits. She donated her time and experience to cultivating future careers for aspiring vocalists. The couple developed a personal and professional association with The Philadelphia Boys' Choir. It was there that Peggy discovered an 8-year old boy whom she recognized had all the talent necessary to become a star. She was right on the money. Justin Hopkins is currently one of the most sought-after young opera singers—an international force in the world of opera today. Justin performs regularly with The Boston Pops, has appeared several times at Carnegie Hall and can be seen and heard handling the leading male role in operatic performances around the globe.

Peggy went into recording studios during the 1980s to create independently-produced albums that received critical acclaim for their artistic approach. These albums, more rooted in jazz than her earlier ones, had modern musical arrangements complementing her still-amazing voice. No longer thwarted by Studio-System honchos, she was free to experiment with her vocal stylizing. No longer was she handicapped by the overwhelming dictatorship of Artist & Repertoire heads at record labels.

When the children grew up, Peggy and Sam sold their large house in Gladwyne, PA, on Philadelphia's tony Main Line. The couple, along with Peggy's mother who lived with them, moved to a 12-room duplex penthouse in The Philadelphian, a condominium complex adjacent to The Philadelphia Museum of Art. The Philadelphian offered them security and access to everything without leaving the grounds. Peggy says that Sam insisted they move there so she'd be safe and not alone if he predeceased her.

With interest waning in the musical genre Peggy always performed—and the unfortunate passing of both Peggy's husband in 1994 and her son Jonathan in 2000, she opted for total retirement. For the second time in her sparkling career, Peggy King disappeared from view, leaving behind legions of fans who still adored her. Following her mother's death and her daughter Suzy's move to northern California, Peggy moved to a cozy one-bedroom unit in her building. With a great view of the city from her panoramic windows on the 19th floor, her grand piano always with her, she became comfortable living alone.

The Philadelphian is a self-contained "city" with every retail service available within the building. She could have her hair done, buy groceries and eat in a great restaurant catering to other residents and locals living nearby. There's a dry cleaner and a bank located in the building. She could also socialize with many retired and middle-aged couples, widowed singles and an increasing number of never-married singles and young professionals—all of whom discovered that a Hollywood star lived right in their midst. It was impossible for her to walk through the complex without bumping into someone greeting her by name. She never felt alone living there. With a full-time concierge staff, 24-hour doorman and security at every turn, Sam was right—Peggy would feel and be safe there.

Over the course of many years, Peggy developed a close friendship with one of her most ardent and devoted fans. Anthony DiFlorio III—involved in the promotion business—began assembling archival material relating to Peggy's career. Through auctions, online resources and intense detective work, Anthony accumulated a huge dossier of photos, articles, vinyl recordings, magazines and disks related to Peggy's miraculous career. Along the way he became her ad-hoc archivist and a very close confidante. When Peggy needed something, Anthony was always there. He took her to personal appearances that he arranged for her and to events where she'd been invited. A bigger fan of Peggy King's cannot be found. The love and admiration Anthony has shown towards her remains unrivaled.

Anthony heard of a concert event being presented on Rittenhouse Square. It was organized by his former colleague, drummer Bruce Klauber and me. Bruce and Anthony had known each other for many years while Bruce was a budding journalist and editor of several regional trade publications and newsweeklies.

The concert was a fundraiser for Musicopia, the Philadelphia institution that brings music curriculum to public schools whose arts programs have been the victims of budgetary cuts. Scheduled for Sunday afternoon, June 2, 2013, this unique event featured both jazz and classical music. A local female jazz vocalist Paula Johns and her trio would be performing, as would the pianist of The Philadelphia Chamber Music Orchestra. Also on the schedule was The All-Star Jazz Trio. Bruce and I were about to engage in a rendezvous of musical destinies.

According to Anthony, Peggy often experienced emotional lows around the anniversaries of the deaths of her beloved husband Sam and her cherished son Jonathan. Anthony did whatever he could during these periods to brighten her spirits. He contacted Bruce Klauber to ask if he could bring Peggy King to the concert. Bruce, of course, was thrilled at the idea of having a real star in the audience. Anthony warned him that at the last minute, she could easily decide not to go. But in this case, Peggy said yes and stuck to it. On that beautiful Sunday afternoon, they were seated in a packed house of nearly two hundred attendees at the Philadelphia Ethical Humanist Society's auditorium. The stage was set for a historic meeting between Peggy King and a couple of seasoned jazz musicians—all of whose lives were about to be altered in a very positive way.

At some point during the concert, Bruce Klauber acknowledged the presence of the star of stage, screen and television and asked Peggy King to stand. Standing and surveying the room filled with people of all ages and musical tastes, she received enormous applause. When the concert was over, The All-Star Jazz Trio—the last act to perform—left the stage to greet people in the audience. I was standing next to Bruce, talking to a number of well-wishers when Anthony, whom I did not know, introduced Peggy to Bruce. I heard a lovely, melodic voice say, "I haven't heard anyone swinging on the drums like you since Buddy Rich asked me out on a date. I said to him, 'Well, if you'd wipe that awful scowl off your face, I MIGHT consider it!'"

Seconds later, she turned to me, and said, "And I haven't heard anyone play the piano like you since I was engaged to André Previn...and I dodged THAT bullet!" Flabbergasted would be one word regarding my reaction as she held up her thumb and index finger—separated by about an inch! We all laughed; Peggy's whole-hearted laugh was the liveliest of them.

Anthony handed me both his card and Peggy's. While I was looking at hers, she put her hand on my right shoulder and said, "Would you please consider giving me a call? I'd really love to sit around a piano sometime with you, if you'd be interested." My answer, of course, was that I'd love to do that. She then said, "But you don't even know if I can still sing!" The rest is a blur for me, as many people from the audience had now congregated around us—all trying to get Peggy's attention. What a scene! It was like a Broadway show's opening night.

Six weeks later in mid-July, I was in Rangeley, Maine. I go there every summer to attend a conference at The Wilhelm Reich Museum—where I also do a solo piano fundraiser for that organization. During a break in the conference, I decided to call Peggy King. I get such a kick hearing Peggy *"sing"* her hello. It's "Hel-O-oh!" in three distinct syllables, delivered in three separate musical notes—EVERY time she answers. This was the first I'd heard it. I hope I hear it for a hundred more years! I told Peggy who I was, and we engaged in the first of hundreds of telephone conversations to come. That one, however, will remain indelibly etched in my memory. While I can't vouch for Peggy's recollections, it was one of such classic dialogue that it's impossible for me to forget even one phrase we exchanged.

"Hel-O-oh!" "Hi Peggy. This is Andy Kahn." *"Hi-eee!"* "We met a month and a half ago, following a concert you attended when my trio performed a fundraiser at The Ethical Society. You came up to us afterward with Anthony DiFlorio that Sunday afternoon. *"Of course! How ARE you?"*

We exchanged pleasantries—connecting on a personal level. Peggy asked me how I knew she could still sing after all these years. I answered I could tell she still had it just from the sound of her voice and the quality of her tone. It was devoid of any garble or hoarseness (unusual for a woman of 83). It had clarity that belied her age. *"Oh? How do YOU know my age?"* she asked. "Well, it's easily found on the internet," I quickly replied. She retorted she didn't use the internet, had no computer and didn't want one. She said there's probably too much information out there about everybody, much more than should be available publicly. She was—as she always is—absolutely correct! It's amazing how someone who doesn't go online could be so astute about the evaporation of everyone's privacy since online data became readily accessible.

I suggested we get together at my home—not far from hers—adding I'd love to accompany her while she sang some songs. *"Oh, I don't sing anymore. I haven't sung in years!"*

"How many years," I inquired? *"Maybe ten or more...I guess. I really don't know."* I assumed she meant she hadn't been performing.

Shocked by her answer, I asked if she sang around her apartment, in the shower, to herself, in the car. *"Car? What car? Ha! You must really be skeptical now if I can still sing at all, aren't you?"* I was embarrassed because, yes, I was skeptical. I answered politely that I was sure she could still carry a tune beautifully. *"Well, I guess we'll just have to find that out when we meet, now, won't we? Hahahahaha."*

That laugh. That Peggy King laugh. It was the second time I'd heard it. The first was when she mentioned André Previn on the day we met. I've heard her laugh now a gazillion times—over the last 5 years. It is a laugh that's nothing less than infectious. Hearty, full, robust, powerful and very funny in its own right—it has a timbre all its own, having evolved from all those years doing live television comedy. It is simply intoxicating. It makes one laugh just hearing it. And it's so easy to make Peggy laugh, especially if something is even *remotely* funny. If it's really funny, her giggling and guffawing erupts, and you begin laughing with her almost endlessly until she stops. Then the next line is uttered, and it may start all over again ending with her stating, "Now, THAT'S really funny!!"

"So, you think you know The Great American Songbook, do you?" Peggy directed this question at me following a discussion of our favorite songs. We agreed there were way too many to enumerate in one session—and that the next time would probably produce a whole new set of tunes that knock us out. We talked about Jerome Kern. *"Jerome Kern's daughter once told me her father would have thought of me as his favorite interpreter of his songs. She just loved the way I performed them on an album of Kern compositions I recorded."* Richard Rodgers and Lorenz Hart came up in our conversation a number of times. *"Well, WHO doesn't love Rodgers and Hart's compositions?! They're all marvelous!"* About Johnny Mercer she said, *"Oh, I knew Johnny. He loved me. And I was crazy about him!"* Of course, I was starting to cream in my pants over what she was saying. Who wouldn't? Harry Warren, Cole Porter, The Gershwins, Irving Berlin—all were part of our

discussion. I suddenly knew there was nothing about the composers and songs that framed the first half of the 20th century that she didn't know intimately.

At one point she devilishly inquired if I thought I could stump her with a tune she didn't know. Having become an ardent fan of one particular song written by Rodgers and Hart for their last Broadway show together "By Jupiter" in 1942, I figured I'd try it out. Recently I'd mentioned this tune to musicians who were very familiar with The Great American Songbook. I'd managed to stump every one of them—no matter how many years they'd been kicking around. NO ONE knew it! Having just added it to my own repertoire—instrumentally and vocally—I loved when I had the chance to deliver Lorenz Hart's amazing lyrics, married perfectly to the exquisite Richard Rodgers melody. (I believe every melody Rodgers composed is exquisite!) So I threw out the pitch to see if Peggy could connect with the ball. "'Nobody's Heart,' Peggy. Do you know that tune?" The prerequisite three-second pause ensued, something she'd learned to execute with precision during her weekly appearances on The George Gobel Show. With her well-honed, timing, she replied coolly, *"Yes. I do. But do you know the verse?"*

"Nobody's Heart" has a verse? I was speechless. I didn't know what to say. Of course, nearly ALL the songs from that age of American music had verses—intros, as they were often called, leading up to the main body of the more recognizable song. I was unaware that "Nobody's Heart" had a verse. Subsequent to our phone conversation, I searched for it; it took me two years to uncover it. It's not a particularly good verse, ergo it's not one that people would know even if they knew the main song—and not many do! Not surprisingly, Peggy King won that round handily.

"Do you know the verse? Are we doing the verse? What about the verse?" These seemingly innocuous inquiries come from the star before just about every song on which I accompany her. It is simply de rigueur, and I've come to expect it whenever we're onstage, in a rehearsal, a recording session or even on the phone just going over a tune she wants to sing. I'd become totally unglued starting a song without Peggy first

asking me whether we were going to do its verse. That's just part of the deal now.

We concluded our first phone conversation with my saying that when I returned from Maine, I'd call her and set up a date for us to get together. She told me how glad she was that I'd phoned and that she'd thoroughly enjoyed speaking to me. About to hang up, she managed to throw another one-liner at me—indelibly etched in my memory: *"Oh, by the way... do I know you?"* Vintage Peggy King. I will never know if she was serious, kidding or both. She knows precisely how to get her audience coming back for more. And after that indelible conversation with her, I was intoxicatingly eager for our next exchange. I knew it had to be soon. I was completely hooked on "La King," the name her daughter Suzy occasionally uses when referring to her mother. And hooked on Peggy King, I shall be—forevermore.

The date was set. Bruce Klauber—not one to miss such an auspicious occasion—would also be there. I offered to pick Peggy King up. *"Oh, I can take a taxi!"* she replied. I would hear of no such thing. I went and retrieved this artist with great anticipation and excitement coursing through me. Bruce was waiting at my front door when we arrived. Inside, she asked if I had a stool. This is Peggy's request upfront—onstage, in a club, anywhere we perform. That day at my home was no exception. I retrieved a bar stool from the basement and witnessed this adorable, little blonde package of authentic Hollywood stardom wiggle herself up onto its swivel seat. We tossed a couple of tune titles back and forth and settled on "Let's Fall in Love," the marvelous Harold Arlen/Ted Kohler jewel. After kicking into a four-bar intro, out came the first notes from Peggy King. My mouth fell open. Had a 35-year-old vocalist just entered my house? I thought I'd brought an 83-year-old star of television, stage, recordings and film there. Yet what I was hearing was a youthful, ageless voice floating in the room I called The Lounge. That first floor room, now-sacred and historic space where Peggy and I performed together for the first time, was witness to many future musical experiences with her.

How could this be, I asked myself? What happened to 50-year vocal-chord aging that wasn't at all apparent in Peggy King? How could an octogenarian sound so perfect? She didn't rehearse, didn't exercise her voice, didn't walk around her apartment singing. And she claimed she hadn't sung for a decade or more. How is it that she could sound just as vibrant and youthful as she did in the 1950s? It was uncanny.

I looked over at Bruce Klauber who was sitting across the room. He was equally astonished. His head was slowly shaking from side-to-side in sheer disbelief at what he and I had both just heard. In our midst was a legitimate American treasure. Bruce and I had previously discussed that hardly anyone was aware Peggy was still around—much less able to perform the way she did. It was 2013 and Peggy King demonstrated the same talent, charisma, ability and professional musical finesse that had endeared her to millions of fans more than five decades earlier. That was during an extraordinary era in entertainment when such things were possible.

She was still Peggy King—no doubt about it. No worse for wear or from life experiences that could have brought her down—or from old age—she was, and still is, at the top of her game. I believe that she'd be considered at the top of anyone else's game who's performing today—regardless of their age, experience or fame. Peggy was the real deal right from the start of her career. And today, Peggy remains as good—if not even better—than ever. Don't just take my word for it. Some well-respected New York music critics like Will Friedwald have written those exact words about her since 2013. She's still an authentic star. Peggy King is simply astonishing!

The All-Star Jazz Trio was booked at Philadelphia's Chris' Jazz Café the following week. Bruce Klauber and I—often of one mind—asked Peggy if she'd like to do a few tunes with us there. She lit up like a 1000-watt bulb and exclaimed "I'd love that!" We began selecting tunes from her list of favorites— they're ALL her favorites, of course!—making certain we'd accompany her in the correct musical keys for her range. We told Chris' that a Hollywood legend would be joining us on August 9, 2013. The promotion-machine wheels began to whir, and the excitement over Peggy King's impending appearance with our group began its ascent. We bombarded Facebook with notices that Peggy King would be joining us at Chris' for our first show at 8 pm. We figured that our second show—scheduled for 10 pm—would probably be too late for her to appear a second time. Word spread like wildfire. Inquiries about Peggy began coming in. We knew it would be an exceptionally exciting night for music in Philadelphia!

Anthony DiFlorio escorted Peggy to Chris' that night, and the two of them sat right up front. She looked adorable in red clothing, her blonde hair coiffed; she exuded star personality from her seat. She looked—and acted—many years her junior. There wasn't an empty seat at Chris' that night.

The anticipation, the sheer electricity of the event about to unfold was pervasive. You could feel the energy—the sense that something magical was about to happen. And it did.

We invited Peggy to take the stage after a few instrumental numbers by our trio. Perched atop a stool next to the grand piano, Peggy found her voice right away and easily slid into the role of star vocalist. She tossed out "Someone to Watch Over Me," "Let's Fall in Love," and "Little Girl Blue" with the kind of practiced professionalism that could only emanate from a true star. The audience went wild. And why not? Peggy King dazzled them with her talent, her exquisite voice, her perfect intonation and exceptional phrasing that could rival that of Mr. Sinatra or Mel Tormé. She took command of her audience. The amazing thing to consider was how many years it had been since Peggy had done this. She was completely at home and at ease with herself from Note One.

Peggy had not performed with a live group before an audience of knowledgeable music fans, critics and admirers for years. Her last recordings had been made more than three decades earlier. She had not done professional appearances for profit or for charity in a long time. Yet here she was, capturing an audience made up of 20-year olds sitting next to octogenarians—with every age group in between. And she won them all over right from her first few lyrical lines. She totally blew them all away.

There was no one more affected by Peggy than The All-Star Jazz Trio—Bruce Kaminsky, Bruce Klauber and me. We were awestruck by this lady now swinging *us* and not the other way around! Peggy was totally comfortable with us onstage, laughing over many things that struck her as comical, telling stories about what life was like in Hollywood and taking full command of our show while she was onstage. She was having so much fun that she said, *"Oh, please, may I come back and sing during your second show tonight?"* Many people stayed for the second show just to hear more of Peggy King.

During the 45-minute break between shows, Peggy and I sat onstage at the piano in front of the nearly packed house. We worked out tunes to do in the second show. When Peggy returned to the stage, those who stayed and those who'd just arrived cheered her on. They screamed with delight. And Peggy once again delivered the goods—beautifully. Her sense of comedic timing was in full form. Her confidence level was at 100%. She kibitzed easily with the three of us onstage—and with audience members who called out to her after each song. She was having the time of her life doing what she was clearly born to do. Her years of being away from the business had not diminished Peggy's ability to dazzle an audience. Her voice was full and steady, supporting her through a romp of George & Ira Gershwin, Cole Porter, Richard Rodgers & Lorenz Hart and Jerome Kern compositions. She performed them all as if she'd been singing them for the last 50 years! *Incredible. Astonishing. Unbelievable.* These words can only hint at the total reality the four of us onstage were experiencing. *"You had to be there,"* could not be a more accurate expression than it was regarding this extraordinary musical event. Peggy King decided to reclaim herself as a star performer that night, allowing the public once again to see what had made her so famous during the 1950s in that final chapter of America's Golden Age of Music.

We knew this was just the start of something unlike anything the four of us had known before. Considering all of Peggy's experiences on television, in theaters, in films, on records, in commercials and on tour with superstars, nothing we would do with Peggy could overshadow her early stardom, of course. But this was 50+ years later, and now she had a swinging trio to back her up. This was something Peggy said she never expected to happen. Well, it was happening!

Clubs began taking notice and asked to book Peggy King and The All-Star Jazz Trio. New York, Washington, D.C., Philadelphia and Atlantic City all wanted to grab a piece of Peggy King, whom they referred to as their "local" star. Appearances at charity events, adult residential communities and television and radio interviews followed quickly. Peggy King was back. Some fans came out just to see if she really could still sing. Rumors circulated about her, insisting that not only could she still sing, but perhaps was singing better than ever!

Playing clubs in NYC (54 Below, Metropolitan Room, The Kitano Hotel) reminded Peggy of her days at El Morocco — back when such clubs existed in Manhattan. Entertainment writers like Will Friedwald of the Wall Street Journal, Gary Giddings of The Village Voice, Rex Reed of New York Post, Joe Regan, Jr. and other notable music critics weighed in. They proclaimed Peggy's voice was beautiful, mature and still possessed the coquettishness that had endeared her to millions of fans during the height of her career. Her self-assuredness onstage was fully intact, they said, remarking that she could still hold an audience in the palm of her hand — notwithstanding her years of absence from show biz. They all raved about Peggy King! The All-Star Jazz Trio appeared with Peggy at The RRazz Rooms in Philadelphia and New Hope, Miller Symphony Hall, The Bethesda Blues and Jazz Supper Club, Sellersville Theater, ACT II Playhouse, Ocean City Library, Cape May Convention Hall and at The Ethical Society on Rittenhouse Square. And all of these performances drew adoring audiences with people of all ages in attendance.

In November 2013, I created "Jazz at Square" a place to hear live jazz in Philadelphia on Wednesday nights. It is located a block from Rittenhouse Square on the second floor of a marvelous, well-established Chinese restaurant called Square on Square. Peggy began performing with us there. She would just appear — often after saying she wasn't coming that night — and sing with the Trio. An eclectic audience congregates to eat, drink and enjoy the music in this relaxed jazz club atmosphere. Peggy became an added attraction to an already stellar jazz evening. Jazz at Square continues to this day.

Planning Peggy's first recordings in more than 36 years seemed to be our next order of business. Bruce Klauber and I set up recording dates for Peggy and the Trio. We decided to record "live" in The Lounge (where my seven-foot Schimmel grand piano was located) in my Philadelphia home. My lifelong pal Fred Reinhart's son Rick had his own professional recording studio setup, specifically geared for remote locations. Two recording dates were arranged. One was for ten songs Peggy would sing with the Trio. The other was for seven songs she would perform with me playing solo piano. We wanted to capture the intimate feel of Jazz at Square. That's where she continued to conquer crowds with ease. Our mutual goals were to record her without using a separate vocal booth and without having to overdub her vocals onto a pre-recorded rhythm track. We simply wanted Peggy to sit on a barstool as she preferred doing when singing. We all agreed that the relaxed environment of my "home studio" would be the ideal way to get the results we wanted.

The Trio session was scheduled for Sunday, March 2, 2015. Upon Peggy's arrival we heard: *"Do you hear that I have no voice today?"* *"I'm sorry,"* she said, *"I won't be able to record anything of value today."* *"Can we postpone this for another week?"* Such words were flying at us from our star singer. We persevered, however, as we always do. We insisted that she sounded great (which she did!) and began to record the American Standards that would become the CD release "Peggy King—Songs a la King." Peggy's voice continually came more alive during the four-hour session as we recorded some of her favorite songs.

Bruce Klauber and Bruce Kaminsky both played superbly. Klauber stuck to brushes for nearly every stroke on the drums. He wanted to maintain his playing as accompaniment for Peggy King—not to overshadow her artistry and performance. The authority, however, of his driving, swinging beat was unmistakable. It was still unquestionably "his" sound—just softer and more reserved than usual. Bruce Kaminsky played admirably. Always the perfect bassist, he laid down a solid foundation on both the ballads and up-tempo numbers. He played with confidence and sure-footedness. As an aside, I should mention that

Kaminsky chose to perform on one of his musical inventions, the KYDD bass—an instrument producing full acoustic bass sound, yet narrow enough to carry on a motorcycle. The list of musical glitterati that have purchased one or more of these instruments from Bruce—artists who perform on them regularly—is impressive. With Peggy perched up on her barstool, Klauber behind his full drum kit, my huge piano and Kaminsky squeezed into a corner, we had just enough space. Had Kaminsky been playing one of his full-body acoustic basses, we definitely would not have all fit into the room!

So many great songs: Harold Arlen's stunning "Let's Fall In Love," Burton Lane's marvelous "How About You?," Mel Torme's haunting "Born To Be Blue," Hugh Martin's exquisite "The Boy Next Door," Jerome Kern's beautiful "Dearly Beloved," Alec Wilder's superb "While We're Young," Richard Rodgers & Lorenz Hart's spectacular "With A Song In My Heart," Jerome Kern and Oscar Hammerstein II's outstanding "Can't Help Lovin' Dat Man" and the venerable "Cry Me A River" (mentioned earlier as having been written specifically for Peggy by Arthur Hamilton). 'Take *THAT* Mitch Miller!" Peggy bellowed after she recorded the song with us. We included Arthur Hamilton's "Any Questions?" mentioned earlier as the only song ever featured in an episode of TV's "Dragnet" series. Before we recorded "Any Questions?" I thought Peggy should tell the story of how this song landed in a "Dragnet" episode. The character Peggy played, a nightclub singer, had witnessed a crime. She was being interrogated by Sergeant Joe Friday (Jack Webb) and his partner Officer Frank Smith (Ben Alexander). Just ahead of "Any Questions?" on the CD, Peggy lets listeners in on the behind-the-scenes decision to include this song in its entirety. Episode #138, "The Big Shot," aired on network television, "Dragnet" Season 5 on November 24, 1955.

We recorded the tunes with Peggy and solo piano the following Sunday, March 9, 2015. Bruce Klauber came to provide inspiration and evaluation. She and I performed Rube Bloom and Sammy Gallup's lovely "Maybe You'll Be There," Irving Berlin's charming "Be Careful, It's My Heart," Richard Rodgers and Lorenz Hart's tearful and poignant "Nobody's Heart" and also their stunning "Wait Till You See Her/Him," Leo Graham and Bix Reichner's heartbreaking "You Better Go Now" and Ira Gershwin and Kurt Weill's perpetual gem "My Ship."

One more song was included on the CD with these recordings. Peggy adored singing Rodgers and Hart's fabulous "You Took Advantage of Me," a song she performed on "The Steve Allen Show" with Pete Rugolo's Big Band in 1956. We show the video of that show when introducing Peggy onstage. We had a recording of her singing it at Square on Square with me on solo piano. For fun—because we mistakenly hadn't included this wonderful song in our two recording sessions, we stuck it at the end of the CD. In this tune, you get to hear the sound of Peggy performing for a "live" nightclub audience—capturing her in a different mood and environment.

Through his personal and professional contacts, Bruce Klauber stimulated interest in Peggy's CD with a top-notch jazz label in Barcelona, Spain. Fresh Sound Records' founder and owner Jordi Pujol was excited to sign Peggy's newest release to his star-studded label. A deal was negotiated, and the CD was scheduled for release in time for the holidays at the end of 2015. Receiving good response and achieving good radio airplay and terrific reviews, Peggy King was now back in the Record Biz!—a wonderful achievement for all of us involved.

Although she was reticent at the start of each of our recording sessions, Peggy King was in marvelous voice. When each take began, Peggy sensed the red On-Air light was lit. Her professionalism took hold and out came performances any vocal artist would envy. Her intonation, delivery, sense of rhythm—*all completely intact*—belie her age by 40 or more years; she doesn't sound at all like a woman about to enter her 10th decade! Clear delivery, not a hint of hoarseness, just clean, sparkling performances from an artist who *knows* how to record. What a joy it was to work with someone who possesses that caliber of musical talent!

Our Trio has always been recognized as a hard-driving, swinging musical group of three minds thinking on the same level. Bruce Kaminsky refers to it as a form of mental telepathy—a connection the three of us sense as one musical stream of thought. Developed over more than 50 years of playing together, we anticipate each other's rhythms and patterns. We mesh together, creating one sound—not as three instrumentalists playing together, but rather playing as one unit. Peggy mentioned this the first time she appeared with us at Chris' Jazz Café. She's often told us that we are the "swinging-est" group with whom she's ever worked—that we inspire her to reach for notes she never thought she could achieve, either in range or harmonic value. The ironic thing about her statement is that Bruce Klauber has observed that Peggy actually swings *us!* Her subtle sense of swing and easy delivery of some of the most difficult standards written is infectious in its own right. As swinging as the Trio may have been before meeting Peggy, she unquestionably helps us to swing even harder today.

Drummers today tend to lag behind the beat, playing in a more relaxed way. This is a style that doesn't satisfy my taste. As of late, bassists also tend not to *push* the beat. Both drummers and bassists have other ways to lay down their solid rhythmic and harmonic foundation, which has always been their main purpose. They also have the option of staying on top of the beat—pushing it forward, hopefully without increasing the tempo. This is an art-form that many rhythm musicians today either don't understand or are incapable of executing properly. Both Bruces I perform with understand the elusive phenomenon of truly *swinging the beat* while holding the line on tempo. As a result, our listeners react by nodding their heads, tapping their feet, snapping their fingers, even swaying to the infectious rhythm we put down. It is my job to overlay arrangements of chordal harmony and written/improvised melody around their solid swing tempo. Peggy says we're the best at doing this, adding *"And, you KNOW I've performed with them ALL!"* Coming from a performer who was both engaged to and accompanied by an artist like André Previn, one can only imagine how proud we are to have become the trio Peggy prefers to work with.

Recently, Peggy was admitted to a senior care facility where she can be watched over better than when she was living alone. With the extra attention, Peggy does much better at keeping herself on track with her personal needs. This does not mean she can't sing a standard song better than anyone

I've ever known. In fact, she can deliver any one of the more than a thousand tunes stored in her head—with instant recall and accessibility. There's simply no more room on her "hard drive" for new material! She has all of the music she's learned and performed safely tucked in her personal vault—one that is both impenetrable and available to her at a moment's notice. Being unsure about when our next engagement with Peggy might occur is discomforting. But this is what happens when someone begins to suffer from short-term memory loss. Peggy King has excellent supervision, ensured personal safety and stability—and she's clearly happy where she's living now. And we couldn't be happier for her.

I told Square on Square owner Stephen Yau that Peggy would not regularly be coming to sing at "our" jazz club on Wednesday nights. He was surprised and asked why. When I explained her situation, he answered in his usual perfunctory manner, *"Pick up Peggy. Sit on stool. Give microphone. She sing."*

Stephen summed it up in those few short phases—something I could never accomplish! Give Peggy the mike. She will sing—as always. And that is the plain and simple truth of the matter. We have the delicious memory of five years performing regularly with Peggy King—learning from her—and Peggy learning from us, making fabulous music along the way. This is music as it should be. Honest. Swinging. Peggy King will always be The Real Deal to me, to my musical colleagues and to ANYONE who's ever heard her—whether it was back in the 1950s or during her reemergence as a bonafide vocal star of the 21st century.

In December of 2017, we brought Peggy back to Square on Square following seven months of her not singing in public. To none of our surprise, she killed it—again! The first two songs were a bit shaky, but this was anticipated. Then she got right into it. She grabbed ahold of the audience and simply did not let go of them until the evening was over. Since then, Peggy has appeared several times with the Trio at Square on Square—performing exactly as Stephen said. The crowd is delighted over how she delivers. She still sings beautifully at 88 with neither no diminishment of vocal quality nor inability to deliver a song. Peggy will continue singing with The All-Star Jazz Trio. Peggy King is still "just about the best girl singer I ever heard."

Long live La King.

THE TIME HAS COME TODAY

As I mentioned earlier, what plagues the music industry today is that musical creative product is available to the public in a way that provides little or no remuneration for those who invest time, energy and money in producing it. When the capability to share music digitally came about, record companies lost their grasp on the very product they sought to create. This, coupled with humankind's shortened attention span, has created the perfect storm—spelling Trouble with a capital "T" for the future of the recording industry. I don't know if anything will ever get the public back into a collective frame of mind in which they'd be willing to pay for something they currently are able to get for very little or at no cost.

In the midst of this chaos, vinyl records are staging a comeback. This is especially true in Europe. Dimitri, a famous and well-respected international club DJ simply will not play a tune unless it's pressed onto vinyl! Some labels press recordings onto vinyl just so he'll consider playing them. And other DJs have limited their playing to club mixes produced only on vinyl so they might achieve some of Dimitri's stature. Are we possibly returning to a musical era in which its creators became so successful?

Digital technology is wondrous. Unfortunately, it has caused the demise of one of the very gifts it promised to enhance: Artistry. How long will it be before the au courant crop of artists—young and old—simply gives up because they can't make a living from their art? The talents they're fortunate to have been blessed with are proving to be of little use because these individuals aren't being paid for their output. Something's gotta give. Let's hope it happens soon. The world will be much poorer without musicians to give it a sweeter spin.

Why would an artist who once sold a million copies of a record expect their record label to put up money for a new set of songs, when a single track now takes hundreds of hours to lay down and mix to satisfaction? Read that as "perfection." Digital has allowed that word into recording artists' vernacular. It has become a mantra to some. Digital tools now available can actually remove the human "feel" from a live performance in the studio. Musical pitch can be corrected. Rhythm can be adjusted. The list goes on. The groove has begun to evaporate. And no one seems to care anymore. Superficially, it all seems to sound terrific. But, unless you're an android, there *just ain't no swing no more.*

Interestingly, a number of artists have returned to recording everything "live" in the studio—with all the instrumentalists performing together. In some circles, there's even been a return to analog recording techniques. Some say its sound is warmer. Others say it has more soul than digital—that it feels more "real." Perhaps they're right. Analog recording is a throwback to times when it truly *was* real—when everyone swung together. Being there to sense the groove actually meant something then.

Digital, by and large—whether in its application to business, defense logistics, communication with family members or the creation of music—*has* certainly allowed previously unimaginable interconnectivity. Transmitting music around the world instantly gives people the ability to sign onto some less-than-legal sharing site and get something for nothing. I personally think that something for nothing eventually equates to *nothing.* Purchasing music gives it perceived and real value. In a world of beings that seem to have an attention span of 4 seconds or less, obtaining music for free is just instantaneous gratification. Then it's over. *Next!* We are overwhelmed each minute with digital information—musical and otherwise. Everything seems to be just for the moment these days. I wonder whether we will ever recover our sense of reality—pausing to take the time to appreciate how art was supposed to be created—by humans.

Bruce Klauber: *Virtually everyone in the entertainment industry—whether involved with audio, video, movies, television, radio or something else—has been affected by this "everything for nothing" attitude. I have written and produced some DVDs through the years about some jazz legends. Not long ago, I found out that most of the footage from my productions has been posted on YouTube and its clones. I had not been contacted about this, I have received no compensation for it and, unbelievably, received no credit nor mention of my work on this* *footage. As Andy says, things you used to have to pay for are now available for free. When I questioned the decency of those who'd posted my clips online, the majority answer was "Music should be free for everyone." The business people who came up with the concept of subscription radio saw the handwriting on the wall: You want to hear Howard Stern's show? You gotta pay for it. Yet getting paid for entertainment is becoming more difficult every day.*

MY WORD

successfully transported two hit-producing disco-era performers—one of them posthumously—back onto the world's
dance floors, in club-goers' ears and into the rhythms that
move their feet. I've made no plans to produce any future remixes of material I recorded back in the day or create new
commercial product that offers little chance of a return on investment. Any recordings I make will be for their artistic value
and not with expectations of turning a profit. Until the world is
willing to truly embrace artistic expression again—and pay for
it, I'll keep playing piano, writing songs to offer artists who might
want to record them, teaching students everything they're capable of learning from me about Jazz and Modern Harmony
and continue believing that music has the power to heal.

Music is the elixir of my life. It's what drives me to face
each day. I want to hear more of it. I want to play more of it.
I want to teach more of it. And I hope to always be able to
appreciate the effects music brings to me and billions of others—as the Universal Language it is.

I'm squarely focused on performing and teaching. As a
jazz pianist and an American Standard song performer who's
never stopped playing, I want to share the talent I've been fortunate to have been given. Audiences of all ages have enjoyed
my "Music by Intention" concert series, which I began in 2010.
Through a deep commitment to preserve America's unique
contribution to the arts, I've designed these concerts to be
both entertaining and educational. To complement a vast repertoire of standard songs I draw on, my performances are also
filled with anecdotes about American composers—whose musical "intention" helped shape our country's ideals. The great
composers and lyricists of the 20th century instilled music and
hope, wit and joy into our lives—through many societal up-
heavals including two world wars, a financial depression and
multiple recessions.

In 2010, I conceived an idea to produce music/dinner
events for The Palm, a privately-owned chain of American
steakhouses with 26 locations across the U.S., in Mexico City

and in London. I approached Palm management in Philadelphia and Atlantic City with my idea of pairing the restaurant's signature steak and lobster dinners—served in their private dining room—with my performing a one-hour concert afterward. These events sold out quickly—proving that good food and live music go perfectly well together. I'm open to bringing my "Music by Intention" dinner events to other restaurant locations. Have music, will travel!

In 2011, I joined forces with Hedgerow Theatre in Rose Valley, PA—an outstanding performance venue just outside Philadelphia's city limits that is the longest-running repertory theater in the United States. They had just celebrated their 88th year as a performing-arts venue. I was booked for a month to perform there—perhaps because pianos have 88 keys—and I play them all. Hedgerow is small and intimate, seating only 130 people. This award-winning theater was constructed inside an old, stone grist mill built in 1840. It's impossible to escape the warm feeling that envelops you upon entering its performance space. Many ghosts of actors, playwrights and legendary performers reside there—well-known artists who graced this historic location with their talent over the last nine decades. Their spirits live on at Hedgerow. What an enlightening experience that was.

I have developed a series of lectures geared toward all grades of school and college students. With an ever-increasing number of students expressing their desire to pursue careers in music, many institutions have added music-industry courses. My presentations describe my experiences in owning and operating a successful, professional, multitrack analog recording studio. They give insights into the transition from analog to digital recording and explain various music production techniques. While I do not perform music in these programs, the content centers on music production, which is on the minds of many students today.

Writing songs is a component of my DNA. I never felt satisfied writing alone, however. One exception was "Rendezvous with Me," which I wrote on my own—specifically for Karen Young—following the success of "Hot Shot." Having a collaborator stimulates my creative energy. Sharing my ideas and integrating them with another person's creative expressions helps me do my best work. During my Disco heyday, Kurt Borusiewicz's ideas were a critical component in the songs we wrote together. Kurt would often come up with a title or provide the first line or two of lyrics. Then I'd jump in, and we'd write the rest of the song together before scoring the arrangements for the recording sessions. Although many times I'd write the lion's share of our songs (my zodiac sign is Leo!), I never considered anything other than an equal split when giving credit and distribution of ownership.

Sometimes Kurt's and my writing and production efforts were not proportionately equal. More than a few times I had to wake Kurt for our studio sessions—following long nights of partying. Sometimes he wouldn't get to the studio until half the session was completed. One time, I had to drive to his apartment, use a spare key he'd given me, lift him out of bed, dress him, stick a cigarette in his mouth, make him coffee and carry him to my car! My father once asked why I was willing to evenly split the ownership of the copyrights he and I held. My brother Walter did not believe in equal economic distribution regarding the creative work he and I produced together. I always did. Perhaps that's why "Hot Shot"—my first record collaboration outside the team Walter and I formed—became an internationally recognized hit song. I truly believe in Karma. And I feel very strongly that without dividing shares in a creative project equally—Karma suffers. All the participants, no matter what their percentage of input is, must feel that they have real "ownership." That only comes when equal shares are assigned to all involved. Fifty percent of something is a whole lot more than 100 percent of nothing. I tend not to care who did more work, spent more time, came up with more ideas or conceived a song's hook line. If it's created by a team, all the teammates should share it in equal parts. That's what keeps things "in the groove!"

As an example, Pamala Stanley's song "The Bank of Love" began with a lyrical idea of mine. I brought it to DJ Zathan Radix, who helped me structure it into song format. It was finished with additional input from musician/engineers Rick Reinhart and Mark Kuryloski. We then produced it together as a demo in Mark's recording studio. Mark engineered the sessions. The four of us worked as a team the entire time we were recording the many tracks it took to create "The Bank of Love." Regardless of the input from the four individuals involved, that song is owned in equal shares—with equal label credit given accordingly. I truly believe that's just as it should be.

During my hiatus from recording, I took up writing songs again. Zathan Radix (who now prefers his given name Jonathan Zubriski) and I wrote together on Wednesdays for more than a year. We'd begin writing sometime in the morning and often finish up around 8 pm. The hours would fly by as we delved into both his ideas and mine—at which point they'd become OUR ideas. Sometimes we'd find ourselves stuck while working on just one "brilliant" idea that was dying to become a new song. We'd agonize for hours over lyrics. Melody and chords continued to clash until we'd both start laughing. And that was the precise moment when we realized we finally made it to the other side.

Jonathan, a quarter-century younger than I am, has ways of structuring a song that, from my perspective, tend to be unconventional. I came from a time when songs were expected to have a basic format consisting of a couple of verses and a repeating chorus. Everything then was typically divided into four 8-measure sections—resulting in a standard 32-measure composition. The thought of adding an extra two measures here and there or changing the rhythmic time signature in order to extend a musical passage was generally frowned upon. Of course, plenty of songwriters deviate from that norm. Dave Brubeck experimented with unusual time signatures—think "Take Five." And composers like Stephen Sondheim are comfortable adding an extra measure here, there or everywhere. And those measures do not necessarily follow the same time signature as the rest of the song! But I used to find that approach too radical. Today, nothing is too radical! Everything goes or, as Cole Porter wrote in 1934, "Anything Goes!" With Jonathan this could not be more true. He hears things in richly-contoured, extended phrases. He goes with his natural flow rather than confining himself to conventional format.

Many successful modern-day composers have broken time-honored songwriting rules. Burt Bacharach and Hal David can claim a huge amount of responsibility for changing the format of standard songs. Listen to their compositions from the 1960s—especially those written for Dionne Warwick. Bacharach changed time signatures in the middle of a phrase or added a measure—depending on the meter and line-length of David's lyrics. Convention was thrown out the window. After they became superstars, the Beatles also did this. Who would question their musical composition formats? These legends helped change the very face of music. What's especially interesting is that these artists have referred to writers of American Standard songs and jazz as having been major influences.

So, songwriting rules have been broken. Composers and lyricists will bend the time, change the tempo and offer irregular numbers of measures in a song. Use of these techniques has become commonplace—perhaps, I must admit, because they work! It's a new musical world order—one about which I was skeptical at the outset. But after collaborating on more than a dozen songs with Jonathan, I've signed onto this freer way of composing. Thinking about it, 12 songs we wrote tell a life story. Perhaps one day they will come together in a new musical.

In our song written for Pamala Stanley, "The Bank of Love," the opening lyrics are *"Change is good, advisors say. But what's the price we have to pay?"* The price is making—and then accepting—the changes that reward us by learning to adapt through uncertain times, evolving styles and oscillating attitudes. As our lives go through changes, we choose to benefit from them or fight them off. The way I see it, accepting change is the only way to go. There's nothing good about a creative mind sitting still. Music is forever changing. And so, I have changed along with it. That doesn't mean I won't continue to pay homage to the classics and standards as their creators conceived them. But there is always another way to sing a tune, turn a phrase, play a melody or improvise a riff. These days, I feel like a passenger aboard a ship that's sailing on a sea of changes. And I'm thoroughly enjoying the ride.

In 2011, a friend of mine from 45 years ago contacted me after I'd written him a note of condolence regarding his mother's death. He told me that while he had been entrenched in the corporate world since finishing college, he has been writing a treasure chest full of songs. He asked if I'd be willing to listen to them. While we were friends during our teenage years, I was totally unaware that Peter possessed any form of musical talent. I told him I'd love to hear what he'd written.

Peter and I have an ironic connection. In 1968, Peter's girlfriend Lisa offered to fix me up with one of her friends, and we arranged to go on a double-date. I had just turned sixteen. The four of us planned to have dinner at a small, popular Italian restaurant—DaVinci in downtown Philadelphia. While not a particularly romantic evening for me, we all had a nice time. Lisa's friend Susan didn't show much interest in me, however. When we dropped the girls off, Peter remarked that he wasn't impressed with Susan. He apologized that Lisa hadn't invited someone who paid more attention to me. The irony of our double-date is that Peter ended up going out with—and ultimately marrying—my blind date Susan! Although she was my date, when she laid eyes on Peter, she set her sights on a future with him. They are still very much together.

Meanwhile, little did I know when Peter came to my home in April of 2011 that his songwriting would fit perfectly into my own style of composing. His lyrical ideas were well developed—and drawn from a similar background to mine. He grew up in a home where Sinatra, popular standards and jazz were the order of the day. His father, an audiophile and music enthusiast, introduced his three sons to the same music that became the beacon for my professional music career. In the years that have passed since we wrote our first song together—on the day he first came to see me, we've completed more than two dozen compositions that could be considered "Modern Standards." They're influenced by the Great American Songbook composers and those modern-day songwriters who relayed the torch—following that amazing period when George and Ira Gershwin, Jerome Kern, Irving Berlin, Cole Porter, Richard Rodgers and Lorenz Hart, Harry Warren, Johnny Mercer, Sammy Cahn and Jimmy van Heusen and dozens of other brilliant composers expanded the world's supply of singable songs. Four and a half decades had slipped by with no communication between Peter Kursman and me. Now, there is no doubt in my mind, we were meant to compose songs together. I love the compositions we've written. I sincerely hope that one day the readers of this book will become familiar with some of them.

For me, it's all about good music. It always has been. The tide seems to be moving toward restoring some quality in music. This is apparent in the overwhelming number of choices listeners have today at their fingertips. Real music will find its own way. In my life's first quarter, it was music and the arts that influenced me in everything I did. The second quarter found me handling my family's personal affairs and running our well-established family business; music took a backseat for me during this period. Now, somewhere in the middle of my third quarter, I'm back in music—right where I belong. It's my destiny to be playing, singing, writing, producing, arranging and now—of course—teaching. It is in my tissues. It's in my blood. It flows through me in a never-ending river of sounds and rhythms, intonation, pitch adjustments, harmonies and melodies all blending together into one stream. On that note, I've determined that for the rest of my life, it will be my musical "intention" to *spread the words and music* to all those individuals who care enough to listen—to people who want to be moved and enlightened, as I have been, by the singular language that everyone understands. It's all about The Groove. None of us ever needs to be taught how to listen to music. It's simply rooted in our human nature.

Bruce Klauber: *Andy didn't use the following phrase, as it's a well-worn cliché—and Andy Kahn doesn't do clichés—but he has, as they say, "returned to his roots." It's a good time for it, in that everyone from Rod Stewart to Liza Minnelli, Sting and Paul McCartney have released recordings of the great American standards. Indeed, Minnelli and Streisand's latest works are being described in some quarters as jazz. Although Andy's success in the record business was astounding and well deserved, I always believed his most significant and long-lasting contributions were, are and will continue to be as a jazz pianist and singer specializing in compositions from the Great American Songbook. His "Music by Intention" concert programs are joyous, touching, vital and educational. His audiences not only* *come away happy after a concert, but they've learned a good deal as well. His knowledge of the great composers' works through the ages is incomparable, as is his lifelong ability to communicate. Most importantly, "Music by Intention" is entertaining. He is, after all, an entertainer.*

I've had the pleasure of hearing Andy's show many times. He has played before packed rooms of fans and music lovers. At the end, the audience is often on their feet in appreciation. At one of them, I decided that something was missing. His "Music by Intention" concept purposely does not emphasize jazz. So I asked my friend of more than 50 years if I might say something to the audience. Always agreeable in impromptu circumstances like this, Andy handed the microphone to me. I mentioned that as great as his concert was, there was a segment of Andy's talent they had not heard. I proceeded to describe Andy's jazz piano stylings, concluding my remarks with "If he will indulge my one request, I would like to have the audience hear another side of Andy Kahn—a giant among jazz pianists." Without hesitation, Andy launched into a Lennie Tristano-inspired version of "Dark Eyes." It was amazing and the audience went wild. I could only whisper to him, sotto voce and with a real tear in my eye, "You've still got it." He does and he always will.

In closing, it's clear the musical canvas upon which I've been painting will receive more brushstrokes—drawn from a rich palette of experiences yet to occur. Music is a composition of life. And there's a lot of music yet to be written, performed and heard.

Life goes on to another song.

ACKNOWLEDGMENTS

Kevin Hinchey, Peter Reinhart, Fred Reinhart, Gary and Gail Krimstock for their invaluable input when I first began to write this book

Bruce H. Cahan for being the love of my life and the next one

Bruce Klauber for his lifelong enduring love, friendship, musicianship and for teaching me to swing

Janice and Kenny Kahn, Jayne Seidman Cahan, Earl L. Cahan, Phyllis Reinhart, Sara and Vito F. Canuso, Jr., Alan M. Kalish, Ronald C. Teare and Leon Perkins for being cheerleaders with never-ending support

Virginia Goff Green for her friendship, musicianship and for editing this book like no one else could

Judge Lynne Abraham for her wisdom, friendship and for conducting the perfect marriage ceremony

Karen Young for always being true to her extraordinary talent and for being a Superstar

Alesia and Cliff Shute, Kurt Borusiewicz, Lloyd Remick, Walter Kahn, Ralphi Rosario, Mitch Goldfarb, Susan Lazarus, Jon Rottier, Frankie Sestito, Wayne Geftman, Legends of Vinyl DJs, Gene Leone, Vince Fay, Ronnie James, Grant MacAvoy, Lorenzo Wright, Daryl Burgee, John Anderson, Ralph Lewis, Sasha-Sonia-Karen D-Carolyn-Karla-Brenda-Karen H-Jackie and Lois, Ted Dormoi, Sahab Daku, Dennis "Hollywood" McTigue, Brian Phipps, Steve West, Robert P. Brown, Darryl Adderly, Larry Lynch, DCA, Second Story, Someplace Else, David Steinberg, Bas van Oers, Jochem Gerrits, Studio 54, Chez Paree, Barry Geftman, The Saint, Ice Palace Fire Island, The Copa Ft. Lauderdale, Catacombs, The Steps, Ice Palace 57 NYC, Limelight, The Cartwheel, The Copa New Hope, Paradise Garage, Bob Pantano, Frankie Knuckles, Robbie Leslie, Phil Mezzatesta, Robbie Tronco, Troy Dougherty, Jimmy DePre, Charlie Buckeye, Michael DeCero, Reenie Kane, Warren Gluck, Jimmy Del Femine, Tony Moran, Shigeki, BeatPort, A House, Studio One, Boatslip, Chester Inn, The Library, Grand Central, Joey The Hatt, Studio Six, Sandy Beach, M & M, Oil Can Harry's, Rendezvous, Girard's, Lost and Found, Zorine's, The Hippo, The Warehouse, John Schultz, Atlantis and RSVP Cruises, Altra Moda Music, High Fashion Music, West End Records, Mel Cheren, Ed Kushins, Alan-Michael Mamber, Jim Burgess, Paul Goodyear, Manny Lehman, Wayne Gibbons, Abel Aguilera, Frankie Knuckles, Bobby Shaw, MaxRoxx Music, Scully Music, Orange Bear Music, Michael Cavalone, Tony Gatta, Chris Tortu, The Pocono Record Pool and record pools everywhere, Morrie Goldberg, Debbie Harry and Blondie, Benny Hill, Reversal of Fortune, The Orchard, Queen Village Recording Studios, Alpha Sound Studios, Sigma Sound Studios, Sterling Sound, Kendun Recorders, Steve Puntolillo, Sonicraft, Kevin Przybylowski,

Acknowledgments

Frankford-Wayne Mastering, Billboard Magazine, Record World Magazine, Cash Box Magazine, Philadelphia Inquirer, Philadelphia Daily News—for delivering the "Hot Shot" heard 'round the world

Bob Craig, Herb Spivak, Alan Eichler, Stephen Yau, Just Jazz Philadelphia, Jack and Ed Manoff, Skewers Philadelphia, Square on Square Philadelphia, The Prime Rib Philadelphia, Sid Mark, Jeff Duperon and Bob Perkins for supporting The All-Star Jazz Trio

Jerry Blavat for being The Geator with The Heater

Stanley and Lisa Weiss, Flora Webber, Howard "Bud" Weiss and Kathryn Fox for their many familial contributions of love

Peggy King for, well…"What Is There To Say?"

Anthony DiFlorio III and Suzy Rudofker for lending Peggy King to me

Neal Goff for his professional legal advice

Evelyn Katz for arranging my first audition as an actor

Nathan Burns for opening the door to my becoming a teacher

Phyllis Lacca for telling everyone in the world about "Hot Shot"

Burnell Brown for showing me how to become a mentor, for his serious devotion to good music and for giving me my first copy of "The Real Book" Volume 1

Bobby Santore and Richard Santore for creating the tradition that is The Saloon in Philadelphia

Chuck O'Brien for being the coolest recording engineer to ever plug into an audio console

Arnie Smith, Al Coury and Michele Hart Winer for believing in Kurt Borusiewicz, AKB and me

Peter Green for giving me my first experience at having a business partner

Bruce Kaminsky, Jimmy Amadie, Al Stauffer, Bernard Peiffer, Thelonious Monk, Lennie Tristano, Bill Evans, Bud Powell, Count Basie, Duke Ellington, Louis Armstrong, Tadd Dameron, Barry Harris, Earl "Fatha" Hines, Oscar Peterson, Charlie Parker, Art Tatum, Dizzy Gillespie, Charles Mingus, Red Garland, Paul Chambers, Scott LaFaro, Eddie Gomez, Erroll Garner, Frank Sinatra, Billy May, Neal Hefti, Quincy Jones, Astrud Gilberto, Pepper Adams, Thad Jones, Jerry Dodgian, Benny Goodman, Mel Lewis, Nelson Riddle, Gordon Jenkins, Gene Krupa, Buddy Rich, Maynard Ferguson, The Gipsy Kings, Stevie Wonder, Ira Tucker, Sr., The Dixie Hummingbirds, Calhoon, Bobby Darin, Chris Connor, Leonard Bernstein, Connie Crothers and Richard Tabnik for their musical artistry that influenced mine on a multitude of levels

David Kay, Joel Klauber, Evan Solot, Don Renaldo, Bernie Lowe and Kal Mann for helping me to learn what real music is all about

Carol Stevens and Norman Mailer for showing their interest in a couple of young jazz cats

Robert Preston and Rex Harrison for portraying two talkative professors, both of whom I wished to emulate at the beginning of my acting career

Princess Grace of Monaco for being the friendliest, down-to-earth royal of a sovereign nation

Peter Kursman and Jonathan Zubriski for their exquisite and creative songwriting collaborations

Roger Choukron and Régine Zylberberg for entrusting The Gipsy Kings to Kurt and me

Paul Cooper and David Myers for being the first two bassists in my jazz trios with Bruce Klauber

Valerie Vogt for knowing that I'd recognize the finest piano in the world and then selling it to me

Steinway & Sons for inviting me to become a Steinway Spirio Recording Artist

Stephen Foster, Victor Herbert, George Gershwin, Harry Warren, Cole Porter, Richard Rodgers, Lorenz Hart, Jerome Kern, Sammy Cahn, Billy Strayhorn, Duke Ellington, Jule Styne, Jimmy van Heusen, Johnny Mercer, Frank Loesser, Antonio Carlos Jobim, Oscar Hammerstein II, Burton Lane, Rube Bloom, Jimmy McHugh, Irving Caesar, Dorothy Fields, Noel Coward, Vernon Duke, E.Y. "Yip" Harburg, Harold Arlen, Irving Berlin, Johnny Burke, Ray Noble, Ira Gershwin, Johnny Mandel, Alec Wilder, Haven Gillespie, Walter Donaldson, Johnny Green, Sammy Fain, Vincent Youmans, Hoagy Carmichael, Arthur Hamilton, Victor Young, Thomas "Fats" Waller, Andy Razaf, Otto Harbach, Richard Whiting, Arthur Schwartz, Ned Washington, Sammy Gallop, Howard Dietz, Ted Fiorito, Eubie Blake, Edward Heyman, Nacio Herb Brown, Victor Schertzinger, Sigmund Romberg, Kurt Weill, Mort Dixon, Al Dubin, Bert Kalmar, Harry Ruby, Paul Francis Webster, Buddy De Sylva, Tom Adair, Mitchell Parish, Matt Dennis, Arthur Herzog, Jr., Jack Lawrence, Bart Howard, Mack Gordon, Ted Koehler, Norman Gimbel, Sonny Burke, J. Fred Coots, Alan Jay Lerner, Frederick Loewe, Meredith Willson, Gus Kahn, Eric Maschwitz, David Raksin, Ruth Lowe, Jack Strachey, Henry Nemo, Charlie Chaplin, Ralph Burns, Sadie Vimmerstedt and their many other colleagues for the timeless songs they've given to the world which I perform, teach and lecture about endlessly

Village Vanguard, The Village Gate, Jazz at Kitano, Metropolitan Room and 54 Below for upholding the gold standard of being a real New York Jazz Club

Acknowledgments

Philadelphia Inquirer, Philadelphia Bulletin, Philadelphia Daily News, Jazz Times, Philadelphia Jewish Exponent, South Philly Review, Philadelphia Gay News, Main Line Times, Main Line Jewish Expression and Philadelphia Jewish Times for writing such nice things about me over the years

Sam Bushman for being the ultimate PR Man about Town

ASCAP for administering my catalogue of musical compositions

John Gummere for being the finest Graphic Designer a first-time author could hope to have onboard

Al Coury for believing in AKB at the very height of The Disco Era phenomenon

Jordi Pujol and Fresh Sound Records for releasing Peggy King's first new recordings in 36 years

Anthony Dean for his excellent sense of photography and capturing extraordinary images

Marty Portnoy for imagining me as the leader of my own society orchestra

Andre Gregory for his direction while I dreamed of advancing my professional acting career

Pamala Stanley, Mark Kuryloski and Rick Reinhart for their collaboration on "The Bank of Love"

Mary Boyd Higgins for loving my music from Day One

ActionAIDS-Action Wellness and MANNA for allowing me the opportunity to perform and raise money for their charitable organizations

Morton Herskowitz for his incredible insight into human nature and for helping those in need

James Strick, David Silver, C. Grier Sellers, Amy Sabsowitz, Phil Eskew, Cat Iordan, Mary and Pete Henderson, Ben Tavares, Kathy Stewart and all those who understand that: "It CAN Be Done"

Beth and Ed Brunswick, Ed Kfoury, Susan and Kelly Ferguson, Margie and Steve Jamison, Severin Beliveau, Kit and Linda Caspar, Gerri and Greg Botka and everyone else who ensured that my visits to Rangeley, Maine were always worthwhile and enjoyable

David Jenson for knowing how to tune an acoustic piano and appreciating a good one

Zack Lehman and Preston Athey for inviting me to perform and lecture at The Hill School

Michael Alexander Lerner, Gregg Spear, Mike DeFulgentis, Ginny Green, David Barsky, Sandee Bengel, Aden Ohayon, Noah Powell, Art Finnel, Jim

Dolan, Bob McHugh, Keyon Elam, Brian LaFreda, Don Smith, Xu Ren, Kris Bartosiak, Isaac Ohayon, Bob Seltzer, Yu Xi Wang, Assaf Patir, Buzz McCafferty, Leslie Greenlee, Lon Gibson, Mina Ratkalkar, Andrew Larzelere, Scott Anthony, Dena Underwood, David Maher, Lin D'Andrea, Mike Bernstein, Paul Berzin, Rosina deLuca Kagel and Dee Redfearn for being my dream colleagues and students

Kathryn Creamer, Tony Ochuida, Leonard Maurio, Greg Sikora, Nellie Serrano, Christy Bates and Marie Schmidt for being the nicest people at Jacobs Music Company

Art Jones, Robert Smith and John Ellis for being the finest piano technicians anywhere

Jean and Tom Rauch for my open invitation to stay in their splendid Royal Oak, MD home, my first ongoing getaway from Philadelphia

King Broder, Lee Rendi, Gerry Glasgow, Bernie Rothbard for being the booking agents who saw the potential in a bunch of talented young musicians and entertainers

The Saloon, H A Winston, The Borgia Cafe, The Rittenhouse Hotel, Not Quite Cricket, The Brasserie, The Prime Rib, The Rathskellar, Skewers, Square on Square and Chris' Jazz Cafe for being Philadelphia venues that offered live music residencies to me as a soloist and to The All-Star Jazz Trio

Resorts Hotel and Casino in Atlantic City for inviting me to headline in their Starlight Room

Artie Singer for giving me my first real singing lessons. So what happened?

Al Rinaldi, Jr., for inviting me to join Jacobs Music Company as its Artist-in-Residence with thanks to The Rinaldi Family

Gino Iovino for his never-ending quest to offer his guests the finest social experience possible

World Cafe Live, Hal Real, Metropolitan Room and Bernie Furshpan for providing emerging and well-known talent a place in which to perform live

Bernie Evans for acting alongside me in my first experience performing in a comedy-drama

Mindy and Kent Gushner, Ilene and Jeff Wachman, Garey Cooper, Palm Restaurant, Karen and Jeff Phillips, Ron Reid, Bruce Bozzi, Jr., and Fred Thimm for their friendship and camaraderie

Bethesda Blues and Jazz, Sellersville Theater, Act II Playhouse, Hedgerow Theatre, Miller Symphony Hall, Theatre of The Living Arts, Painters Mill Music Fair, Westbury Music Fair and Shady Grove Music Fair for providing excellent live performance venues

Acknowledgments

Sam Rulon for his belief and guidance shown to me as an aspiring child-actor

Beth David Reform Congregation for allowing Janice Kahn to produce "The Music Man" with children playing all the acting parts

Lorry Finkel and Avra Bershad for being my third grade teachers who arranged for me to participate in Temple University's "Psychology of The Gifted Child" program

The Auspitz Family's Famous Delicatessen in Philadelphia for feeding everyone who came through Queen Village Recording Studios

Chuck Darrow, Peter Binzen, A.D. Amorosi and all of those contributing writers at newspapers and magazines who thought enough about my accomplishments to write something about them

Local 77 American Federation of Musicians of which I am a Lifetime Member

Andy became Music Director for veteran performer Peggy King in 2013 as she embarked on her singing career comeback. He co-produced the CD of Ms. King's first new recordings in 36 years and continues to appear with her onstage. His group The All-Star Jazz Trio and vocalist Peggy King create excitement wherever they perform.
— *Alan Eichler, Talent Manager and Producer*

Andy Kahn's piano playing has long been a fixture on the popular music scene in Philadelphia. His professional roots in Swing and Jazz go back to his teenage years. Andy's broad knowledge and infectious enthusiasm for The Great American Songbook have made him a welcome guest during radio programs I host on WRTI in Philadelphia. As a performer, he contributes a great deal to keeping American Standard Songs alive!   — *Bob Craig, Radio Host WRTI Philadelphia*

One of Philadelphia's diamonds in our own backyard is Andy Kahn. His family story of emigrating to America to seek a better life is fully explored in his book, reaffirming the promise that is our country. Andy is a consummate musician and entertainer with none of the egocentric baggage carried around by so many others. His sojourn into his family's longtime paint and decorating business, along with his becoming a highly sought-after recording, show business and musical entrepreneur is an odyssey to marvel at.
— *Lynne Abraham, Esq., Former*
Philadelphia District Attorney and Judge

I've watched Andy Kahn perform at nightclubs, concerts, special events, academic institutions, private parties and audio recording sessions for CDs, radio and films. I consulted closely with Andy on the music for a documentary film I finished in 2017. For two decades, Andy has entertained me and others with his wonderful stories, many of which are collected here in his page-turner of a memoir that's as engaging, energetic and fun as being in the same room with him.   — *Kevin Hinchey, Filmmaker and Professor*

33946145R00175

Made in the USA
Middletown, DE
20 January 2019